T4-ADF-335

MAJORITY LEADERSHIP
IN THE
U.S. SENATE

MAJORITY LEADERSHIP
IN THE
U.S. SENATE

Balancing Constraints

ANDREA C. HATCHER

Politics, Institutions, and Public Policy in America series
Series editors: Scott A. Frisch and Sean Q. Kelly

CAMBRIA PRESS

Amherst, New York

Copyright 2010 Andrea C. Hatcher

All rights reserved
Printed in the United States of America

No part of this publication may be reproduced, stored in or introduced into a retrieval system, or transmitted, in any form, or by any means (electronic, mechanical, photocopying, recording, or otherwise), without the prior permission of the publisher.

Requests for permission should be directed to:
permissions@cambriapress.com, or mailed to:
Cambria Press
20 Northpointe Parkway, Suite 188
Amherst, NY 14228

Library of Congress Cataloging-in-Publication Data

Hatcher, Andrea C.
 Majority leadership in the U.S. Senate : balancing constraints / Andrea C. Hatcher.
     p. cm.
 Includes bibliographical references and index.
 ISBN 978-1-60497-703-5 (alk. paper)
1. United States. Congress. Senate—Majority leaders 2. United States. Congress. Senate—Leadership. I. Title.

  JK1227.H38 2010
  328.73'0762—dc22

2010008652

*To my parents,
Dewey and "Millie" Hatcher*

Table of Contents

List of Tables and Figures   xi

Acknowledgments   xiii

Abbreviations   xv

Chapter 1: Introduction   1
    What Do We Know About Senate Leadership?   3
    Balancing Constraints   10
    Expectations for This Research   17
    Caveats and Qualifications   22
    Organization of the Study   22

Chapter 2: Institutional Constraints: Job Description of Senate Majority Leadership   25
    The Office Emerges   27
    Organizing the Senate   29
    Setting the Agenda   32
    Managing the Floor   37
    Mobilizing the Majority   39
    Campaigning and Fundraising   40
    Speaking for the Party   42
    Networking With Elites   45
    Conclusions   46

Chapter 3: Party Constraints: Selection of Senate Majority Leaders   49
    How a Senator Becomes Majority Leader   51
    Factors in Leadership Selection   53
    Conclusions   68

Chapter 4: Party Constraints:
Ideological Placement of Senate
Majority Leaders   **71**
   Competing Expectations of Leaders' Voting Behavior   72
   Median Voter or Extreme Partisan   75
   Stability or Change   82
   Majority Matters   85
   Interpretations and Implications   90
   Conclusions   93

Chapter 5: Extra-Institutional Constraints:
Presidential Expectations
of Senate Majority Leaders   **95**
   The Logic of Unified Government   97
   Early Leaders   102
   The Modern Moment—Lyndon B. Johnson (D-TX)   108
   The Post-Johnson Era—Mike Mansfield (D-MT)   111
   Republican Presidents and Republican Senate
      Majority Leaders   116
   Interpretations and Implications   121
   Conclusions   123

Chapter 6: Extra-Institutional Constraints:
State Expectations of Senate
Majority Leaders   **125**
   Great Expectations   127
   Howard H. Baker, Jr. (R-TN)   137
   George J. Mitchell (D-ME)   142
   Interpretations and Implications   148
   Conclusions   151

Chapter 7: Conclusions   **153**
   Constrained by Multiple Constituencies   153
   Constrained by the Development of the Office   160

Appendices **163**
    A. U.S. Senate Majority Leaders, 1913–2007   163
    B. A Note on Sources   165

Notes **169**

References **183**

Index **205**

List of Tables and Figures

Table 3.1.	Contested selections for U.S. Senate majority leader.	54
Table 3.2.	Ideological comparison of candidates for contested selections.	55
Table 3.3.	Prior leadership positions of U.S. Senate majority leaders.	59
Table 3.4.	Robert C. Byrd (D-WV): U.S. Senate majority leader, 1977–1980 and 1987–1988.	65
Figure 4.1.	U.S. Senate majority leaders: At first Congress.	76
Figure 4.2.	U.S. Senate majority leaders: At selection.	78
Figure 4.3.	Republican U.S. Senate majority leaders: Ideological placement as leader.	79
Figure 4.4.	Democratic U.S. Senate majority leaders: Ideological placement as leader.	81
Figure 4.5.	Career ideological change of U.S. Senate majority leaders.	83
Figure 4.6.	Immediate ideological change of U.S. Senate majority leaders.	84

Table 4.1.	OLS estimates of leaders' voting behavior.	88
Table 5.1.	Unified government: U.S. Senate majority leaders and presidents.	101
Table 5.2.	Divided government: U.S. Senate majority leaders and presidents.	101
Table 6.1.	Number and amount of earmarks by U.S. Senate majority leader, 1995–2005.	129

ACKNOWLEDGMENTS

For support of many varieties, I extend professional and personal thanks to: Bruce Oppenheimer, Sean Kelly, Scott Wilson, Claudia Anderson, Addy McCulloch, reviewers known and unknown, Vanderbilt University, the Dirksen Congressional Center, the Lyndon B. Johnson Foundation, and Sewanee: The University of the South.

Abbreviations

GJMA   George J. Mitchell Archives
HHBA   Howard H. Baker, Jr. Archives
LBJL   Lyndon Baines Johnson Library and Museum
MMA   Mike Mansfield Archives

MAJORITY LEADERSHIP
IN THE
U.S. SENATE

Chapter 1

Introduction

[W]e have no really adequate model of party leadership as it exists in Congress, and...none can be constructed because we lack simple descriptions of many of the basic working parts of the system. (Huitt, 1961, p. 334)

It may be a little difficult to envision just what a representative or senator does in Washington; the added title of majority leader compounds the complexity.
—Senate Majority Leader Mike Mansfield, 1962[1]

Since 1913, U.S. senators have recognized one position among themselves as majority leader.[2] The first incumbent, John W. Kern (D-IN), began the gradual process of converting the position into an office. He and his colleagues also set other precedents that, as this research will show, endure nearly a century later. Notwithstanding such a long period of experience, and despite the profusion of political scientists' accounts of Congress and journalists' daily observations of the legislative branch, no comprehensive study of the Senate majority leader has found its way into the annals of American politics. This book aims to correct the anomaly.

The study examines Senate majority leadership in terms of the constituencies, both electoral and functional, of the Senate majority leader. These constituencies—state, party, Senate, and president—are found to represent constraints on the Senate majority leader as their demands often compete, and the ways in which Senate majority leaders balance them form the contours of Senate majority leadership. It might seem obvious for there to be much variance as Senate majority leaders and their constituents change over time, and, to be sure, differences in leadership styles emerge. However, what is more striking is not the change but the continuity that guides the institutional development of Senate majority leadership. The path dependence is one of constrained Senate majority leadership, not for the conventional wisdom that the majority leader operates in a supermajoritarian institution (Sinclair, 2001b), but for the broader reason that a plethora of intra-, inter-, and extra-institutional forces pull at the leader.

The scope of inquiry is comprehensive, beginning with an identification of trends in the selection of senators to become majority leader. There is no stepping-stone pathway to leadership, but there does seem to be one constant factor in leadership selection: ideological orientation. The idea that senators, before their selection, are universally "middlemen" (Truman, 1959) within their party provides a baseline for the measurement of change in their voting behavior once they become majority leader. This linkage of preleader to leader voting behavior enlarges the compass of the present study from becoming leader to being leader. In addition to looking at voting behaviors, this study enumerates many of the other tasks that are required of Senate majority leaders, noting changes in expectations from the emergence of the office to the present. It also drafts something of a job description for the position of Senate majority leader. Still, voting remains the single activity by which the leader represents, or balances, multiple constituencies. This work, then, traces the voting behavior of Senate majority leaders, analyzing by way of statistical findings how the leader represents his party constituency by roll-call voting. One key, but often overlooked, variable that this study examines is the size of a leader's majority.

Introduction

The effort goes further to explain how Senate majority leaders fulfill their representational obligations to state or electoral constituencies with "distributive benefits," or those federal funds or projects distributed by members of Congress to a particular locality or constituency. In addition to service to party and state, Senate majority leaders, as the functional head of the upper chamber of the legislative branch, maintain institutional service to the Senate. Moreover, demands to maintain the institutional prestige of the Senate are heightened under divided government and, at the least, complicated by unified government. Thus, the president introduces an extra-branch constituency to the electoral, partisan, and institutional audiences of the Senate majority leader.

Each of these lines of inquiry is not entirely without precedent in the literature of Congress. Nevertheless, they have not been asked of Senate majority leaders and leadership, and an examination of what we know about congressional leadership makes the omission of knowledge about Senate majority leaders glaring.

WHAT DO WE KNOW ABOUT SENATE LEADERSHIP?

While leadership in the U.S. House of Representatives has been studied extensively (e.g., Sinclair, 1983, 1995) and intensively (e.g., Peters, 1995, 1997), there exists no comparable body of research of U.S. Senate leadership, in general, and of the Senate majority leader, in particular. Indeed, much of what we know is House-bound, but if the Senate is an "exceptional" body (Oppenheimer, 2002), meriting a different understanding, so too should we expect the leader of that body, with his multiple constituencies, to merit specialized attention. To be sure, many of the prominent findings of congressional research have been extended to the Senate, albeit mostly in a piecemeal fashion.

A Senate Framed by the House

Because we know more information about the House, scholars tend to generalize those findings to the Senate, treating the Senate as an addendum to the House (for evidence of this, look no further than any standard textbook on American government or legislative processes). Accordingly, much of what is known, or thought to be known, about the demands and constraints of Senate leadership comes from auxiliary chapters or even briefer token comparison paragraphs in House studies.[3] A conference sponsored by the Dirksen Congressional Center noted this disparity in interest and research between the House and Senate and suggested increasing knowledge about the Senate as a next step in understanding congressional leadership (Mackaman, 1980). That suggestion has yet to yield a groundswell of research.

Two decades later, Bruce Oppenheimer (2002) reinforced the "exceptionalism" of the Senate, emphasizing that apportionment and size differences make an altogether different body from the House. In addition, the Senate's norms, processes, and its party leadership operate in different institutional and political contexts than are found in the House. Therefore, if assumptions about the Senate are based on studies of the House, conclusions may be flawed. Furthermore, initial premises may be misdirected. Rather than using findings from the House as a benchmark for findings on the Senate (e.g., "Does Y also apply to the Senate?"), scholars should tailor research questions specific to the institution that is the Senate (Oppenheimer, 2002, pp. 6–7). Because of the structural and political context in the Senate, members' goals are specialized to produce institutionally specific conditions for the Senate majority leader and thus shape behaviors unique to those demands.

Leadership Selection
There have been a handful of studies examining the selection of congressional leaders. Garrison Nelson (1977) provided perhaps the most comprehensive review of partisan influences on leadership selection. Robert Peabody's work (1967, 1976), which devoted half a volume to descriptions of select battles for whip or minority leadership positions in the Senate, stands as a benchmark for cross-sectional analyses of specific races. His finding of "leadership ladders," or a hierarchical ascension up leadership ranks (Brown & Peabody, 1992), obscures other individual-level factors that contribute to the emergence of certain members of Congress

as leaders in their respective chambers. However, his work fathered other studies of leadership races and outcomes that analyzed the extent to which the rank and file choose leaders to advance individual or collective goals (Green, 2006; Green & Harris, 2007; Harris, 2006; Oppenheimer & Peabody, 1977).

Alone among these studies, Sean Kelly (1995a, 1995b) examined leadership selection in the Senate. Why Senate leadership selection has been understudied in comparison to the House defies explanation. Data are just as readily available, and any results would be substantively interesting (especially as Sinclair [1989] has described the "transformation" of the body which would make leadership less a matter of inheritance). It is decidedly easier, and more meaningful, to explain the value of studying Senate leadership. Understanding the types of leaders that members select illuminates not only the goals the members find salient (Green & Harris, 2007), but also reveals the expectations they have for the office and its holder—expectations, which, in turn, place demands and constraints on leaders in carrying out the duties of the office.

If we are lacking in scholarly understanding of how senators choose leaders, thanks to Gerald Gamm and Steven Smith (2000, 2002a, 2002b, 2004), we do know how the office of Senate majority leader came about. With a renewed interest in the historical Congress (e.g., Brady & McCubbins, 2002, 2007), Gamm and Smith offered historical accounts of the development of leadership positions in the Senate and their contribution to the creation of the modern Senate. The office of Senate majority leader is not formally specified in the constitution, nor is it established in the elaborate Senate rules. Using content analysis of major newspapers of the day, Gamm and Smith were able to pinpoint the emergence of the "official" leadership positions in the Senate and to link it with strong party competition. They noted that as formal leadership positions emerged, leaders became chief spokesmen for their parties and in so doing, provided "policy leadership," affecting not only how the Senate conducts business (process and procedure) but also what business the Senate conducts (setting agendas and passing legislation). These remarkable efforts of research identified conditions under which Senate majority leadership emerged and became institutionalized. Yet, there still is a lacuna in the literature about how individual senators emerge as leaders, specifically the unique office of majority leader.

A focus on the distinctive selection processes of the majority-leader post, which this study undertakes, will help us understand not just the processes involved in becoming but also those involved in being majority leader. Being majority leader entails different goals, and thus different behaviors, than being whip or minority leader. As leader of the majority party, he must fulfill the expectation to pass legislation whereas minority leaders are expected to thwart the agenda of the majority—a task made easier by the minority-oriented rules of the Senate. And it is this partisan distinction that informs so much about how Congress works.

Theories of Leadership
In the form of conditional party government (Aldrich & Rohde, 2001) and party cartel theories (Cox & McCubbins, 1993), political scientists have a strong theoretical grasp of how the majority party works to produce preferred outcomes. These works derive from the contemporary cycle of House leadership studies that began with Barbara Sinclair (1983).[4] Sinclair (1983, 1995), describing majority leadership in the House, relied on principal-agent theory to frame majority leadership's influence on lawmaking in the House after the adoption of several reforms in the 1970s. With the strengthening of parties in Congress, she noted a more active and centralized leadership. She argued that since leaders are agents of the membership that chooses them, leadership styles derive from principals' expectations, which in turn are shaped by changing political and institutional contexts.

David Rohde also concentrated on the postreform period, noting the distinct changes in parties and leadership that reforms brought. He, too, traced a bottom-up and somewhat circuitous development of centralized leadership, beginning with the class of 1958. This influx of junior Democratic members was almost immediately frustrated by the lack of movement on key policies and thus reclaimed much individual power from both committee chairs and party leaders. With the reforms of the

1970s, the rank and file subsequently returned it en bloc as necessary to meet their legislative goals; that is, they granted to their party leaders the authority to whip votes on key issues. This is party government (American Political Science Association, 1950; Schattschneider, 1942) conditioned to important issues, or "conditional party government," and over the years, that issue base has grown. Rohde advanced the view that membership homogeneity determines leader power, which, in turn, determines leadership style. The result is a leadership responsible to its members and one capable of party-line policymaking. This line of party cohesion is formalized as the "party cartel theory" by Gary Cox and Matthew McCubbins (1993, 2005). As parties in Congress have strengthened, indicated by an increase in intraparty cohesion, the majority party has acted like a cartel, writing the rules of the game and setting the agenda, which has given them advantages in the legislative arena. Leaders, then, are like police, meting out rewards and punishments based on party loyalty. The result is party-line lawmaking and policy, framed by admirers as pure party government and by critics as majority run amok.

That being said, and keeping in mind the distinction between a majoritarian and supermajoritarian institution, Sinclair observed that majority party leadership may be impossibly constrained with supermajoritarian rules. Sinclair (2001b) noted that leaders, in the Senate as in the House, must meet members' demands—specifically their legislative or policy goals. But, as she so aptly described earlier (1989), the transformation of the Senate, from one characterized by mid-century institutional folkways to one known for its late-century individual-oriented practices, makes party government in the Senate hard to achieve. Rather than the almost feudal structure of the 1950s, in which committees were led by their chair-barons, the institution Sinclair wrote about is one of individuals who use public arenas, such as floor speeches and media statements, to freely voice their positions. This increased activity, she noted, has changed the nature of influence in the body. No longer are committees the primary bases of influence, but neither has that influence become concentrated within party leadership. Instead, influence is widely dispersed among individuals who seek it out, and that individualism is compounded by the several supermajoritarian rules of the Senate as well as individual prerogatives such as "holds" (Evans & Lipinski, 2005; Sinclair, 2005). Sinclair highlighted, but did not resolve, this dilemma of legislating that requires some support of the minority party in order to pursue majority party goals. These partisan and institutional demands illustrate the value in studying the Senate separate from the House and provide prominent constraints on the power of the Senate majority leader.

Individual Leaders
Tales of individual congressional leaders, both formal and informal, are replete with outsize personalities who have established themselves in the lore of Congress (e.g., Cheney & Cheney, 1996; Davidson, Hammond, & Smock, 1998; Peters, 1995, 1997). While a general and theoretical understanding of Senate majority leadership leaves room for attention, scholars do know something about a few Senate majority leaders, especially about Lyndon B. Johnson (D-TX). Probably because his tenure and personality were so extraordinary, his is a notable case that draws scholars' attention. Ralph Huitt (1961), writing at the end of Johnson's tenure, instructed about Democratic party leadership in the Senate, but he did so through a case study of Johnson, and it is now widely appreciated that Johnson is an exceptional case. Recently scholars, mostly historians (Caro, 2002; Conkin, 1986; Dallek, 1991), have produced biographies of Johnson and found a rich trove of activity in his Senate years. John Stewart (1971) offered comparative cases of Johnson and his successor Mike Mansfield (D-MT). But other, later leaders, such as Howard H. Baker (R-TN), have found interest as well (Annis, 1995; Bobic, 1996; Welborn, 1993). Richard Baker and Roger Davidson (1991) assembled a volume's worth of profiles of Senate party leaders and their tenures from which we can glean the problems and achievements, the opportunities and constraints, faced by each individual leader. Over two decades, Norman Ornstein, Robert Peabody, and David Rohde (1977, 1997) "reconsidered" trends in Senate development, including turnover of leaders. Their snapshots began with the contrasting styles of Johnson and Mansfield and ultimately profiled the tenures of George J. Mitchell (D-ME) and Tom Daschle (D-SD). However, an individualized

focus on the men who have held the office of Senate majority leader clouds the office itself and the extent to which the office shapes the behavior of the man rather than how the personality of the man shapes the office. A focus on the position rather than its holder allows for a more systematic treatment of behaviors common to Senate majority leadership.

HOW TO STUDY SENATE MAJORITY LEADERS?

This brief review of congressional scholarship answers the question, "why study Senate majority leaders?" but the question, "how to study them?" still remains. A current approach to the study of leadership, legislative and otherwise, is what may be called the contextual view. This lens recognizes that leadership does not exist in a vacuum and thus emphasizes variables within the broader political environment. Among congressional researchers applying this lens, Lawrence Evans and Walter Oleszek (1999) identified multiple themes—among them, preferences of leaders and parties, prerogatives of the office, and interactions with members, chambers, and administrations—to contour congressional leadership.[5] However, Randall Strahan (2002) found the contextual view to be insufficient to explain the development of House leadership in the 19th century. For him, the environment in which leaders operate is secondary to the "personal motivation and political skills" (p. 238) of the leader himself. Leadership, after all, depends on the variability of leaders. Recognizing the value of both influences, Matthew Green (2007) defined the legislative leadership of the speaker of the House by looking at such contextual variables as norms of behavior, presidential interests (both institutional and partisan), and congressional interests (both institutional and partisan), as well as by considering individual speaker interests.

The present study of Senate majority leadership similarly examines actors that contextualize leadership—namely, the multiple constituencies of the Senate majority leader—in addition to the personal proclivities of individual leaders. However, in the process of examining what have become familiar contextual variables, like party and president, this scholarship returns to considerations of power.

Historically, and in a variety of disciplines, students of leadership tend to approach the topic by looking at the power gathered by, awarded to, or exercised by leaders. A leader, in other words, is someone who holds power, and scholars have studied power to understand leadership. To understand the presidency, Richard Neustadt (1960) examined the power of the office. About the Senate, Randall Ripley (1969b) included party-leadership positions in a discussion of power distribution in the Senate, but stressed much more heavily the power of committee leaders—a distribution much changed in the postreform (or post-"transformation" [Sinclair, 1989]) Senate. Huitt (1961, p. 334) offered a glimpse at the power of party leaders in the Senate, acknowledging that the principal actors, including Senate majority leaders, had ignored academic prescriptions for congressional reform because they exhibited "too much violence to the political context in which members operate." In other words, the balance of power was the focus of interest for practitioners and scholars. Still others have looked at leaders to understand the nature of power. Political theorists like Machiavelli to Hobbes have pointed to leaders in both their works, *The Prince* and *Leviathan* respectively, to understand the structures and functions of political power.

Contemporary scholars also have followed this line of inquiry. Although Robert Dahl's (1961) "theory of community power" broadened the object of inquiry to emphasize a plurality of leaders rather than a single leader, he still equated power with position and position with power.

This book, however, rather than being a tome about the leadership of power or the power of leadership, is an investigation of the limits of leadership. By looking at the context of Senate majority leadership in terms of the multiple constituencies it must satisfy, it is a study of constraints.

BALANCING CONSTRAINTS

The idea or concept of balance is an old one in political science, often formulated in terms of equilibrium (Russett, 1966). As either metaphor or concept, it captures interactions between the leader's discretion and the constraints imposed by the multiple constituencies and ambiguities of the office.[6] In an interview not long after his selection as Senate majority leader, Bill Frist (R-TN) said almost plaintively, "Majority leader sounds good…but people assume you've got a lot of power…. There's no power to it. You learn quickly that there's no power" (Gann, 2003, p. 72). Perhaps Mike Mansfield (D-MT) revealed the limitations of the office most directly: "I didn't want the job. I prefer being just a senator because when you are majority leader, you lose a certain amount of independence you have when you are just a senator."[7]

A focus on constraints, counterintuitively, reveals the full extent of power. Peter Bachrach and Morton Baratz (1962) added nuance to discussions of power by describing its "two faces." The "overt" face of power consists of the more obvious forms of decision making and power exercising (e.g., the Senate majority leader using his "right of first recognition"[8]). The "covert" face of power is the ability not to persuade someone to do something they otherwise would not do, as Dahl (1961) defined power, but to prevent them from "doing something" in the first place. As multiple actors are introduced in political institutions, the covert power of one actor influences the overt power of another. In the context of the Senate, one cannot understand the power of the Senate majority leader (say, the "right of first recognition") without an understanding of the conditions within the party caucus or the Senate that may limit the application of that prerogative.

A focus on constraints also reveals more about the nature of the Senate majority leader, from which emerge inferences about the types of leaders that have held the office and the types of leaders that caucuses (and senates and presidents) will select to lead them. Specifically, an emphasis on constraints of Senate majority leadership reveals the requirement for balance inherent in the office. As the present study unfolds, it becomes apparent that majority leadership revolves around balancing multiple constituencies on which the leader depends and to which he assumes obligations. These include: the state that elected him to the Senate, the party that designated him as its leader, the Senate as a whole, whose members entrusted him with institutional responsibilities, and the president with whom he must compete, whether under unified or divided government.

State

Senate majority leaders have, essentially, dual electoral constituencies—their state and their party. And while all senators owe allegiance to both, the leaders face unique cross-pressures because of their sequential elections, first by state, then by party; their reelections depend on successful balancing of the varying demands of the different audiences. They must be senators before they are Senate majority leaders; the leaders must represent the interests of their states. These interests are defined in the context of the campaign and, in the heterogeneous environment of a state, can range from localized concerns to national policy (Abramowitz & Segal, 1992; Fenno, 1996; Jacobson, 2009). Leadership complicates the task of representation. Despite the partisan sorting of the past few decades (Abramowitz, Alexander, & Gunning, 2006; Bishop, 2008; Oppenheimer, 2005b), there are cases in which the policy preferences of the Senate majority leaders' states may conflict with the policy preferences of the party they lead (e.g., Tom Daschle). However, a Senate majority leader may find state demands take the more tangible form of distributive benefits as he assumes leadership. That is, one way of balancing conflicting expectations is to use his party and institutional clout to "bring home the bacon."

As party and institutional head, a Senate majority leader may be positioned to get more federal dollars for his state. The leading players in pork barrel politics (the appropriations committee, for example) may be willing to supply the Senate majority leader with appropriations or earmarks he can "claim credit" (Mayhew, 1974) and the Senate majority leader, in turn, can assist with their needs of agenda setting and scheduling. This trade is more than a quid pro quo, however, because quality state representation (if in benefits rather than policy) secures the reelectoral prospects of the Senate majority leader and diminishes uncertainty for a party needing leadership.

Party

On an individual level, reelection may be the underlying goal of every member of Congress (Mayhew, 1974). But as a collective, congressional parties have as their proximate goal the passage of policy which can help with individual reelection efforts. Thus, the Senate majority leader's party demands policy outcomes that will help fulfill the electoral goals of members (Rohde, 1991). However, party caucuses are rarely monolithic in preferences or behaviors, and partisan demands on Senate majority leaders are rarely uniform. Instead, partisan constraints fluctuate with the size of the Senate majority leader's majority. A narrow majority places the Senate majority leader in the position of negotiating with the minority to accomplish the policy goals of the party. However, that narrow majority also places a burden on the caucus to remain unified for a narrow win. This incentive is the principle of the "minimum winning coalition" (Riker, 1962). As the margin of majority increases, greater numbers by definition mean greater interests. With more heterogeneity, the partisan coalition tends to fracture as the risk of losing a vote lessens and thus defection carries fewer consequences. But the prospect of defections leads to other defections—why should one faction be excused on principle from the coalition while another must remain because the party cannot afford to lose any more votes? Plus, party factions tend to activate others in an action-reaction response. Thus, the Senate majority leader is constrained by his own partisans.

Senate
The Senate majority leader is more than a senator and more than a partisan. As functional head of the upper chamber of the legislative branch, the majority leader must act to preserve institutional prestige that is the currency of legitimacy. In an era in which public opinion of Congress is exceedingly low (Hibbing & Theiss-Morse, 1995), the Senate majority leader must preserve the legitimacy of the body. From Washington's explanation to Jefferson's ideas about the tempering nature of the upper chamber, the Senate is perceived by members and observers alike to be the more deliberative body, the stalwart against the passions of the House. However, many perceptions of the Senate as a collegial, orderly club have been transformed in recent decades (Byrd, 2005; Sinclair, 1989), while the idea of the Senate as wiser, fairer, and less partisan than the House remains.

Even though the office, unlike the speaker of the House, lacks a constitutional charge, it is no less significant. As chief administrator of the Senate, the Senate majority leader is responsible for upholding order with scheduling and agenda setting. The institutional structure and rules require a supermajority for most major actions, effectively mandating an institutional role to the Senate majority leader. The necessity of minority support de-emphasizes overt partisanship by the Senate majority leader. Even as a large margin of majority may lessen the need to consult with relevant members of the minority, the demand for institutional preservation constrains the Senate majority leader to that role still.

President
For the Senate majority leader, balancing the different factions within his own party against the centrifugal forces of the minority, while attending to the needs of the state that elected him in its service and while preserving the institutional prestige of the Senate, is no mean feat. Add to that juggling act an extra-branch constituent—the president. Whether under unified or divided government, the president and Senate majority leader have a reactive relationship. Under unified government, the Senate majority leader is beholden to the policy demands of the national figurehead of his party—a man who was elected on a slate of campaign promises he now has to enact. In fact, one scholar (Munk, 1974) tied the emergence of the office of Senate majority leader to the demands of the president—he needed a leader to push his platform. Presidential influence, thus, may be evident in the selection and operation of Senate majority leaders. Divided government perhaps gives the Senate majority leader more leeway to originate policy and set agendas, but the leader remains constrained by the threat of presidential veto, if not presidential popularity. The result is an office obliged to so many interests, there is no clear understanding by participant or observer as to what the role is or what it should be.

Ambiguities of the Office
During the throes of the Vietnam War, President Lyndon Johnson, himself the previous occupant of the majority leader's desk, pleaded with Senate

Majority Leader Mike Mansfield (D-MT), "I would appreciate some support from my majority leader." Mansfield replied, "Mr. President, I'm not your majority leader. I'm the Senate's majority leader" (Valeo, 1999, p. 215).[9] Thus, inherent in the balancing of constraints are ambiguities surrounding the office, its occupant, its function, and the conditions under which the Senate majority leader will strike the balance in favor of one constituency over another.

A reflection of leaders' own words shows disparate perspectives on leadership, on both searching for balance and coping with ambiguities. Howard Baker (R-TN), in a memo directed to his constituency or media, but in either case to the public, wrote that his first "duty and responsibility" is "to represent the interest of my Tennessee constituents, [and] to study the many and varied issues confronting our country as a whole."[10] Baker's ranking fits with Mike Mansfield's refrain that he, first, was a senator from Montana:

> I am, however, fundamentally a Senator from the State of Montana, and you may rest assured that as long as I have the honor to represent the people of our State, I will do everything I possibly can to see that they are given the type of representation which they deserve and are entitled to and which I have tried to give them over the past 20 years.[11]

Each time a constituent questioned his role of majority leader, he reminded him or her, "I was elected by the people of Montana. It is my job to represent them."[12] Baker's and Mansfield's clear philosophy of majority leadership as secondary to their functions as senators is quite different from that of George Mitchell (D-ME), who viewed the post as a national responsibility, and by that time, the prevalence of media ensured that he spoke to a national audience, in addition to his state and the Senate. Mitchell's Senate agenda was a function of "personal interest and where problems are that need to be addressed."[13] "Maine concerns" made the list but were not at the forefront as Baker's and Mansfield's home-state concerns were.

Perhaps it was Lyndon Johnson who philosophized most about his office. With regard to his state, Johnson was nothing if not diplomatic in an era in which state and regional divisions defined political stances:

> [T]here could be no real conflict [between being a senator from Texas and Senate majority leader], since every member of the Senate represents a state and every state has certain regional problems all its own. The U.S. is a Nation made up of states and every senator is confronted with the problem of representing his own constituents and at the same time looking after the interests of the Nation as a whole.[14]

He described his political philosophy elsewhere: "I am a free man, an American, a United States Senator, and a Democrat, in that order. I am also a liberal, a conservative, a Texan, a taxpayer, a rancher, a businessman, a consumer, a parent, a voter,...and I am all these things in no fixed order."[15]

Johnson's frequent writing and ruminating on his role belie his fundamental philosophy of pragmatism. He was continually searching for ways to keep his "even political balance."[16] And the path to balance is paved with such ideas: "A true [majority] leader consists of a man who can get people to work together on the points on which they agree and who can persuade them that when they disagree there are peaceful methods of settling their differences."[17] "The concept that the Lyndon Johnson type of leadership precludes the use of the Senate as a public education forum for the definition of issues is one of the latest conversation stoppers."[18] "I think that the majority leader is more than the leader of the majority. He is actually the leader of the Senate."[19] Constraints remain, no matter how leaders rank order their constituencies and obligations.

> The basic problem is a widely held misconception as to the authority of the majority leader in the Senate. Actually, as the term 'authority' is understood in executive or management circles, he has none at all...The real 'power' of the Senate leader depends upon his skill at brokerage between various blocs.[20]

These viewpoints, to which others could be added, offer glimpses into the ambiguities and constraints of Senate majority leadership. Ambiguities mean that there is no standard for Senate majority leadership. There is no blanket concept, no regularized measure of what a majority leader does or should do. The purpose of this book is to explain Senate majority leadership as the balancing of multiple constituencies—state, party, senate, president—which act to constrain behaviors of the leader.

Expectations for This Research

To Focus on the Senate Majority Leader

Rather than studying congressional leadership by looking at the speaker of the House, which has been the trend among political scientists (Green, 2004, 2006, 2007; Peters, 1995, 1997), this research focuses on the Senate majority leader. As head of the upper legislative chamber, the Senate majority leader lacks a constitutional mandate but does not lack expectations, as this study will show. That the majority leader carries them with the burden of the chamber's egalitarianism and without the aid of majoritarian procedures demonstrates the merit of studying the office and counters the conventional wisdom that the Senate majority leader is less important—in government and for scholars—than the speaker.

Rather than a broad study of Senate leadership, which may consider majority and minority leaders, whips, policy and steering committees, and so forth, this inquiry focuses exclusively on the Senate majority leader. Although the leaders of the two major parties in the Senate share many similar tasks and responsibilities, they differ by their structural placement and purpose. For example, although there are sure to have been and to be many exceptions to this rule of thumb, consider the majority leader to be active and the minority leader reactive. As the leader of the majority, the majority leader bears an expectation to push his party's agenda and policy. Since he does not command a majority of membership, the minority leader carries no such expectation. Instead, he is to check the will of the majority, to respond to its agenda with alternatives of his own. Moreover, the majority leader is the leader of the entire Senate. This institutional position requires him to protect the institution on the way to advancing his state and party interests. And while his tasks as leader of the Senate may be more figurative than literal, they nonetheless provide a check, if by expectation only, on his otherwise strictly partisan behavior.

To Fill a Void

The Senate is understudied compared to the House, particularly on the topic of leadership; and what is known about Senate leadership derives largely from House studies, much of which is anecdotal and erratic. The goal of this research is to take a step toward filling that void in understanding. In his article on Democratic party leadership in the Senate, Huitt wrote:

> [T]he preoccupation with reform has obscured the fact that we have no really adequate model of party leadership as it exists in Congress, and that none can be constructed because we lack simple descriptions of many of the basic working parts of the present system. (1961, p. 334)

While scholars have rendered the point moot with regard to the House, it remains applicable to the Senate. On the way to ameliorating Huitt's lament, this study offers general trend reporting and descriptive statistics combined with the leaders' own words to present an introductory and broad portrait of becoming and being Senate majority leader. The result is an appreciation for the unending search for balance among constituencies and the limited discretion available to one dependent on multiple constituencies.

To Use a Multimethod Approach

This topic necessitates a multimethod approach. Neither "hard" nor "soft" data alone are adequate to describe Senate leadership. For that reason, perhaps, the principles and practices of leadership in the Senate have eluded researchers. As emphasized earlier, the Senate is a distinctive legislative body. Its elaborate, formal, supermajoritarian rules governing a chamber of 100 individuals have created an atmosphere that is a "club" for insiders (Matthews, 1960) and a "citadel" for those outside (White, 1957). As such, most of the politics in the Senate historically transpires via interpersonal interactions. Party cloakrooms have for decades been the places where deals are made, bargains are struck, and votes are traded. A handshake in the hallway counts for more than a formal discourse on the floor. These norms and mores that contribute to and thrive on a sense of egalitarian membership made leadership offices, and the study of them, late to emerge. Senate leadership is hard to grasp, hard to model, and impossible to ascertain without knowledge of the individuals that fill the roles. It is in this way, via a multimethod approach, that this book makes a contribution to understanding and to scholarship.

Statistical inferences have been derived from the DW-NOMINATE scores (Poole & Rosenthal, 1997) of individual leaders; these scores are systematic measures of ideology which gauge movement over time, comparing behaviors of senators before and during tenures of leadership. But undoubtedly the most original part of this study is its reliance on archival data.[21] In the process of researching this project, I have made use of four paper collections of former Senate majority leaders.[22] My work began at the Howard Baker Jr. Center at the University of Tennessee, Knoxville. From there, I looked into the mammoth compilation at the Lyndon B. Johnson Presidential Library, University of Texas, Austin, after which I searched the collection of Senator Mitchell housed in the Bowdoin College Library, Brunswick, Maine. I examined the papers of Senator Mansfield at the Michael J. Mansfield Library at the University of Montana, Missoula. These are perhaps the most extensive papers, given Mansfield's extraordinarily lengthy tenure both in the Senate and especially as majority leader. In addition to these archival collections, I have relied on numerous transcripts of oral-history interviews with leaders, staff, and relevant participants in the Senate and in presidential administrations.[23]

Archival materials, unlike any other data set, show the politics of political interactions. Memos, hand-jotted notes, phone slips, letters, and reports provide evidence of "who got what, when, and how" (Lasswell, 1936). These and other documents detail interactions with constituents—state, party, and Senate alike. An examination of these papers for the years prior to leadership and for those years as leader also shows noticeable differences in activities and styles before and after. Research of interactions is the only way to "measure" leadership by interactions.

One line of inquiry of this research focuses on federal aid to states and the majority leader's particular capability to funnel funds to his state or pet projects. Data on distributive benefits, specifically earmarks in annual appropriations bills, are available for many years from the watchdog group Citizens Against Government Waste.[24] While readily accessible, numbers and raw dollar amounts are unhelpful in linking the majority leader to such expenditures. There are, in most cases, increases in federal outlays to state governments about the time that state gains a majority leader. However, pinpointing the hand of the majority leader in those increases is a difficult, if not impossible, task. Other factors, such as inflation, the efforts of the leader's state colleagues in the Senate or House, or even authorizations appropriated years earlier, may be the proximate cause for the increase. Therefore, reliance on archival collections is the key to this project; these archives left a paper trail of the leader's case and the project activities to follow. From these, I was able to see which projects kept the leader's attention, why they did so, how he used his influence within and without the Senate to advance the causes, and with what outcomes. The result is a broad picture of the politics of leadership, especially its demands and constraints, and what it means for representation.

Of course, archives suffer from problems with both validity and reliability. No collection is exhaustive, so that gaps in record keeping may yield a biased sample. Moreover, a researcher must take special care to collect evidence in a standardized manner, so that findings are generalizable rather than anecdotal. And yet, given the small universe of Senate majority leaders ($N = 21$), any study of Senate majority leadership must rely on anecdotes, and so does this book. But it does so as systematically as possible, looking at similar or dissimilar events across tenures of leaders. Variations from collection to collection inhibit, to an extent, research. Records are kept differently within each office, and one collection may be heavy on administrative files while another is replete with project files. Still, an examination of several archives, like this work undertakes, ensures that no one collection is assumed typical. That is, systemization comes as each set of information counterbalances the others. The validity of the data increases with sample size.

Archival and content data are unified by the comparative method, in which case studies illustrating empirically evident outcomes are "used to generate new conceptual schemes" (Ragin, 1987, p. ix). Cases presented are wide ranging. Because the scope of the study is historically comprehensive, yet topically defined, the presentation of cases is not chronological. Rather than an historical narrative of Senate majority leadership, the following study identifies constraints on Senate majority leadership by offering cases linked by a unique variable. The result might appear to some to be a selective look at both the tenures of specific Senate majority leaders and the operation of Senate majority leadership. However, I must issue some qualifiers. First, any apparent selection bias is the result of data availability. The availability of usable data varies, naturally, across historical eras and with the peculiarities of Senate majority leaders themselves. Confidence in conditions analysis increases when multiple cases are presented to illustrate the factor in question. Chronological gaps only strengthen the universality of the application.

This research is made strong by its multimethod design. Archival findings paint a picture which statistical analysis cannot sketch alone; and an established data set on roll-call voting provides a framework to systematize otherwise anecdotal evidence. In its approach, as in topic, this study is distinctive.

To Treat Leadership as an Independent Variable

Lastly, this work merits attention for its novel treatment of leadership, not just as an outcome but also as an explanatory variable. Rather than considering only the tenures of specific leaders or what results from their leadership (e.g., policy), this study examines leadership, concomitant with the demands accompanying it, for its effects on senatorial behavior. This juxtaposition from dependent to independent variable is seen in the dual roles of senator and leader. That is, how does being a leader affect being a senator? How does being leader alter his representational style and his interactions with his constituencies? These questions and others are the subjects of the remaining chapters; it is a highly descriptive and theoretical treatment of constraints on Senate majority leadership and, thus, its effect on senatorial behaviors. This study creates assumptions from which propositions and hypotheses can be derived and tested; as such it is hypothesis generating rather than hypothesis testing, although both quantitative (from large-n data sets) and qualitative (case studies from archival data) methods will be employed to support the assumptions presented.

CAVEATS AND QUALIFICATIONS

Leadership is an ambiguous term, with roots in psychology, management, and other academic fields as much as politics.[25] The present work defines leadership in terms of its function; that is, to function as a leader is to manifest leadership.[26] In other words, leadership is what a leader does. "Leadership style" can describe, like Fenno (1978) on representation, that pattern of behavior (Stratton & Hayes, 1998) in which Senate majority leaders are home bound, policy driven, or institution oriented.[27] That is, some leaders are more attuned to state concerns than are others. Likewise, some are intent on producing policy in keeping with party preference, while still other leaders are to a greater degree oriented to maintaining the Senate as an institution. These types are not mutually exclusive. While a Senate majority leader may more often favor one constituency above the others, he demonstrates different leadership styles in different contexts.[28] As such, this research emphasizes the duties, functions, activities, and behaviors of Senate majority leaders to an empirical rather than normative end. No attempt is made to evaluate who is an "effective" or "ineffective" leader or even to explicate criteria for such an appraisal, much less a ranking. In the sense that all Senate majority leaders function as leaders, they all exhibit leadership.

ORGANIZATION OF THE STUDY

As a comprehensive examination of Senate majority leadership, the chapters of this book present a view of Senate majority leaders from becoming leader to being leader. Chapter 2 offers a job description for U.S. Senate majority leaders. As the first full-fledged account of what a majority leader does, it explicates legislative duties, such as scheduling votes, and institutional ones, such as diplomatic receptions and social events. These administrative and managerial tasks represent Senate constraints on Senate majority leadership.

To introduce partisan constraints, chapter 3 presents a discussion of leadership selection. The selection calculus includes factors such as prior leadership and regional balance; media acumen is also a growing requisite. A necessary but not sufficient condition to a senator's selection to majority leadership is ideological placement within his party. Comparison of the ideological placement of candidates in every contested selection of Senate majority leader indicates that successful candidates are median voters within the party caucus. This finding generates competing hypotheses for the behaviors exhibited by leaders that are explored in chapter 4. One hypothesis, based on a projection of ideological convergence, states that a majority leader, if not a middleman at selection, becomes one with leadership; the other is one of divergence, hypothesizing that a majority leader becomes more extreme with leadership. An examination of voting trends of Senate majority leaders from their first Congress, to the Congress immediately prior to selection, to all congresses during their tenure as leader allows for analysis of ideological stability or change. Findings here respond to conventional wisdom and help to overturn conclusions espoused a generation ago. Future leaders begin as median voters in their party, but drift in response to the size of their majority upon becoming leaders.

Chapter 5 presents extra-institutional constraints by the president on Senate majority leadership. The Senate majority leader bears an expectation to serve as presidential broker to the chamber. Heightened under unified government, such a relationship constrains the majority leader from policy innovation and from deviation from the presidential or party agenda. This expectation originates with the position of Senate majority leader, and its continuation evidences the path-dependent evolution of the office.

Chapter 6 emphasizes the dual roles of senator and leader through broad analysis of earmarks designated to a Senate majority leader's state before, during, and after his leadership as well as through targeted case studies of senators Baker and Mitchell. Drawn from archival evidence, these cases demonstrate that leadership induces a transformation in the representative relationship between senator and state. With leadership, the Senate majority leader becomes a patron to his first electoral constituency. Being leader allows him access to resources by which he can provide distributive benefits that states have come to expect.

Chapter 7, by way of summary, provides some observations and conclusions pertaining to a Senate majority leadership constrained by multiple constituencies; it also addresses the ambiguities of an office that informally emerged and developed in response to competing demands and expectations.

CHAPTER 2

INSTITUTIONAL CONSTRAINTS

JOB DESCRIPTION OF SENATE MAJORITY LEADERSHIP

There is in fact not even any fixed and general concept of just what a leader is and just what he *ought* to do, except that when the Senate is in characteristic mood and tone there is general agreement on what he is *not* and what he ought *not* to do. (White, 1957, pp. 95–96)

One cannot draw up for this post a neat list of authorities and prerogatives that describes its power adequately, if not exhaustively, as one can for a place in a tightly structured hierarchy. (Truman, 1959, p. 104)

Senate leadership in the 1980s remains an unformed commodity. Despite certain imperatives, the post still depends largely on the personality and priorities of the individual occupant. (Davidson, 1985, p. 249)

Davos, Switzerland, is a small town in the Alps that derives notoriety once a year in January for hosting a global economic summit. The World

Economic Forum was instituted in 1970 and has consultative status with the United Nations Educational, Scientific, and Cultural Organization (UNESCO). Leaders in government, business, and even Hollywood converge here for a week-long series of panels and talks related to world developments and crises on a range of issues from the economy, to the environment, to the health-care system. In short, it is model cooperation among intergovernmental and nongovernmental organizations. The result is networking and photo opportunities at the highest degree. In 2005 caught among the flashbulbs, was U.S. Senate Majority Leader Bill Frist (R-TN). Senator Frist moderated a panel, entitled "Funding the War on Poverty,"[29] that included entrepreneur and philanthropist Bill Gates, economist Jeffrey Sachs, British Prime Minister Gordon Brown, Italian Finance Minister Domenico Siniscalco, and Tanzanian President Benjamin Mkapa. The audience was no less varied or star studded. Movie actress Sharon Stone, long affiliated with AIDS foundations and research, was in attendance. Before the meeting was concluded, much in revival-style fashion, she rose from her seat and pledged $10,000 to help purchase bed nets that would guard against disease-carrying mosquitoes and challenged others to do the same. Within 10 minutes, $1 million was raised (O'Brien, 2005; Smith, 2005, February 4). In the middle of all the fundraising, news making, debating, and philanthropy was Senator Frist. How the roles and expectations of the Senate majority leader have changed in 90 years; the leader went from being a part of the party caucus, to the well of the Senate, to a player on the world stage, with a genuine Hollywood starlet in the supporting role!

This chapter describes the emergence of the office of Senate majority leader and its subsequent development, highlighting required tasks such as agenda setting and media managing. It is remarkable to observe the constraints of duty that have changed over time, and more importantly, how many of them persist from leader to leader. Together, they amount to a job description for senators who may aspire to becoming the leader of a majority.

The Office Emerges

At the first Senate in 1789, there were 26 members—two senators from each of the 13 colonies turned states. Initial membership was fully a quarter of what it is presently, and this small body reflected and contributed to expectations of individualism, tempered with high-minded collegiality. Processes of thoughtful debate were to yield outcomes for the public good (Haynes, 1938). To that end, the framers left the rules of the Senate to be decided by the body itself and, most notably of all, did not specify a leader, akin to the speaker of the House, to merge individual interests into collective action. The inference of this constitutional omission is that a senator is a senator is a senator and that therefore operations of the upper body would be informally arranged among these egalitarian individuals. And for much of the 19th century, the Senate was indeed guided by these dual principles of individualism and informality (Haynes, 1938).

Committees provided some structure for conducting business. Standing committees were rare at the outset for fear of the formation of powerful factions (Deering & Smith, 1997). Instead, select committees, which had been the norm during the continental congresses, were created and adapted to the new Senate. But ironically, it was not committees that yielded powerful factions but powerful factions, acting as incipient parties, that overtook the committee system.

The emergence of a form of party-based leadership structure was incremental and rooted in the loose formation of party caucuses. Early party caucuses of Jacksonian Democrats and Whigs were no more unified than the floor, and the primary organizational problem they faced was the makeup of committees. In 1833 the Senate voted to elect members to committees rather than allowing the president pro tempore to appoint them, an action prompted by the anti-Jackson coalition majority against the pro-Jackson officer (Gamm & Smith, 2002b).[30] This proved to be a watershed event, for three years later, Jacksonian Democrats, now in the majority, followed precedent as the problem of committee composition plagued both party caucuses. In 1845 four Democrats defected to the

Whig minority and voted to have committees elected by ballot (Hatfield, 1997). Gamm and Smith wrote: "That decision, more than any other single event, created the modern party caucus" (2002b, p. 223). The need for unified action, called for in and out of the Senate by papers such as the *New York Evening Post*, prompted caucuses to meet and assemble committee lists. Soon, the Democratic caucus created a committee on committees, and the Republicans decided to do the same.

Two decades later, Republicans began to use ad hoc steering committees to manage the business of the caucus, and the Democrats soon followed suit. But it was not until 1879 that partisanship officially bled into Senate offices. The Democrats gained control of the chamber for the first time in 20 years and replaced the Senate's secretary and clerk as well as other lower officials, maintaining that such patronage was the purview of the majority party. While the Republicans resisted at the time, they cemented the precedent four years later when they took the helm again (Gamm & Smith, 2002b).

By now, both party caucuses regularized their respective steering committees, both in attempts to corner the electoral advantage—the Republicans to maintain the majority, the Democrats to try to regain. Both committees were charged with organizing a partisan legislative agenda. At this time, however, the parties diverged. The Democratic caucus merged the functions of their committee on committees and the steering committee; the Republicans kept them separate.

It was in the 1890s, under the chairmanships of Nelson Aldrich (R-RI) and Arthur Pue Gorman (D-MD), that these caucus committees became instruments to manage the Senate, and not just vehicles through which the position of floor leader emerged. The position of floor leader developed with the personal, not official, leadership of Gorman and Aldrich. Gamm and Smith (2002b, p. 229) wrote, they "did their work quietly." But as chairs of their respective caucuses, they also chaired their parties' steering committees and, via those, Senate operations. Inwardly, they prodded their party members; outwardly, they negotiated and cooperated to expedite the Senate's business (Gamm & Smith, 2002b). They worked in the cloakrooms, committee rooms, and on the floor. And, by example, the two of them established practices that are still followed today. Both men had become so effective in their unofficial capacities that after Gorman's retirement, journalists and other watchers of the day cemented expectations for continuity in operations by speculating on a successor. At the turn of the 20th century, the Democratic caucus chair was referred to as Senate "minority leader," and by middle of the first decade, references turned to "floor leader" (Gamm & Smith, 2002b). Thomas S. Martin (D-VA) won the first open contest for leader of the Democratic party in 1911. But it was John W. Kern (D-IN) who, in 1913, captured a divided caucus and was first called "majority leader" (Gamm & Smith, 2002b).[31]

Kern both drew from and contributed to expectations for the office. As the first Senate majority leader, his actions established the pattern that others would follow. Successors emulated his strategies, and his failures served as lessons of what not to do. Nearly a century later, the precedents and innovations of Kern's short tenure survive. It is commonplace to find that Lyndon Johnson (D-TX) transformed the office and that Mike Mansfield (D-MT) reversed some Johnsonian changes (Stewart, 1971). But as we shall see, the constraints emphasized in this research—the central ideological position of the leader, the size of his partisan majorities, his inherited obligations to the president—have their origins with the first Senate majority leader and are recurrent factors in becoming and being a leader.

Organizing the Senate

Perhaps the principal purpose of majority-party leadership is to organize the chamber. Most congressional scholars (e.g., Sinclair, 1995) now view leadership in terms of service; that is, leaders serve members or "principals," providing information and other benefits as a coalition that members could not obtain individually. This logic of collective action is best evidenced in the organization of the Senate.[32] At the start of each Congress, the majority leader sponsors an organizing resolution that specifies committee ratios, funds, and staff. The majority party, of course, has control of the chamber and positions a numerical majority on each committee, chaired (usually but not always) by the majority member most senior in years in the Senate.[33] Committee assignments are made in respective partisan committees, the Democratic steering and coordination committee and the Republican committee on committees.

For most of the 20th century, the Democratic leader was also chair of the steering committee, so the leader had ultimate say in who sat where. The power over committee makeup was perhaps the greatest tool in his arsenal, giving him both a carrot and a stick to ensure senators' loyalty to the party. At the same time, however, the power was not universally effective because the norm of seniority prevailed, and the "old bulls" knew their positions were secure in spite of the coaxing of their younger leaders. On the other side of the aisle, the Republican practice of decentralized leadership made the leader a member, but not the chair, of their committee on committees. The leader's control over committee assignments was influential but not absolute. However, after a century of centralization for Democratic leadership and decentralization for the Republicans (Smith & Gamm, 2005), the parties have crossed paths. Beginning with the tenure of George Mitchell (D-ME), the Democrats have opened leadership to their ranks so that, at present, the party leader does not simultaneously chair the steering and coordination committee.

For Republicans, however, their evolution has tended to be one of consolidation, with the effect of giving their leader more power over committee assignments. Each Congress, a committee on committees within the Senate Republican conference makes recommendations to fill vacancies incurred by the last election and any vacancies that occur throughout the upcoming Congress. The leader then has the authority to fill all other vacancies (*Rules*, 2004). Moreover, as a result of party-rule changes adopted in November 2004, the Republican leader has the authority to appoint half of party members on "A" committees—appropriations, armed services, finance, and foreign relations. Others are filled on the basis of seniority among requesters (Ota, 2004). And given the term limits Republicans imposed on themselves during a fit of reform-mindedness in the 1990s,[34] there are more turnovers, and thus more vacancies, for the leader's approval. Republican senators freely granted this power (although moderates demurred), curbing individualism in the name of party unity, to their majority leader, who has another instrument whereby to enforce adherence to party preferences.

The party leader is the single most influential member of his party. Whether or not he chairs the steering or committee on committees, he often has the final say, or at least the final veto, on an assignment. Archival collections of Lyndon Johnson, Mike Mansfield, Howard Baker, and George Mitchell are replete with requests from senators to their leaders to move from one committee to another.[35] And often such requests are worded to express how such an assignment can enable the senator to help his state and, in turn, his party. More than the others, the Johnson collection evidences a greater number of these requests, for Johnson was the ultimate chief, as leader, chairing the Democratic caucus, the policy committee, and the steering committee. His successor, Mike Mansfield, began the trend toward decentralization for the Democrats, and, while he also chaired the steering committee, he charged the committee to vote a slate of assignments so that in the end, his approval was largely pro forma.

These observations fit with findings presented by Scott Frisch and Sean Kelly (2006), who likewise used archival data to examine committee-assignment requests for Democratic leaders from 1953–1994. Their analysis of factors predicting success of senatorial requests found a significant role for leaders among other expected influences, like seniority and ideology. The effects of leadership are not uniform but are tempered by individual leadership style as well as caucus constraints. Thus, the centralized method of the Johnson leadership meant that Johnson exerted more personal influence in the committee-assignment process while Mansfield's decentralization after Johnson was reflected in his "hands-off" approach to committee assignments (Frisch & Kelly, 2006). Both leadership styles were reflective not only of personality differences between the two majority leaders but also of the makeup of their caucuses. The Democratic caucus under Johnson was smaller, at least until 1959, and less fractured. Under Mansfield, Senate Democrats had larger majorities and were more scattered in policy outlook, beginning the "transformation" of the Senate that Sinclair (1989) so cogently describes.

The Senate majority leader fills not just party assignments but also Senate offices. The Senate majority leader is the chief administrative officer of the chamber. He is ultimately responsible for assigning and rearranging office spaces, usually primarily to the satisfaction of his party rather than the opposition. In this administrative role, he nominates the secretary of the Senate, chaplain, sergeant at arms, parliamentarian, and other staff that serve both parties. Although the majority leader selects and nominates them and the entire membership votes on them, these officers are nominally and generally nonpartisan. For the past two decades, however, partisanship has pervaded even these organizational appointments. When the Republicans took control of the Senate in 1981, they ousted Parliamentarian Murray Zweben from his post of six years, under both Mansfield and Robert Byrd (D-WV), and filled the vacancy with his assistant Robert B. Dove (Hook, 1987). Six years later when Democrats regained the majority, Byrd replaced Dove, who joined the staff of then-minority leader Bob Dole (R-KS), with Alan S. Frumin (Hook, 1987). Frumin served until the next partisan turnover in 1995 when the Republicans reappointed Dove. But the partisan switching took a twist in 2001, when Senate Majority Leader Trent Lott (R-MS) dismissed Dove after confrontations over several parliamentary rulings on tax and budget bills. In his place, Lott brought back Frumin with both sides decrying the politicization of the office (Taylor, 2001). While the job of the parliamentarian may be likened to an umpire calling plays (Hook, 1987; Taylor, 2001), the effects of those rulings are the creation of partisan alignments, in that they favor one side or the other. As a result of procedural outcomes carrying partisan effects, filling and refilling the post has become one more tool by which the majority leader can further the majority party's goals.

Setting the Agenda

First and foremost, like successive leaders, Kern sought to control his party's agenda and, in the process, to manage the Senate floor; and like so many leaders to come, he had to do it with the party divided ideologically between progressives and conservatives. But the Democratic legislative program did not originate from John W. Kern. While he managed the agenda, he did not create it.

Unlike leaders before him, such as senators Gorman and Aldrich, Kern did not wield personal power. He did not have a political base from which he derived his power. His activities during his first two years in the Senate were marked with quietude. He introduced only a single public bill—an early version of campaign finance reform, stemming from his failed run for vice president with William Jennings Bryan in 1908. He rarely took the floor, and when he did, it was usually on matters administrative, such as staff organization and pay, rather than political issues. So it is no surprise that as majority leader the Democratic legislative agenda did not come from his hand but was set by President Woodrow Wilson.

For the first time in roughly 20 years, the White House and Congress were under unified Democratic government, and Kern deferred to the president in setting a national program. At the time, this "executive-legislative alliance" was not questioned, and in fact, was planned and supported by a recent influx of Progressive senators: "Never before had the president's party in the Senate intentionally elected a floor leader for the primary purpose of implementing an executive-initiated legislative program" (Munk, 1974, p. 31). While we know virtually nothing from Kern about his perceptions of his role and expectations as leader, as his wife disposed of his papers, we do have evidence that Kern met regularly with Wilson; and, according to his biographer, he often went under the cover of night with explicit instructions to his aides not to publicize his whereabouts (Bowers, 1918).

Clearly, Kern saw no conflict between his activities and the constitutional principle of separation of powers—here was the leader of the Senate, the upper chamber of the legislative branch, receiving and/or seeking legislative directives and discussing strategy with the chief executive, at a time when it was not accepted practice. He served as Wilson's "leader of the House," much as Wilson described party leaders in the British House of Commons in his many works admiring the British cabinet system (Oleszek, 1991). Perhaps, as Lewis Gould (2005) affirmed, Wilson's dominant role in legislative affairs stems from his training as a political scientist and from his extensive research in the workings of legislatures, both here and abroad. In his work *Congressional Government* (1885), he had no dearth of opinions on how Congress should operate. And perhaps Kern's deferential treatment to Wilson stemmed from his quiet, behind-the-scenes working style, or from the fact that after only two years' distance from selection (by Indiana's state legislature), he was still a novice in the Senate, though not in politics, having been a vice-presidential candidate. Whatever precipitated this relationship, the expectation for the majority leader, when he is of the same party as the president, to be the president's "salesman" became so firmly entrenched that it remains today.[36]

However, even if the majority leader shirks responsibility for outlining his party's legislative policies, he is responsible for adjusting them. Adjustments often are products of consultation with individual senators and with party committees. Committees varied in names and titles in the first half of the 20th century, but both parties had codified and standardized a committee structure by 1945. Both the Democratic and Republican policy committees (DPC and RPC) were established by the Legislative Reorganization Act of 1945, and the evolution of policy committees has been of great interest and concern to majority leaders and their closest colleagues. Demands for such agencies were resisted by leaders in the House as well as the Senate, understandably so, because proponents of policy bodies usually were junior members outside "the club" or inner circle of the Senate. Somehow, however, perhaps as an oversight, policy committees survived in the Legislative Reorganization Act of 1945 (Bone, 1956).

Policy committees act as legislative platform committees in which members discuss their partisan agenda and formulate strategies for accomplishing it. Usually, they meet weekly in respective luncheons, presided over by the majority and minority leaders. The majority leader's primary mission, under unified control with the White House, is to sell the president's proposals to his own caucus. Their support is not a given, and negotiations may require as much bargaining and compromise as with the opposition party. On this policy agenda, there is continual adjustment according to the political winds. Support varies, as do strategies for framing the issue to the opposition, to the media, and to the electorate. There is continual updating to moves and countermoves by the minority party.

Policy committees have varied over time in function and power. Democratic leaders at first relegated the innovation to low levels of activity and infrequent meetings. Republican leaders, notably Robert A. Taft (R-OH), co-opted their policy committee and made it a base for personal and coalition agendas in the 80th Congress, 1946–1947. Democratic leaders similarly restricted the committees by taking them over, but differences in party rules concerning the structure and governance of the body have tended to make the Democratic policy committee more powerful than its Republican counterpart. From the inception of the committee, the Democratic majority leader was automatically and simultaneously the chair of the DPC; and the staff of the leader staffed the DPC as well (Petersen, 2009), thus binding loyalty and offering "personalized service to the leader rather than provision of service to all Democratic members" (Baumer, 1992).[37] This body gave the leader great clout in formulating official party positions on issues. Gradually, however, both parties supplemented the staffs of standing committees and delegated individual senators to meet the demands of media innovations. In due course, the policy-committee apparatus became unimportant to the leader's public advocacy (Bone, 1958). Moreover, not until Lyndon Johnson had the dual authority of majority leader and chair of the policy committee was the latter position fully exploited; in the post-Johnson era, there was a concerted effort to make the DPC more representative of Democrats as a party. There was also less of an inducement for the majority leader to use the panel to achieve his goals and to break up the majority leader's consolidated grip by selecting another member as chair of the DPC.[38]

George Mitchell, for the first time, altered the leadership structure of the DPC when, upon his selection as majority leader, he appointed Senator Tom Daschle (D-SD) to co-chair with himself (Kelly, 1995a). The change was said to be a relaxing of the traditional hold by his predecessor, Robert Byrd; but with the Daschle appointment, he rewarded the senator for his help in organizing the freshmen bloc to get Mitchell selected leader. Daschle continued the practice by appointing Harry Reid (D-NV) as co-chair when Daschle was selected to succeed Mitchell as leader.[39] And, when Reid assumed Daschle's place as party head after his electoral defeat, he chose Byron Dorgan (D-ND) as chair, ending the bifurcated leadership of the committee. With this move in 2005, the Democratic leader abdicated official control of the policy committee, signaling to party members a more open structure. Homogeneous party membership made this decentralization possible.

What once was a fractured caucus, requiring tight control to unify on key issues (e.g. Democrats in the Johnson era), is now more cohesive than any time in a century, affording the leader the freedom to cede control without splintering his caucus. The breakdown of the hierarchical structure of the DPC has made the committee emerge as an arm of the party rather than the arm of the leader; the distinction is subtle but important when assessing constraints on the majority leader. As the structure of the DPC decentralized, the functions of the committee were revitalized and recentralized, creating "nurturing consensus among Democrats, building public support for Democratic policies by developing message strategies...and publicizing Democratic accomplishments" (Kelly, 1995a, p. 134). In times of party cohesion, these functions have the appearance of collective leadership, but the enhanced role of the DPC has "established a centralizing mechanism" (Kelly, 1995a, pp. 134–135) that further limits the discretion of the leader and thus introduces a further constraint on his power.

Unlike its Democratic counterpart, the Republican party organization historically has been dispersed with the leader prohibited from chairing any party committees. This has, at times, left a Republican majority leader without the necessary power to accomplish the party's legislative priorities. The Republican policy committee hosts weekly luncheons for all their membership in which the majority leader provides updates on legislative issues.

Beyond the official charge to express party policy preferences, policy committees currently function in this media age to supply information to their party membership and beyond. There is a research arm of the committees to conduct polls, calculations, and general fact finding for each legislative proposal to be considered. This information is then neatly packaged and graphically represented in concise pamphlets and distributed to party members. And especially before each vote, each party member is given a "scorecard" providing pertinent information related to bill number, timing, party position, and even talking points to discuss with the media and/or constituents afterward. The RPC has activated an in-house cable channel where members and staff can stay attuned to current legislative status. In these ways, policy committees are storehouses of information for members—information that otherwise would be cost-prohibitive to obtain—and therefore, they help to solve the collective action problems of a party coalition.

Managing the Floor

While he was not innovative in creating policy, Kern instituted practices whereby the leader tries to persuade and promote policy, and these are established expectations that survive today. The majority leader's primary duty to the Senate is to schedule floor business; the majority leader's primary duty to his majority is to schedule such business in a way that furthers his party's agenda. Scheduling, then, requires strategic behavior. It is more than the job of clerks, for the ordering of bills and proposals can help determine their outcomes. In the words of a pioneer student of agenda formation: "The shape of an agenda influences the choices made from it...Making agendas seem just about as significant as actually passing legislation" (Riker, 1993, p. 1). Unlike its counterpart in the House of Representatives, the Senate rules committee does not function to organize and shepherd bills. And in his capacity of scheduler, the Senate majority leader acts as a one-man rules committee. It is the leader who may prod the assigned standing committee to report it or table it favorably for his party's advantage. It is the leader who, once the bill comes out of committee, schedules it on the calendar and subsequently calls it off the calendar to the floor.

The majority leader, by necessity, works in close consultation with the minority leader in this function. No leader wants to be surprised; complete information reduces uncertainty and makes for more favorable outcomes. So, the leader shares and gleans information regarding votes and vote counts with the other party. This sharing of information is particularly necessary in a supermajoritarian institution (Sinclair, 2001b) where the rules of the Senate, namely those concerning the filibuster and cloture, demand a three-fifths vote for action.[40] Leaders rarely have ruled a filibuster-proof majority, so their capacity for majority leadership is limited by the need to carve away a couple, or as many as 10, votes from the minority.

In later congresses, these administrative tasks of the leader have been primarily handled by unanimous consent agreements (UCAs). Gould (2005) credited Lyndon Johnson with using UCAs so frequently that they became routine. Like the rules assigned by the House rules committee to accompany bills, these are agreements hammered out by the majority and minority leaders, in consultation with interested senators; although in earlier years, individual senators themselves negotiated and prepared UCAs. These vary in specificity—some outlining the number and types of amendments, as well as the length for debate. UCAs act as precloture; by setting terms for debate, they limit the possibilities for filibusters and may preclude them by setting dates for votes (Oleszek, 2007; Watkins & Riddick, 1964). The rise of obstructionism in the Senate (Evans & Lipinski, 2005), not only outright in the form of filibusters but also in the hidden form of holds, or nonpublic signals from individual members to party leaders that they seek to block floor action on a specified bill (Evans & Lipinski, 2005; Sinclair, 2005), has created inducements for the leader to bargain out differences before bringing measures to the floor.

Before scheduling a bill, with or without a UCA, the Senate majority leader typically consults with the presidential liaison if he is of the same party. Or, it may be oftentimes that the president consults first with the leader to ensure a coordinated campaign for or against the proposal. As the executive has gained in power, in part a result of "going public" (Kernell, 2006), the leaders' scheduling or not scheduling is as much a function of external politics, such as public opinion and White House plans, as internal politics. The leader times the Senate calendar according to public sentiment. If an issue is particularly salient, the leader may press ahead and call the bill. If not, he can avoid a vote until later in the session, or even the next Congress to keep it alive.

The leader uses scheduling not only to further party success but also to arrange opposition defeats. Calling a minority party bill that is sure to fail can be as important as passing a piece of his party's legislation. And putting up for vote a party initiative that is popular with its electoral base but baits the opposition to filibuster enables the leader to frame the minority as obstructionist. Majority Leader Frist employed this tactic during heated debates over some of President Bush's judicial nominations during the 109th Congress. Such strategic scheduling is, in effect, a variant of "position-taking" (Mayhew, 1974), in which the majority leader forces senators to take sides on a vote, with the hope that his position and timing benefit his party to the detriment of the opposition.

Mobilizing the Majority

Before, but especially after, a leader has a working calendar, he begins the process of mobilizing his members for the vote. At this point, the leader, as chief information officer, is on exhibition. Senate Majority Leader Howard Baker created an office to consolidate this information and make it available to members.[41] The papers of George Mitchell showed evidence of refinement with weekly bulletins prepared by the Democratic policy committee listing the bills being considered that week along with summaries of each, and the party line for all. As policy committees have added presidential preferences to independently generated bills, they now serve more as information sites, producing pamphlets and disseminating information via their large staff to members regarding their party and even personal state interests.

The job of mobilization entails more than making sure the members know when and where to show up. It also means making it worth their while to show up. At this point, personal leadership skills come into play. Oftentimes the leader meets privately with interested members to ensure their support or opposition if that is how the bill is framed. He can cajole or deal; the "power of persuasion" (Neustadt, 1960) is not limited to the president. The leader works by both indulgence and deprivation, using either a carrot of pledged support or a stick of withdrawn support from the member's upcoming sponsored legislation (Ripley, 1969a). The leader has an extensive whip system, first created by Kern in 1913 (Gould, 2005) to "count noses" and keep a running tally of where the votes are on each issue, but sometimes the leader can persuade when no other can. Kern found his fellow Democrats "balky and hard to manage" (Gould, 2005, p. 59). A half-century later, Howard Baker likened majority leadership to "herding cats" (Annis, 1995), a description Trent Lott (2005) adopted and further analogized to "keeping frogs in a wheelbarrow" (Cloud, 1996).

Campaigning and Fundraising

Among the most visible acts of majority leaders are campaigning and fundraising to keep and enlarge their majority. While this role has taken on new significance in current times of burgeoning campaign expenses, Lyndon Johnson, as party leader, traveled around the country before the 1954 elections, dispensing cash to Democratic candidates (Caro, 2002). Both George Mitchell and Bill Frist used their respective party campaign committees (Kolodny, 1998) as a stepping stone to party leader, and their stints as chairmen no doubt were an advantage to them, providing beneficial experience that could be applied to leadership. The majority party leader is the highest-ranking and, thus, most visible face in the Senate and carries much weight in appealing to partisan voters, especially activists, donors, and lobbyists.

The majority leader may even help recruit candidates to run for his party, and he has assumed an obligation to travel and speak out on behalf of its candidates, assuring voters in the state that "X" is "someone I can work with in the Senate." On these campaign travels, he hosts fundraisers, breakfasts, lunches, and dinners to raise money for the candidate. The leader also works in tandem with his party's senatorial campaign committee and also with individual senators to loosen the purse strings on their personal political action committees (PACs) and dole out funds to needy races.

In 2004 Senate Majority Leader Frist made headlines when he, in his regular fundraising newsletter, identified his counterpart Tom Daschle as a "must defeat" candidate in the election cycle. He wrote of Daschle's vulnerabilities and pleaded for funds to turn the race in favor of his opponent, John Thune (R-SD), a novice from the House of Representatives. Majority and minority leaders had typically refrained from targeting each other directly, at least so openly. Media were eager to report Frist's treatment of Daschle (e.g., Hulse, 2004), and Senate Pro Tempore Emeritus Robert Byrd quickly pointed out that as majority leader he never would have besieged Howard Baker. Moreover, Frist did not end with fundraising. He made a personal trip to South Dakota to declare his support for Thune and drew even more fire from the media and from Democrats for this "unprecedented" move. However, archival data show that the majority leader as campaigner, even against his chief rival in the Senate, is not without precedent. Byrd obviously overlooked a legislative memo sent to Democratic senators identifying, among other electoral speculations, Senate Majority Leader Baker as a possible target for defeat in the next election cycle because members of the incoming class of conservatives were likely to question Baker's ideological credentials.[42] A newsletter put out by then-Senate Majority Leader George Mitchell, not long before his retirement from leadership and the Senate in 1994, revealed that his resignation was partly related to the massive campaign operations Republicans, Bob Dole included, had planned to try to unseat him (Campbell, 1993). After losing a naval base in Maine during the last Base Realignment and Closure (BRAC) round, he felt vulnerable and chose to exit the Senate rather than face a tough campaign. Frist's efforts against Daschle may have been personal, may have been a sign of the further polarization of parties in the Senate, and may have been the latest sign of the decline of comity and senatorial courtesy, but it was not unprecedented, except for the visit to the opponent's home state. And we can be sure that the favor will be repaid, not to Frist, who completed a self-imposed term limit in 2006, but to future Republican majority leaders.

Speaking for the Party

As evidenced by the unprecedented resignation of Robert Byrd from the office of majority leader at the end of the 100th Congress,[43] the role of party spokesman has been increasingly important for majority leaders. As the importance of media has grown in politics, so has the expectation for leaders to be effective at using the media to communicate chamber and party stances.[44] Douglas Harris (1998) wrote of the changing nature of the speakership to become more public. As context changed, so too did members' expectations for more public leadership (Harris, 1998). For the task of spokesman, much like the president, the leader has a press secretary and an entire press office to maximize coverage when he wants it and neutralize it when he does not. Having too many voices for the party diffuses rather than compounds the message. As Robert Taft said upon becoming leader, "You can't have a lot of fellows running down to the White House and then coming back to the Senate to speak for the president. That voice has got to be one voice" (Gould, 2005, p. 211). So the majority leader is the single most important voice for articulating chamber and party plans and policies. And more than any other individual senator, he can command media attention at will. Speaking in sound bites, distilling complicated policy matters and intricate rules of proceedings into 30-second nuggets is a virtual requirement for the job.

The role of party spokesman varies in times of unified and of divided government. When the Senate majority leader is in the same party as the president, the majority leader must speak the message set by the White House;[45] but in times of divided government, the Senate majority leader bears responsibility not only to speak but to create the party line. The Senate majority leader as party spokesman is shaped by whether or not the speaker of the House belongs to the same party as well as the level of the speaker's activity before the media. With unified party control of both chambers, and especially with a vocal speaker, the Senate majority leader may have to compete with the speaker for the role of party spokesman. To whatever degree he is constrained by president and speaker, the Senate majority leader must speak for the Senate but also the party line.

Engaging the media to his party's advantage first requires the leader to tell the issue in a way that is at once understandable to the average voter and framed so that his party's position seems the most logical and beneficial. In short, he points out the benefits of his solution and the costs of the opposition. The majority leader speaks for his party in a variety of formats according to season (election year or not), according to issue ("hard" or "easy"[46]), and according to personal preference and demeanor (the flowery oratory of Robert Byrd versus the one-word responses of Mike Mansfield).[47] The majority leader may give speeches or interviews or write editorials.[48] But in recent years, the leader's regular method of communication is on the Sunday morning talk-show circuit. Television is perhaps the quickest and most efficient method for reaching elites, those with high levels of political interest and therefore knowledge, both in government and in the electorate. And, of course, the advent of C-SPAN has given leaders daily access to cameras whenever the Senate convenes.

However, majority leaders also have been innovative in creating opportunities for press coverage. Lyndon Johnson held what came to be known as "dugouts." These were 10- to 15-minute press conferences situated by his desk in the well of the chamber before the beginning of each day's events. The practice continues off and on, with varying regularity, according to personality and leadership style. Tom Daschle tried to replicate Johnson's ritual, and both he and Trent Lott, during their leadership, met regularly with press in a conference room just off the Senate floor. Bill Frist convened the press corps, with a bank of microphones and recorders, in a Senate hallway to give statements and accept questions after key events on the floor. Lott did the same regularly after the Republican policy committee luncheon each Tuesday.

Most recent innovations include Web sites created to communicate with multiple audiences. The majority leader has his personal Web site, as does every other senator, which serves as a basic tool of communication to his state constituents. It provides pertinent information about office locations along with instructions for contacting appropriate offices and departments. But the majority leader also sponsors a Web site for the party that links the various components of the leadership hierarchy (from the conference to the policy committee and beyond) and summarizes current issues of interest. Since the Web site user must be the one to initiate and seek out the information, these Web sites serve to speak primarily to highly interested partisans.

In this political climate, not only the president, but also other political actors benefit from "going public," or gaining advantage by presenting their cases to the public through the media and challenging the opposition to respond (Kernell, 2006). Public opinion is now so influential that the majority leader also uses the media to marshal public sentiment to his side as a way to negate the minority or perhaps even the president. In so doing the leader must not only get his message out but he also must formulate strategies to ensure maximized reception of his message. That may mean creating or changing conditions if they are not presently ripe. Or he may simply wait for the tide to turn in his favor.

By 2005, the trend in media strategy was to form party task forces, dubbed "the war rooms." First formed by the Democrats at the beginning of the 109th Congress, this method is based on and named for a similar organization used in presidential campaigns. The minority leader brought together about 20 staff members under the leadership of about half a dozen senators and charged them with preparing strategies, talking points, and responding to President Bush and the newly expanded Republican majority. This rapid-response operation, called the Senate Democratic Communications Center, acts as a permanent "war room," anticipating and reacting to Republican actions. Its purpose is to hone and unify the party message as well as sharpen its delivery.

Despite what its name may suggest, the structure is not transient; the center is fully established under communications and staff directors, both of whom are seasoned media aides tried in the heat of presidential campaigns. In addition, the center has a specialist devoted to Internet coverage and a blogger to post daily messages of party perspectives on current issues. The center became all the more focused, first, when overhauling Social Security topped President Bush's and Senate Majority Leader Frist's agenda, and yet again, when the debate over judicial nominations came to the forefront. The effort was so successful that soon Republicans were holding their own "bull sessions" to try to win back the public relations tug-of-war, noting, however, "having a war room inside the Capitol is unprecedented" (Bolton, 2005). And two months later, Senate Majority Leader Frist announced the formation of a new Republican task force "whose mission is to help define the GOP's agenda and message in the coming months" (Preston, 2005).

The GOP task force started much like the Democratic center did, under the direction of a handful of senators, notable among them former Senate Majority Leader Trent Lott. It was planned to buttress the existing press operations of the Senate Republican conference and to focus on issues that may have gotten sidetracked in the recent hoopla of the "nuclear option," such as energy, health care, and, of course, Social Security. History leaves us with little doubt that such an operation will become institutionalized in light of initial success and the burgeoning role of the media in political life.

NETWORKING WITH ELITES

As functional head of the Senate, the majority leader also has expectations to maintain a presence at certain social affairs. Lyndon Johnson was a regular at parties hosted by Katherine Graham, publisher of the *Washington Post* and doyenne of the Washington social scene (Graham, 2002). Mike Mansfield, as terse as he was in the press and on the floor, also made the rounds at black-tie affairs.[49] And Howard Baker's daily schedule cards show a marked increase in diplomatic functions and ambassadorial meetings after he became majority leader.[50] For Bill Frist, his social interests as majority leader were not limited to the Georgetown circuit but were global. There was the appearance at Davos in January 2005, and once he became majority leader, the physician continued his annual trips to impoverished areas of Africa to provide medical care and surgeries. As majority leader, however, his trips took on greater significance, no doubt aided by greater press coverage.

While the vice president is the titular head of the Senate, the majority leader is more prominently linked to the body. He may be the voice of his party, but he is the face of the Senate, and as such, he has certain duties to represent the Senate from the not-so-casual reception to a state dinner. While others may accompany him, he is the head of any congressional delegation. Frist showcased multiple demands on a majority leader when, upon the death of Pope John Paul II, he had to lead a delegation to Rome and also to select which senators were to fill a designated number of seats for the trip. He did so in consultation with the minority leadership and according to religious affiliation. At the papal funeral, he appeared with the president and a delegation from the House, and we saw evidence of the majority leader fulfilling not only legislative but also social obligations.

These affairs, while seemingly distant from his work within the Senate, may be equally as important as his legislative and partisan operations. Such appearances are networking at the highest degree. At these dinners, meetings, and receptions, he is able to communicate with other members of the elite, at once picking up and floating trial balloons to legislative plans. And oftentimes, the media will give more coverage to such events than to a regular speech on the Senate floor. Fulfilling this expectation, then, becomes a way by which the leader meets a more demanding responsibility—crafting and expressing a partisan message and learning details (read: gossip) that can aid him in strategizing legislative maneuvers.

Conclusions

The job of majority leader is varied. It may carry him from the well of the Senate to the halls of the Vatican. The influence of the majority leader lies, first, in his task to set the agenda. Scheduling votes, by way of order, oftentimes controls outcomes. Never mind that by the time a bill reaches the majority leader it is a circumscribed proposal that has survived a larger set of "feasible" alternatives—mostly never seriously regarded and only "considered" alternatives. These alternatives are mostly rejected, leaving a limited, narrow, small set of "admissible" alternatives for the majority leader to manage and among which the Senate may choose (Riker, 1993, p. 2). The leader's influence stems also from his ability to command media attention. The effects are cross-cutting to be sure, in that unwanted media attention can be as damaging as positive coverage is advantageous; but more than any other senator, the majority leader can capture an audience to express his party's side of an issue.

If a job description were to be posted for the office, it would require a majority leader to: manage, if not create, an agenda; mobilize a coalition behind it; create a strategy for passing it with scheduling finesse or parliamentary maneuvering; sell it to the public through the media; and promote it to elites most likely at some social occasion. And the job description would detail the importance of following these procedures almost daily, continually adjusting and updating strategies based on current political context, and for every issue. All the while, the majority leader performs these tasks to his greatest partisan advantage since he is responsible for basic Senate administration and maintenance. These managerial tasks of the office of majority leader reflect institutional constraints activated by the leader's Senate constituency. Moreover, not only do these tasks constrain majority leaders in being leader, but they also affect the criteria for becoming leader.

CHAPTER 3

PARTY CONSTRAINTS

SELECTION OF SENATE MAJORITY LEADERS

> Campaigning for a leadership post is an exercise in retail politics. Issues count for little, subtle leadership skills are prized, and friendships can be invaluable. (Doherty & Langdon, 1996, p. 1361)
>
> The race for majority leader is as intimate and uplifting as a New England town meeting; as bloody and conspiratorial as dinner at the Borgias. (Rogers, 1984, p. 1)

A generation ago, Robert Peabody's (1967, 1976) work on leadership selection in Congress recognized the dependent nature of leadership on the leader. He also justified the importance of focusing on who fills those offices and how they are chosen. He specifically studied alterations in party leadership under conditions of interparty change (turnover from majority to minority status), intraparty change (replacement of incumbent leaders), and congressional reform (creation of new or revision of existing offices) (Peabody, 1976, p. 10). Among his "narrative case histories" (p. 11) describing these different paths to leadership, Peabody distinguished leaders in the House and leaders in the Senate only by providing case studies from each chamber, and he did not conceptually distinguish between contests for lower-level leadership offices (whips) and heads of party (minority and majority leaders). That pattern has since varied with particular emphases on the speaker (Green, 2004, 2008), House majority leader (Green, 2008), and whip (Harris, 2006), but the familiar focus on the House remains. Scholars have examined House leadership selection on both individual (Green, 2006; Harris, 2006; Oppenheimer & Peabody, 1977) and factoral (Green, 2008; Green & Harris, 2007; Harris & Nelson, 2008; Nelson, 1977) levels of analysis.

While scholars have studied in great detail leadership contests in the House, no comparable study exists on the selection of Senate majority leaders. To be sure, Sean Kelly (1995b), based on his participant observation as American Political Science Association Congressional Fellow with the Democratic policy committee, has provided unique insight into the selection of Senator Tom Daschle (D-SD) as Democratic leader in the 104th Congress. That treatment alone in recent years sheds light on the leadership-selection processes in the Senate. The scholarly neglect of the Senate, especially the unique role of the Senate majority leader, is perhaps understandable. Peabody wrote his work during the apex of Mike Mansfield's (D-MT) lengthy tenure as leader of the Senate. Mansfield had been "promoted" to the office from whip after Lyndon Johnson (D-TX) became vice president and had, by the time of Peabody's writing, served 15 years as majority leader—the longest, then and now, continuous service as leader. At the time, there had been only two cases of contested "selections" for Senate majority leader, leaving us with few generalizations about what it takes to fill the position except that selections had usually been uncontested.

Since then, there have been contested selections for both Republican and Democratic majority leaders (see table 3.1). Beyond that, we have experienced a heretofore unprecedented challenge to a sitting majority leader.[51] And beyond that, we have witnessed the resignation of a Senate majority leader and his replacement, selected, according to conventional wisdom among both reporters and scholars (e.g., Bumiller, 2002; Oppenheimer, 2005a), by persons in the White House and not the Senate.[52] Much has transpired in the selections of Senate majority leaders, with the primary development being that selections are increasingly contested. Contested selections mean we can infer from the challengers and the job description outlined in the previous chapter certain qualifications for majority leadership of the upper chamber. The tasks required of the job suggest the criteria on which senators choose a majority leader; thus, what we know about the duties of the office can enlighten us to the types of men chosen to fill the office. The job description applied to specific contests provides a clearer picture of why some senators are selected to lead the majority and others are not.

This chapter addresses contested selections in greater detail, highlighting both antecedents and precedents. From these cases, which reflect the universe of contested selections of Senate majority leader, some recognized pathways to majority leadership are apparent. Thus, it is possible to elucidate some prerequisites for majority leadership, noting that the weight of each criterion varies with institutional, partisan, and personal contexts. The result is the first comprehensive outline of the making of a Senate majority leader.

How a Senator Becomes Majority Leader

The campaign for leadership in many ways resembles any other campaign for office. Usually after an initial "nose count" to make sure he has enough base support to give him a chance, a senator announces his intentions to seek a leadership post. And oftentimes, a significant number of pledges are enough to stave off any competition.[53] On at least one occasion, the candidate for leadership gained support by forming a ticket with another senator to be his running mate for whip. Mitch McConnell (R-KY), assistant leader under Majority Leader Trent Lott (R-MS), agreed to remain in his post to support Bill Frist's (R-TN) 2002 candidacy as majority leader and thus perhaps provided a precedent-setting tactic for future would-be majority leaders.

The nose counting continues throughout the contest as the senator works to build momentum going into balloting. He makes his case by calling in individual favors, and in recent years, there has been a trend of campaigning before subgroups, such as freshmen, in the Senate. These events are part old-fashioned stump speech, part job interview as the candidate makes his case for selection and entertains questions. Bloc voting is an especially effective way for smaller groups to have their voice heard when individuals might not. In the race to replace Robert Byrd (D-WV) in 1989, the 11 freshman Democrats who were elected in 1988 interviewed candidates Daniel Inouye (D-HI), Bennett Johnston (D-LA), and George Mitchell (D-ME). They gave their support en masse to Mitchell after he promised to be more inclusive in the leadership ranks than his predecessors. He fulfilled his pledge right away by appointing one of their organizers, freshman Tom Daschle, as co-chair with himself of the Democratic policy committee.

Formal procedures are similar for both parties. On the day of balloting, the entire party meets in conference without press or other recorders of the proceedings. The meeting opens with supporters of the candidates giving nominating and seconding speeches. After an official nomination, the candidates themselves make remarks for one last minute push for votes, and then voting begins on secret ballots that are color-coded by round. Balloting proceeds in rounds as the candidate who pulls in the fewest votes is dropped in the subsequent cycle. The winner is the first candidate to obtain a majority of the caucus.

For most of the century, these proceedings were pro forma as majority leaders came by promotion or otherwise without challenge and were elected by acclamation. The earliest exception was in 1937 after the sudden death of Joe Robinson (D-AR).[54] Jockeying to replace him began on the funeral train from Washington, DC, to his home in Little Rock, Arkansas (Ritchie, 1991, p. 127). In the end, Alben Barkley (D-KY) won the votes to replace him over Pat Harrison (D-MS), finance committee chair, in the first of two contested ballots for Senate majority leader in 50 years. And in 1951, the Democratic caucus chose Ernest McFarland (D-AZ) over Joseph C. O'Mahoney (D-WY) by a margin of 30–19 (McMillan, 2004). Not until 1984, when Howard Baker (R-TN) retired and opened up a five-way race for his replacement, did balloting occur for a Republican majority leader. Four years later, the Democrats held the contest among three senators to replace Robert Byrd.

These procedures are not as straightforward as they seem, for they are not played out in the public eye but are "confined to the intricate maze of offices, subways, hallways, and hide-a-ways that constitute the Byzantine world of Senate politics" (Kelly, 1995b, p. 1). An aide to former Majority Leader Byrd described the selection process this way: "It has the most to do with relationships and a level of trust" (Hager & Hook, 1994). Still, the selection of Senate majority leaders is more than a popularity contest, and there are identifiable factors beyond "trust" in the decision-making process of leadership selection.

Factors in Leadership Selection

This analysis focuses on the only six contested elections for Senate majority leader as listed in table 3.1.

Using both reporting in the moment and analyses since, I examined these races for the prevalence of certain factors that seem, to varying degrees, to affect the decision making in the selection of majority leader. Not all factors are evident in every contest; instead, factors appear with contexts both endogenous and exogenous to the Senate. Moreover, factors other than those discussed surely are present, but these criteria reflect recurring themes common to contest selections.

Ideology

Among factors contributing to the selection of Senate majority leaders, an obvious influence would be ideology; after all, the fundamental task of the Senate majority leader is to lead the majority party in the Senate. Ideology implies a continuum of predictable positions or preferences or a set of issues held by voters, in this case senators (following Poole & Rosenthal, 1997). Conventionally speaking, positions range from left to right or from liberal or progressive to moderate to conservative (Freeden, 2003). To measure ideological placement of senators, I relied on first-dimension DW-NOMINATE scores, widely accepted indicators that are

TABLE 3.1. Contested selections for U.S. Senate majority leader.

Year	Party	Candidates	To replace
1937	Democratic	*Alben W. Barkley (KY)* Pat Harrison (MS)	Joseph T. Robinson (AR), deceased
1951	Democratic	*Ernest W. McFarland (AZ)* Joseph C. O'Mahoney (WY)	Scott Lucas (IL), defeated
1984	Republican	*Robert J. Dole (KS)* Pete Domenici (NM) Richard Lugar (IN) James McClure (ID) Ted Stevens (AK)	Howard H. Baker, Jr. (TN), retired from Senate
1988	Democratic	Daniel Inouye (HI) J. Bennett Johnston (LA) *George J. Mitchell (ME)*	Robert C. Byrd (WV), resigned from majority leadership
1994*	Democratic	*Thomas A. Daschle (SD)* Christopher J. Dodd (CT)	George J. Mitchell (ME), retired from Senate
1996	Republican	Thad Cochran (MS) *C. Trent Lott (MS)*	Robert J. Dole (KS), retired from Senate to run for president

Note. Successful candidates appear in italics.
*Democrats had a majority when Mitchell announced his retirement before the 1994 elections, but Republicans gained control of the Senate in those elections and ensured Daschle served as minority not majority leader. However, Daschle campaigned for majority leader, so his selection is included here.

comparable over time (Poole & Rosenthal, 1997). As an ideological requisite, members appear to want a majority leader in the party mainstream (see table 3.2).

The role of ideology was not a significant factor in the very first contest for Senate majority leader. The death of Majority Leader Robinson came at the height of a divisive battle in American politics—Democrats in the Senate, led by Robinson, were divided over President Franklin Roosevelt's "court-packing" plan. The strain proved to be too much for Robinson, who succumbed to a fatal heart attack the evening following a particularly bitter debate on the Senate floor. The contest to fill his position immediately took shape with the candidates restraining themselves and

TABLE 3.2. Ideological comparison of candidates for contested selections.

Candidate	DW-NOMINATE Score	Party Median
Alben W. Barkley (D-KY)	−0.375	−0.182
Pat Harrison (D-MS)	−0.401	
Ernest W. McFarland (D-AZ)	−0.209	−0.192
Joseph C. O'Mahoney (D-WY)	−0.244	
Robert J. Dole (R-KS)	0.303	0.273
Ted Stevens (R-AK)	0.149	
Richard A. Lugar (R-IN)	0.347	
Pete Domenici (R-NM)	0.229	
James D. McClure (R-ID)	0.578	
George J. Mitchell (D-ME)	−0.391	−0.354
Daniel Inouye (D-HI)	−0.367	
J. Bennett Johnston (D-LA)	−0.150	
Thomas A. Daschle (D-SD)	−0.397	−0.361
Christopher Dodd (D-CT)	−0.414	
C. Trent Lott (R-MS)	0.471	0.347
Thad Cochran (R-MS)	0.286	

Note. Successful candidates appear in italics. Scores are for the Congress immediately preceding selection.

power brokers lobbying for their selection (Ritchie, 1991). Alben Barkley emerged as the candidate for the moderate liberals and Pat Harrison as representative of the Southern conservatives. Ideology seemed to play little role in the public debates between the two, and their DW-NOMINATE scores show Barkley and Harrison crossing voting paths just as the contest was taking shape—Barkley grew more liberal as Harrison slightly moderated. Although a Southern Democrat, Harrison was no archconservative; scores covering his career varied from −0.476 to −0.401. Barkley, on the other hand, fluctuated during his preleadership career from −0.321 to −0.375. Relatively speaking, Barkley was the mainstream candidate in the race.

In the second contested selection of Senate majority leader, ideology played a prominent if not decisive role. Scott Lucas (D-IL) was the first sitting Senate majority leader to be turned out of office by his state electorate.[55] He had served only two years as majority leader but was targeted in a McCarthy-era election and defeated by Everett McKinley Dirksen (R-IL), who soon would lead the Republicans in the minority for a decade. For the leadership vacancy, Richard Russell's (D-GA) name was floated only to be taken out of contention by Russell himself who recognized that formal leadership would only draw attention to a Southern caucus that heretofore had flourished as a breakaway, or "blocking" (Riker, 1962), rather than mainstream coalition (McMillan, 2004). Russell himself chose McFarland in what was widely surmised as a "conservative tactic of using a cooperative moderate" (McMillan, 2004, p. 197). At the Democratic caucus on January 2, 1951, Russell and a majority coalition of Southerners and Westerners, including Carl Hayden (D-AZ) and Bob Kerr (D-OK), drafted McFarland for the vote. At the last moment, liberals put forth their own candidate, O'Mahoney, whose DW-NOMINATE scores (−0.244 at balloting) show him drifting toward, if not fully ensconced, in the liberal faction. McFarland, on the other hand, had moved rightward over the course of his career to be positioned at −0.201 when he was selected. McFarland appears to have been elected and O'Mahoney defeated on the assumption that the latter was more liberal than he actually was. To the extent ideology played a role in the fronting of these candidates and subsequent balloting, it was as a proxy war between competing factions in the Democratic party.

Although his race to be majority leader never came to an official ballot, the selection of Robert Byrd is an example of the intermittent relevance of ideology. Byrd's ascension to majority leader after Mike Mansfield retired was billed as a return to the mainstream (Hook, 1988). In 1977 Byrd, who earlier had successfully challenged Edward M. Kennedy (D-MA) for the whip position, sought to fill Mansfield's chair. The alternatives to Byrd were, again, Kennedy and Hubert H. Humphrey (D-MN). Both were leaders, though unofficial, in the liberal wing of the Democratic party. While Kennedy withdrew his name (in the face of personal scandal, he counted noses and came up short), Humphrey stayed in until "selection day," but facing a tougher fight than he had expected and battling an illness that soon would claim him, Humphrey withdrew on the day of balloting. Byrd was chosen without challenge and by acclamation.

The race to replace retiring Majority Leader Howard Baker was the first contested election in over 30 years, and the first ever among Republican senators, and it ushered in a new norm of contested leadership races as the decades that followed witnessed four sequential challenges. Bob Dole's (R-KS) selection in 1984 was a victory for the moderate wing of the Republican party (Granat, 1984; Rogers & Shribman, 1984). In the presidential-nominating convention earlier that year, Dole and others were pushed aside in the platform committee. But when it came time to replace Baker, himself a party moderate, Senate Republicans showed a different face of the party. They chose Dole and filled the slate of other supporting leadership roles with the likes of John Chafee (R-RI) and John Heinz (R-PA). Moreover, the first candidate to drop on the initial ballot was James McClure (R-ID), the most conservative with scores (0.583) more than double the party mean; Senator Pete Domenici (R-NM), with a score of 0.232, was the next to fall, and although Richard Lugar (R-IN), just beginning his second term, had moderated from 0.363 to 0.339, he dropped on the third round. Dole's closest competitor was Ted Stevens (R-AK), whose voting behavior was even more moderate (0.160) than Dole's (0.311) but perhaps too much so, having begun two terms earlier at 0.084.

Four years later, in the first Democratic race to come to a vote since Ernest McFarland was designated to succeed Scott Lucas in 1951, Democrats chose a new majority leader at the retirement of Robert Byrd. George Mitchell, Daniel Inouye, and Bennett Johnston announced as candidates for the post. Each was distinct and brought his base of support. Inouye, the most senior of the three, was billed as the "institutional man," who would continue the traditional leadership style of Byrd (Elving, 1988). His ideological leanings (−0.360) were somewhat to the left of the party and so he appealed to the "old bulls" and liberal bloc. Mitchell also was left-leaning ideologically (−0.403) and roughly matched Inouye. Johnston was different still—he was chair of the energy and natural resources committee and had become influential on the powerful appropriations committee, dominating two subcommittees (Elving, 1988). Ideologically (−0.159), he was further from the Democratic mean (−0.332) than either of his two opponents, with a base of Southerners and conservatives. Inouye was the better ideological fit with the party, yet at balloting, the caucus gave Mitchell 27 votes on the first ballot, one shy of a majority of the 55 members. After Inouye and Johnston tied with 14 ballots each, they moved for Mitchell's selection by acclamation. Clearly, there appears to be more to selection than ideology. While centrist ideology may be a necessary condition to being selected majority leader, it is not sufficient.

Prior Leadership or Seniority
Although ideology is crucial, perhaps foremost, among requisites of leadership, it alone does not a majority leader make. Maybe even most obvious in leadership selection is seniority, or prior leadership experience. Midway through the history of leadership posts, selection was a stepping-stone process, as early on, there were few leadership slots to provide experience (see table 3.3). As the ranks of leadership developed and professionalized (Canon, 1989), prior leadership experience became a requisite for Senate majority leader. There was much overlap between "leadership subsystems" of institution and party (Hinckley, 1970, p. 271), and those senators with the most experience (defined by lengthy tenures) were favored for party leadership slots, and once within the "leadership ladder" (Brown & Peabody, 1992), they were likely to be promoted within the ranks. David Canon (1989) measured the increasing years of Senate service before leadership as evidence of the establishment of boundaries in the Senate. These boundaries are themselves signals of institutionalization of leadership in the chamber (Canon, 1989; Polsby, 1970). But this stepping-stone pattern existed when the norms of seniority and apprenticeship reigned in the chamber. Barbara Sinclair (1989) described how the decline of these customs in the 1970s and 1980s changed the nature of the Senate and instituted an aura of individualism in which junior senators are no longer willing to wait their turn.

TABLE 3.3. Prior leadership positions of U.S. Senate majority leaders.

Name	Position	Date
John W. Kern (D-IN)	None	
Thomas S. Martin (D-VA)	None	
Henry Cabot Lodge (R-MA)	None	
Charles Curtis (R-KS)	Whip	1915–1924
James E. Watson (R-IN)	None	
Joseph T. Robinson (D-AR)	None before minority leader	1923–1933
Alben W. Barkley (D-KY)	None	
Wallace H. White, Jr. (R-ME)	None before minority leader	1944–1947
Scott W. Lucas (D-IL)	Whip	1947–1949
Ernest W. McFarland (D-AZ)	None	
Robert A. Taft (R-OH)	Chair, Republican Policy Committee	1947–1951*
William F. Knowland (R-CA)	Chair, Republican Policy Committee	1951–1953*
Lyndon B. Johnson (D-TX)	Whip Minority leader	1951–1953 1953–1955
Michael J. Mansfield (D-MT)	Whip	1957–1961
Robert C. Byrd (D-WV)	Secretary, Democratic Conference Whip	1967–1971 1971–1977
Howard H. Baker, Jr. (R-TN)	None before minority leader	1977–1981
Robert J. Dole (R-KS)	None	
George J. Mitchell (D-ME)	Chair, Democratic Senatorial Campaign Committee	1985–1986
C. Trent Lott (R-MS)	Whip	1995–1996
Thomas A. Daschle (D-SD)	Co-chair, Democratic Policy Committee Co-chair Democratic Conference Minority leader	1989–1999 1989–1999 1995–2001
William H. Frist (R-TN)	Chair, National Republican Senatorial Campaign Committee	2001–2003

Note. *These majority leaders maintained these posts as Senate majority leader.

However, it should be qualified that inasmuch as prior experience is a consideration, a seniority rule, strictly defined, does not operate in selection. The longest-serving member does not automatically ascend to the post. In fact, the first Senate majority leader, Kern, was selected leader in only his second year in the Senate. Margaret Munk (1974) has pointed out that since Thomas Martin (D-VA) took over for Kern, neither party has strictly used seniority to select leaders,[56] a pattern which extends to the present. This observation is extraordinary in a tradition-bound institution in which seniority held the chamber in the vise of Southern Democratic committee chairs for decades. Munk (1974) claimed that members saw that reliance on a seniority rule for leadership would only promote their most aged to tasks requiring great stamina. Even as age is not the infirmity it once was, a more likely reason is that more senior members, by the time party leadership positions opened up—especially the post of Senate majority leader—already had gained status via committee leadership and were unwilling to risk the uncertainty of giving up committee chairs that accepting the office of Senate majority leader would require.

It was to Alben Barkley's advantage to succeed Joe Robinson because Barkley had acted functionally, and nominally, as assistant leader to Robinson in the fight to push Roosevelt's plan for the court. At Robinson's death, Democrats looked to Barkley to manage the floor, and he began acting as leader. That presumption was enforced by Roosevelt's "My Dear Alben" letter, which spelled out the administration's favored position on the court-reform bill and which addressed Barkley as "the acting majority leader in the Senate" (Barkley, 1954, p. 155). Anti-Roosevelt Democrats "seized upon it as 'proof' that the president was interfering with their choice of majority leader to succeed Senator Robinson" (Barkley, 1954, p. 155). However, the presumption had been in his favor; Barkley moved from acting leader to majority leader.

In the past two decades, for both Democrats and Republicans, the chairmanship of the senatorial campaign committees has been something of a stepping stone to the leader's chair. Both George Mitchell and Bill Frist earned their bona fides there. Recently, chair of the campaign committee has become inimitably advantageous for majority-leader aspirants. In that role, senators raise and dole out funds to their colleagues who are unlikely to forget such assistance when the chair is running for majority leader. The Senate, in general, and leadership selection, in particular, may turn on personal relationships, but such relationships are forged in large part through the ultimate favor exchange—fundraising and spending.

As far back as 1953, after Ernest McFarland's defeat with the loss of a Democratic majority in the Senate, Lyndon Johnson, who had only been elected to the Senate five years earlier, campaigned and cajoled his way from whip to party leader before the close of his first term. He won his second term and a majority in the Senate a year later. His youth and inexperience were the subjects of debate, but he succeeded in his quest with the blessing of his "sponsor," Richard Russell. This "generational" experience (Kelly, 1995b) of Johnson was cited when Tom Daschle announced his intentions to follow George Mitchell as majority leader.[57] Daschle had been co-chair (the first to bear such a designation after Mitchell, in an unprecedented move for an otherwise centralized party organization, splintered some power to those who helped get him selected leader) of the Democratic policy committee, but he had never chaired a committee or even a subcommittee. Unlike Johnson, he was untested as a legislative manager. His competition was James Sasser (D-TN), who was a decade ahead of Daschle in seniority and at the time was chair of the budget committee. Their ideological positions were roughly equivalent, and their stands on particular key issues were the same—in line with the then-current Democratic leadership. In his race, Daschle urged his fellow partisans to choose a younger, media-friendly leader and, along the way, criticized the Senate's inefficiencies. But his push toward party rejuvenation did not entirely convince his party—at least immediately. Sasser had the votes of his party on the run up to balloting day, but he did not have the votes of his state constituents on election day. A political newcomer, Bill Frist, defeated Sasser. After Sasser's loss, Chris Dodd (D-CT) stepped in and inherited much of his support but raised some discomfort by his geographical similarity to Mitchell.

By way of context, Trent Lott, like Alben Barkley, followed a more conventional path to leadership by serving as whip, or assistant leader, to Bob Dole. In that post, he operated as deal-maker and vote-counter while building a constituency that would support him as majority leader. Connie Mack (R-FL) confirmed, "His main advantage is that he's been operating as whip of Republican senators for a year and a half" (Doherty & Langdon, 1996). Lott's experience began in the House of Representatives, where he also served as party whip, and his Senate leadership résumé began with a stint as conference secretary, the fourth-ranking leadership slot, from 1992–1994. His senatorial career was one of aggregation of experience in which Lott established strong credentials that masked what many outsiders viewed as a hard core of conservative ideology. While his DW-NOMINATE scores may seem to bear witness to an ideologue (0.466 to 0.511) beyond the party mean (0.303 to 0.388), insiders note "a pragmatic streak," his push "for Republicans to put aside their hope for sweeping change, tone down the partisanship, and get results," and his tendency to serve a bridge between "old-school Republicans" and "the rebellious conservatives" (Cloud, 1996). But the extent of prior leadership in Lott's success is complicated by the fact that his challenger, Thad Cochran (R-MS), held a lower leadership post. The careers of these same-state colleagues are remarkably parallel, beginning as cheerleaders at Ole Miss and law students at the same, followed by overlapping stints in the House, and subsequent elections to the Senate. Cochran was chair of the Republican conference when Lott was secretary, and when Lott upset Alan Simpson (R-WY) for majority whip, he leaped over Cochran in the leadership rankings. The race for majority leader was another confrontation in their parallel careers.

Region
Just as seniority seems obvious among factors in the selection of majority leaders, so too does region in an institution established to absorb and thus absolve differences among distinctive geographic areas. The push to elect Ernest McFarland exemplifies the influence of region. The balance of power lay with Southerners who recognized that to have one of their own as leader would draw increased scrutiny to their interests. Richard Russell, the unofficial leader of Southern Democrats, demurred to run: "To have a southerner as majority leader would cause criticism of his acts to fall upon the South as a whole" (McMillan, 2004, p. 196). Russell chose McFarland, an Arizonan with a Southern background, and soon McFarland's colleagues, Carl Hayden and Bob Kerr, began rounding up Western votes for McFarland. A last minute challenge by another

Westerner, Joseph O'Mahoney, obscured backing by Senator Brien McMahon (D-CT) and other Northern Democrats. These Northern liberals recognized the Southern tactic of using "a cooperative moderate" to mask their conservative aims and, lacking the numbers to nominate a Northerner, found a cooperative moderate in O'Mahoney to hold the liberal line (McMillan, 2004, p. 197). Thus, the West became a battleground for a proxy war between the Southern and Northern factions of the Democratic party that would last for several decades. With the ideological homogenization of the Democratic party that signaled the end of the conservative coalition and the diminution of race as a crosscutting issue in senatorial politics, regional balance became far less important.

While region has been declining in importance since mid-century when maintaining the proper balance between Southern, Northern, and Western factions in leadership and in committees was an art and a science, remnants of regional influence did play a part in the Daschle-Dodd race. Like Sasser, Dodd had no major ideological disagreements with Daschle, and the 1994 race became one in which geographical and generational factors dominated. Daschle made his case that majority leadership in the 1990s required a new face, and some senators—among them Harry Reid (D-NV), who would co-chair the Senate Democratic conference and the Democratic policy committee—questioned the wisdom of back-to-back leaders from the Northeast with its usual qualifier of "liberal" (Doherty, 1994). Reid argued that "as a 'fresh face' from the Midwest, Daschle can provide a new image for Democrats and that this is what the party desperately needs. The party has been taking a pretty good beating in the West...It's seen as a northeastern liberal party" (Doherty, 1994). On the day of selection, the caucus cast their ballots to a tie: 23 to 23, whereupon the lone proxy vote was opened and read. The vote was for Daschle, cast by Senator Ben Nighthorse Campbell (D-CO), who in a year's time would switch his affiliation to the Republican party.

Effects on Committee Chairmanships
Other considerations in voting for majority leader can be deemed "complicating factors," including the effect a candidate's selection may have

on committee chairmanships. Unlike the speaker of the House, the Senate majority leader retains his committee assignments, but both parties' rules prevent the leader from being chairman. As a consequence, a fairly senior senator who is already chair of a committee would have to relinquish his seniority in that committee if he were selected majority leader. This sacrifice can actually inhibit support for his candidacy. Senators appear to be risk averse (Kahneman & Tversky, 2000) and, like most rational actors (Downs, 1957), prefer certainty (Fenno, 1978), but a vacant chair on a prime committee opens up a chain reaction throughout the Senate, reordering committee and even subcommittee assignments throughout the chamber and disrupting a carefully arranged structure of seniority and favors. If the empty chair can be a bargaining chip for a candidate for majority leader, it can also be his albatross if his likely successor as chair is unpopular among members. These complications were evident in the five-way bid to succeed Howard Baker. Three of the contenders were chairs of powerful committees: Bob Dole of finance, James McClure of energy, and Pete Domenici of budget. A fourth, Ted Stevens, was chair of the important appropriations subcommittee on defense, and another candidate Richard Lugar, was in line to chair foreign relations or agriculture. The next ranking Republican senators in these committees were "a different political complexion" (Rogers, 1984) and promised to upset the policy paths of these committees. Lugar's candidacy was particularly hampered by the anticipated chain of events: If Lugar were selected Senate majority leader, Jesse Helms (R-NC) would then chair the foreign relations committee. Described as "hero" of the "New Right" (Rogers, 1984), Helms was well known for being an ideologue and demagogue, even by himself (Helms, 2005, p. 64), and his chairmanship would be inconsistent with recent moves toward the center by Senate Republicans (Granat, 1984; Rogers & Shribman, 1984). Thus, Lugar's candidacy never gained momentum.

Ability to Serve as a Spokesman
The Senate majority leader is the voice of his party—on the floor, in print, on talk shows, to the president, with the House—and though this public

Party Constraints 65

role for any senator did not exist before the development of the formal position, it became quickly entrenched in expectations for the majority leader (Gamm & Smith, 2002a). Henry Cabot Lodge (R-MA) evidenced the leader-as-spokesman when he stood in vociferous opposition in the Senate debate over the Treaty of Versailles and refused to work to pass the treaty without reservations—reservations that President Wilson would not abide. The role of majority leader as speaker for his party and the chamber became institutionalized and professionalized with the leadership of Alben Barkley who regularized his meetings with reporters (Gamm & Smith, 2002a). Majority senators look to their leader to provide policy leadership, not only to formulate a legislative agenda but also to design and implement strategies for bringing it to fruition (Gamm & Smith, 2002a). A contemporary strategy for brokering policy is to move beyond the cloakroom to before the cameras, to "go public," to garner support from voters to use as leverage against their colleagues of the other party.[58] This means the majority leader must be nimble in speech so that the public is left with a sound bite, an identifiable position on the issue at hand.

Therefore, perhaps most of all, a candidate's ability to be a spokesman for his party may be the deal breaker for his candidacy for majority leader. In no other case is this demand more apparent than that of Robert Byrd (see table 3.4).

TABLE 3.4. Robert C. Byrd (D-WV): U.S. Senate majority leader, 1977–1980 and 1987–1988.

1977	Selected majority leader to replace Mike Mansfield (D-MT), who retired from the Senate (Edward M. Kennedy [D-MA] and Hubert H. Humphrey [D-MN] withdrew before balloting.)
1984	Challenged by Lawton Chiles (D-FL) (survived 36–11)
1986	Challenged by J. Bennett Johnston (D-LA) (Johnston withdrew one week before balloting.)
1988	Resigned as majority leader to assume chair of the appropriations committee

Almost from the beginning, he was criticized for his lack of media acumen. Byrd is a classical orator, in the great tradition of "stump" speakers. His flair for the dramatic is unmatched in his ability to pepper his statements on the floor with examples from Roman history, our constitutional founding, and even poetry, including Appalachian folk tales. However, his style could not translate from the stump to the television camera. He also had a penchant for calling press conferences at 8:00 on Saturday mornings when capitol hill reporters had the day off. Even if the move was more tactical than tactless, it did not endear him to the press corps on which he depended to carry his party's message. Coincidentally, but unfortunately for him, media became all the more important to the delivery of political information and to Congress during his tenure as majority leader, especially with the 1986 introduction of C-SPAN into the chamber—a move he had supported. This changing context altered expectations for the role of Senate majority leader. Mike Mansfield, noted for his single-word responses to interviewers, was more taciturn and every bit as uncomfortable when facing the camera.[59] But what was endearing for Mansfield was problematic for Byrd. Context had changed. Media were not only more pervasive but also more relevant as the tool by which leaders were to shape and sell their party's message both to elites and citizens.

Dissatisfaction with Byrd and his media relations mounted until he was challenged for his position by Lawton Chiles (D-FL) in 1984 (Cohadas & Tate, 1984). Never before had anyone contested an incumbent majority leader. Byrd won fairly handily, but the open challenge itself sent a message. And two years later, he again was challenged for his post, this time by Bennett Johnston (D-LA). Johnston dropped out of the race two weeks before voting for lack of support. It was widely supposed that this second attempt to replace Byrd floundered because Byrd had intimated that he planned to resign within two years anyway (Hook, 1988). And he did. Byrd announced his resignation as leader on April 12, 1988, effective at the end of the 100th Congress. He stepped down from majority leadership and claimed the chair of the Senate appropriations committee.

In replacing Byrd, members sought to remedy his weakness, and they found a ready successor in George Mitchell. Also in the race were Daniel Inouye and Bennett Johnston, who had challenged Byrd two years earlier. But their styles could not have been more different. Daniel Inouye was an institutionalist much in the mold of Byrd, whereas Bennett Johnston was something of a party maverick. Mitchell provided a TV-friendly persona that appealed to the newest generation of senators, and he had already established himself as a ready spokesman for the party during the Iran-Contra affair. Convening after Thanksgiving in 1988, Democrats selected Mitchell to succeed Byrd. Most important to the new class of Democratic senators were media capabilities, and the freshman class proved to be the most influential bloc (Ornstein, Peabody, & Rohde, 1997). It was their election in 1986 that had restored the Democrats to the majority and Robert Byrd to the majority leadership. Moreover, it was under Mitchell's service as chair of the Democratic senatorial campaign committee that they were elected. He had provided the freshmen with resources that brought them electoral success, and they repaid the favor by aligning to support him as majority leader. He became their spokesman.

For the Republicans in 1984, Bob Dole was selected Senate majority leader in large part for his media skills (Ornstein, Peabody, & Rohde, 1997). He had four opponents in the race (Ted Stevens, Richard Lugar, Pete Domenici, and James McClure), only one of which could compete with him ideologically—Pete Domenici. McClure (0.583) was too far right, and Stevens was below the Republican mean, but Lugar (0.339), Domenici (0.232), and Dole (0.311) tracked closely in their ideological placement. Lugar was fettered because of his committee placement (Granat, 1984; Rogers, 1984; Rogers & Shribman, 1984), and initially that concern inhibited support for Domenici, who was dropped in the second round only two votes shy of Lugar (Rogers & Shribman, 1984). However, Domenici's supporters then divided among Stevens and Dole, ensuring that Lugar lost in the third (Rogers & Shribman, 1984). As Gerald Ford's vice-presidential nominee in 1976, Dole was not only ideologically more in keeping with the party mainstream but also proven on the training ground of a presidential campaign as a spokesman. He was sharp tongued and quick witted on the floor and before the press (Granat, 1984).

And, when it came time to replace Dole after his resignation in 1996 to run for president, the pattern repeated itself. Republican senators chose between same-state colleagues from Mississippi, Trent Lott and Thad Cochran. Both were in party leadership positions at the time, with Lott as whip and Cochran as chair of the conference. Cochran (0.293) and Lott (0.489), on the conservative side, were almost equidistant ideologically from the party mean (0.372). But Lott had undeniable media skills, and moreover, he enjoyed exercising them. He was comfortable holding forth after the weekly policy committee luncheons. He did not shy away but sought out the media; he had a "talent for self-promotion" (Doherty & Langdon, 1996). He was aggressive and partisan in his media appearances, much more so than the "courtly" Cochran (Kalb, 1996), and those traits were seen as a boon rather than a hindrance for a Senate majority leader that would be operating in the shadows of House Speaker Newt Gingrich's (R-GA) Republican Revolution and "Contract with America."

Conclusions

Based on a job description of Senate majority leadership, this chapter has listed contributing factors in the selection of Senate majority leaders. From the universe of contested selections, it is evident that senators choose majority leaders to fit not only relevant tasks of majority leadership but also the institutional, partisan, and personal contexts of the time. For example, institutional considerations related to committee reassignments seem to have prohibited Richard Lugar from leadership. And Byrd's personal style inhibited cooperation with media, a necessary part of the majority leader's job in the era of the perpetual news cycle. Among these contexts, ideology makes an observable difference. Selected leaders are almost without exception closer to the ideological median of their party than other candidates. The universality of this trend merits further investigation, not least of which because ideological placement can be concretely measured. Roll-call voting scores provide tangibility that other factors lack. Moreover, a measurement of ideological placement of senator and party speaks to the demands of party on majority leadership. Just as the ideological placement of a senator to his party can anticipate his selection as majority leader, so too can the ideological location of a Senate majority leader in his party explain his leadership behavior. Both measures should reveal partisan constraints on majority leadership.

CHAPTER 4

PARTY CONSTRAINTS

IDEOLOGICAL PLACEMENT OF SENATE MAJORITY LEADERS[60]

Ideology is the single consideration common to all contested selections of Senate majority leaders. Thus, an examination of the ideological placement of majority leaders at various points throughout their Senate careers should present a number of findings relevant to the selection of majority leaders as well as to the partisan tasks of the leader and constraints thereon. Unlike the speaker of the House, who rarely casts a vote and never sits on committees, the Senate majority leader retains all privileges and duties of a senator.[61] One act universal to all senators is voting, primarily recorded calls of the roll. In this elemental behavior, we observe a Senate majority leader answering the demands of at least two constituencies—his state and his party. The positions he takes on roll calls must simultaneously reflect the interests of both; his goal of reelection to both offices demands nothing less. Roll-call voting, then, can tell us about a senator becoming a leader and a leader being a senator.

As an extension of the descriptive statistics presented in the previous chapter, this chapter yields findings that are two-fold—first, locating senators who would become majority leaders within their parties and, second, tracking changes (if any) toward and during leadership. The primary, and not necessarily obvious, finding is that Senate majority leaders are located at or near their party medians. However, some Senate majority leaders drift toward their party's ideological extreme over the course of their tenure. Although median voting may contribute to selection as majority leaders, regression analysis shows that other factors, endogenous to the office, pull them toward the extreme as leader. These findings contradict the traditional "middleman" (Truman, 1959) hypothesis of party leadership and offer new perspectives on party constraints on Senate majority leadership.

Competing Expectations of Leaders' Voting Behavior

Studies of congressional roll-call behavior are prolific. There is a rich tradition and forceful debate about the sources of a member's voting behavior—whether constituency or party more influences voting styles. But before a judgment on the source of voting behavior proceeds, one must make a descriptive judgment about voting behavior. On that too there is debate. Some scholars note stability in a member's roll-call voting behavior over the course of his career (e.g., Poole & Rosenthal, 1997);[62] others see variation in his voting behavior, perhaps as he adjusts it to meet the demands of constituency, party, or even presidential veto (e.g., Krehbiel, 1998). Based on assumptions of congressional ambition or careerism (Black, 1972; Brace, 1984; Herrick & Moore, 1993; Hibbing, 1986; Rohde, 1979; Schlesinger, 1966), observers might expect a senator when in pursuit of leadership or when he becomes leader—that is, when he takes up his party as a constituency—to alter his voting behavior accordingly.[63] If he is "agent" in service to his party as "principal(s)," he may move to serve party demands—toward either the median or extreme of his party (Sinclair, 1995).

Expectations are contradictory. David Truman (1959) purported, and others (e.g., Peabody, 1976) reiterated, that leaders (principally, but not only, majority leaders) will be *centrists* within their party. This claim suggests Anthony Downs's (1957) theory of party ideology: the Senate majority leader would move toward (or be located at—if his voting behavior is indeed stable over the course of his career) the median position of his party. Positioning himself as a moderate enables him to appease factions within his party. He is able to establish solid party preferences that are neither too provocative nor too conciliatory but appeal to most in his party and, thus, are easier to pass in a supermajoritarian institution (Sinclair, 2001b). John Aldrich (1995, p. 185) provided support for this expectation in his model of a legislature with leadership to solve collective action problems: "...leadership is ordinarily in the mainstream."[64]

On the other hand, classical bargaining theories (Raiffa, 1982) would expect the Senate majority leader to be *extreme* in his voting behavior. Indeed, Duncan McRae (1958) and Samuel Patterson (1963) explored the extremist tendencies of leaders in state legislatures. David King and Richard Zeckhauser (2002) modeled leadership using, as Barbara Sinclair (1995) did, principal-agent theory. They found that at least for the 100th Congress onward (1990–2002), party leaders (caucus chairs, whips, majority and minority leaders, etc.) tended to be more extreme than their parties. And moreover, these representatives and senators were extreme before joining the leadership (King & Zeckhauser, 2002). An important task for all legislators and especially for leaders, as agents to principals, is negotiation or bargaining (Baron & Ferejohn, 1989). The logic of extremity suggests that in the game of bargaining, the negotiator offers a position more radical than his true preference in order for the final product, after compromise, to end up closer to his true preference. King and Zeckhauser (2002) described this process as "punching and counter-punching," and they were quick to caution that, in fact, a too extreme leader-negotiator would cause gridlock. Thus, leaders should be near the extreme but not beyond the pale.[65]

The first explicit tests of Senate leadership found evidence of this tendency toward the ideological extreme—leaders, in fact, occupied the far right or left (respective of their party) end of the spectrum (Sullivan, 1975). Moreover, Jack Van Der Slik and Samuel Pernacciaro (1979), allowing for the possibility of movement toward the middle by these future leaders in anticipation of a candidacy for a post, still found no evidence of accommodation among leadership aspirants. Instead, their findings echoed those of William Sullivan (1975) and contradicted the explanations of Truman (1959) and others—leader-hopefuls tended to be extremists.[66]

And yet, Robert Peabody (1976, pp. 470–471) expressed a slightly different hypothesis for consideration: party leaders are "middlemen;" if not at selection, they soon become so. I call this the *convergence hypothesis*. It posits that, if not on the way to becoming leader, then with (or after) selection,[67] he alters his voting behavior to meet his party. This moderation occurs for all the reasons Downs (1957) and Truman (1959) described: the prime task of the majority leader is to build and hold coalitions, and the fulcrum from which he operates, within and beyond his party, is in the middle. He is the bridge between factions. Sullivan (1975, p. 37) provided an implicit test of this proposition by considering "whether the leadership role moves individual leaders to exhibit more moderate...positions within their congressional parties compared to preleadership behavior." He found some adjustment in voting behavior toward the center after senators have been selected to leadership positions, illustrating a trend of convergence just as Peabody predicted. On the other hand, Van Der Slik and Pernacciaro (1979), interested in ambition effects, briefly surveyed voting behavior of senators moving out of leadership. As ambition goals changed, they expected decreasing moderation. This expectation can be called the *divergence hypothesis*. They found some support for their expectations: although he would not leave leadership until 1977, Mike Mansfield (D-MT) "safely established as majority leader for three previous Congresses, was increasingly liberal over the period especially on Vietnam policy" (Van Der Slik & Pernacciaro, 1979, p. 216).

These contradictory findings from varying research designs merit new examination.[68] Where does the majority leader stand in relation to the party he leads? Does his voting behavior change as he is leader? Does this voting pattern that perhaps contributed to his selection continue once he becomes leader?

Median Voter or Extreme Partisan

To answer these questions, I examined the locations of Senate majority leaders within their parties at three key points in their senatorial careers: their first Congress, their Congress immediately preceding selection as leader,[69] and their terms as majority leader. Ideological placement is measured by DW-NOMINATE scores, widely accepted indicators that are comparable over time (Poole & Rosenthal, 1997).[70]

First Congress

The first term in the Senate must be a difficult one for any senator. Getting accustomed to "the citadel" (White, 1957) takes time, so I would expect that during one's first Congress, any senator, with leadership aspirations or not, would closely hew the party line. And, indeed, this is the case for future Senate majority leaders.

Figure 4.1 shows the voting scores of leaders in relation to their party means and medians for their first congresses in the Senate.[71] Standard deviations from the mean are designated by vertical lines. Negative scores indicate Democratic leaders, means, and medians; positive scores indicate the same for Republicans. During their first term in office, future Senate majority leaders are closely aligned to their party's mean and median, with most within one standard deviation of the party mean. Only three would-be leaders lie outside one standard deviation of their party mean: Henry Cabot Lodge (R-MA) in the 53rd Congress; Robert A. Taft (R-OH) in the 76th Congress; and William F. Knowland (R-CA) in the 79th Congress. All three are Republicans.

Figure 4.1 reveals another trend in voting behavior—with the exceptions of Knowland and Charles Curtis (R-KS) for the Republicans and Lyndon Johnson (D-TX) and Robert Byrd (D-WV) for the Democrats, future leaders are all on the "party side" of their party's midpoint. That is, these four lie between absolute zero, the demarcation line between the two parties, and their party's mean. And, in fact, Knowland and Johnson are closer to absolute zero (or the other party) than to their own party's mean or median.

76 MAJORITY LEADERSHIP IN THE U.S. SENATE

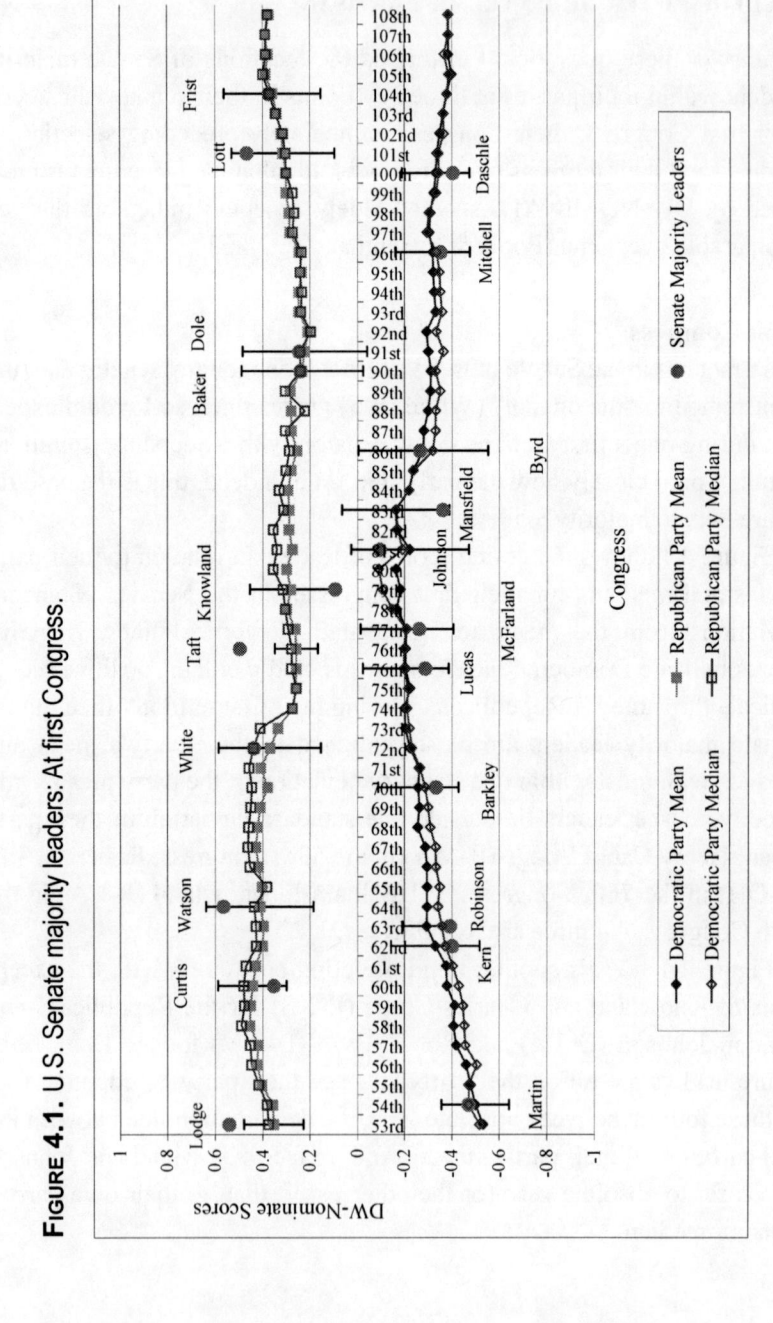

FIGURE 4.1. U.S. Senate majority leaders: At first Congress.

At Selection

The selection of a leader says as much about the party that selected him as the leader himself. Peabody (1976) presented the most detailed examination to date of the selection and succession of Senate leaders. In a series of case studies of decided leadership races, he induced criteria for selecting a leader. The trends reported in figure 4.2 highlight the role of voting behavior in that selection decision (see Sullivan, 1975).

Figure 4.2 shows the placement of Senate majority leaders in relation to their parties for the Congress immediately preceding their selection as majority leader. With a single exception (Joe Robinson [D-AR]), every would-be leader was within one standard deviation of his party mean at the time of his selection as majority leader. Moreover, most had actually moved (however slightly) closer to their party means since their first term (see figure 4.1). This certainly was the case with the outliers, Lodge, Taft, and Knowland. Clearly, the voting behavior of leaders about to assume the office is one of centrism. If voting behavior plays any part in the selection decision, it surely can be assumed that party members want a party loyalist, or at least a moderate not prone to extremism in either direction.

As Leader

The picture as majority leader is somewhat more complicated, so I divided the nearly a century of Senate majority leaders by party.

Figure 4.3 shows the trend of Republican leaders and the party means and medians since Lodge, the first Republican majority leader, in the 66th Congress. Vertical lines indicate one standard deviation from the party mean. Although Lodge and Trent Lott (R-MS) are on the conservative end of the range, it is clear that every Republican leader is within a single standard deviation. This portrait is fairly stable in the aggregate. During the course of the century, the Republican party moved within a range of roughly 0.22 units (from a mean high of 0.429 in the 67th Congress to a low in the 92nd Congress of 0.209), while leaders themselves varied within about 0.35 units. And there is similar stability in the individual voting behavior of Republican Senate majority leaders, although leaders who served multiple congresses did become slightly more conservative

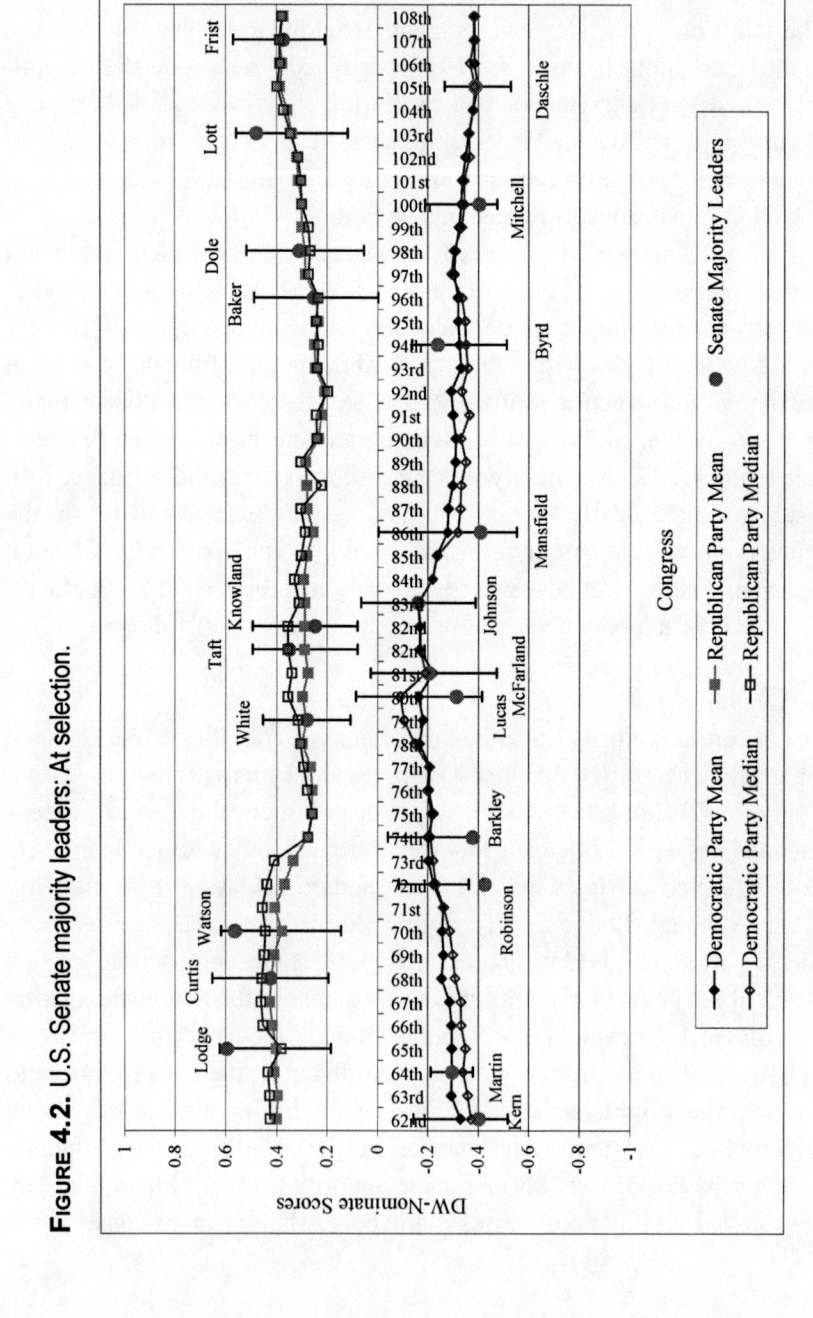

FIGURE 4.2. U.S. Senate majority leaders: At selection.

Party Constraints 79

FIGURE 4.3. Republican U.S. Senate majority leaders: Ideological placement as leader.

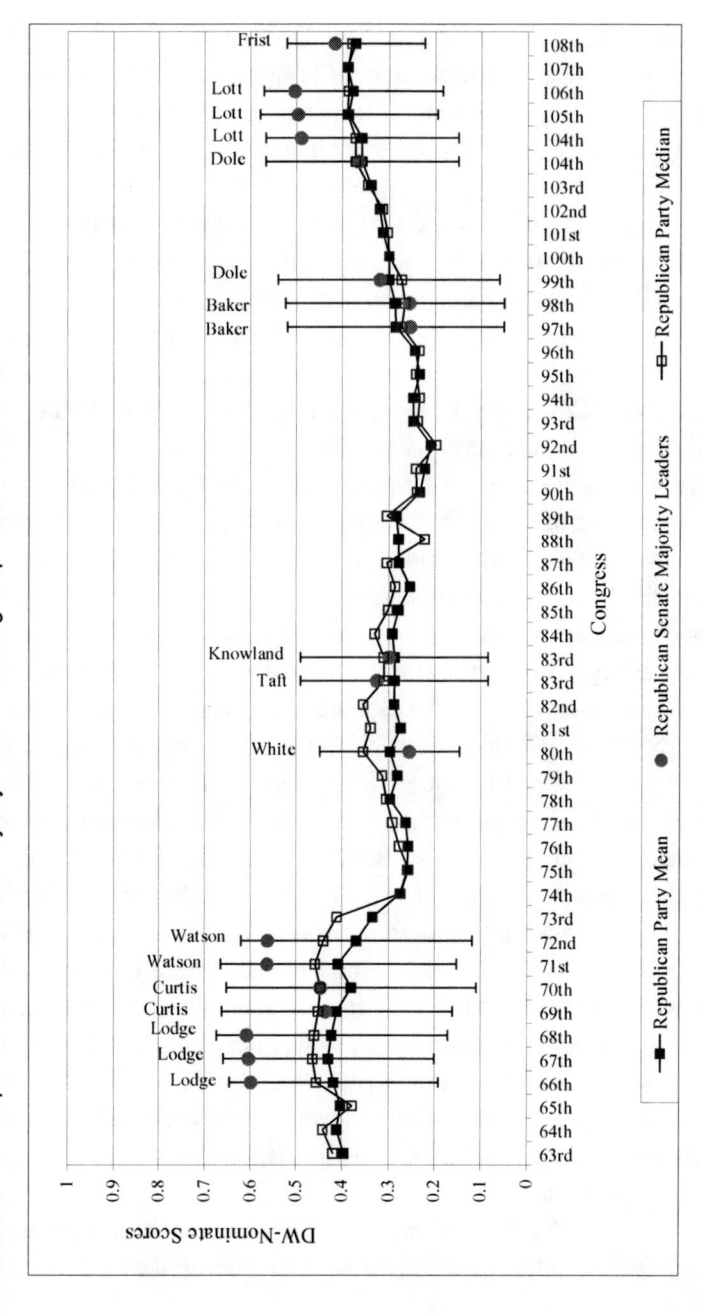

as their tenures progressed (e.g., Bob Dole [R-KS] and Trent Lott). Even earlier Republican leaders, such as Lodge and Curtis, showed a slight tracking to the right during their leadership. Dole's movement to the right closely matched that of his party, such that in his final Congress as leader, he was the median Republican senator. Lott, who took the helm when Dole resigned to run for president, was to the right of the party's "middleman" and moved further in that direction. But he remained within a single standard deviation of Republican members.

Figure 4.4 shows the voting trends in Democratic majority leadership. With the exceptions of John W. Kern (D-IN), Robinson, and Alben W. Barkley (D-KY), every Democratic majority leader is within one standard deviation of the party mean.

Kern is on the cusp of the midrange at the Congress of his selection and is outside the marker during his second Congress as leader. However, the marker moves, not Kern. The standard deviation from the mean shrinks as Democrats become more cohesive. As leader, Robinson showed movement leftward and, in so moving, further diverged from his party. He began his career closely aligned with the party mean (although never as conservative as his Southern credentials would suggest) in a strongly unified Democratic party. By the time he was elected majority leader, his party had become slightly more conservative, but he kept to the left. And during his tenure, he and the party remained ideologically distanced. Upon Robinson's death, Barkley, a border-state, if not Southern, Democrat took the reins. Like Robinson, he kept to the left of a steadily conservative Democratic mainstream. Notable are the last three congresses of Barkley's tenure—he had been steadily voting more liberally, while the mean of his party took a rather sharp spike to the right. In all the century, the Republican party had never been as far to the left as the Democrats had been to the right than during the 81st Congress. By this time, the conservative coalition was in full force, and the Democratic party was fractious and scattered (its standard deviations cover fully a quarter of the scale).

Like that of the Republican party, this is a picture of comparative stability. However, the aggregate trends are reversed: the median varies over

Party Constraints 81

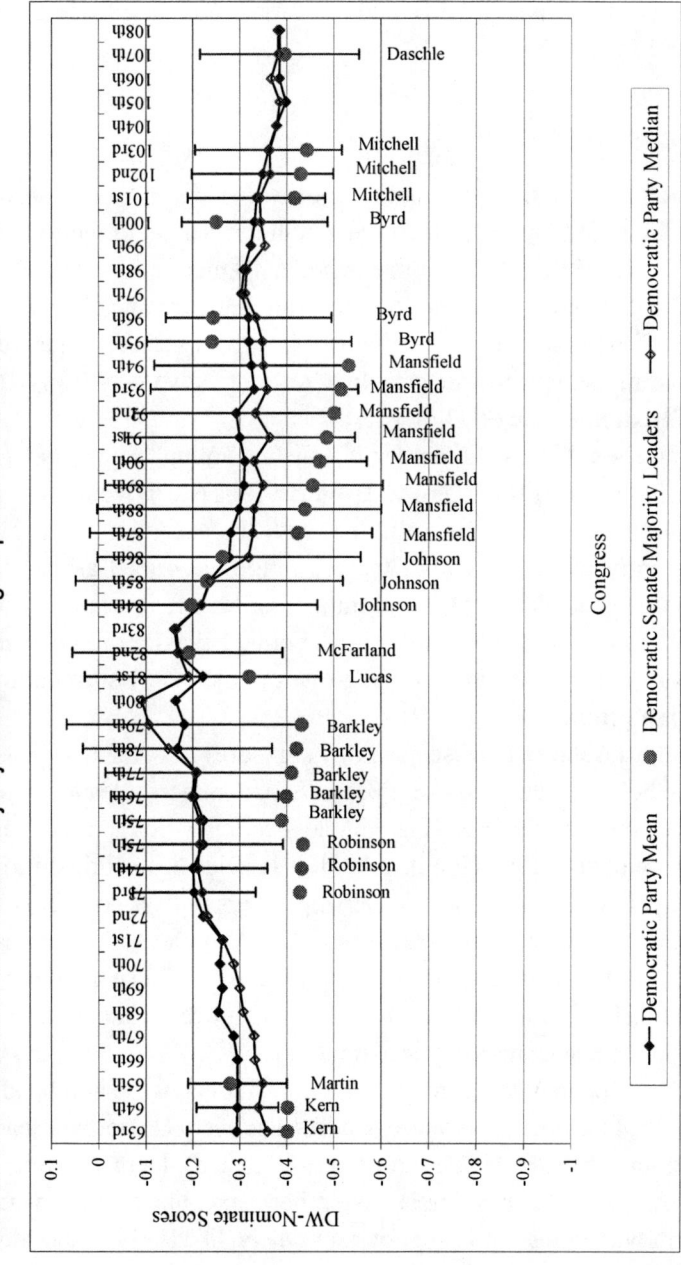

FIGURE 4.4. Democratic U.S. Senate majority leaders: Ideological placement as leader.

a slightly larger range (0.35), and the variation among leaders is smaller (about 0.25 units).

Stability or Change

The voting behavior of Senate majority leaders is remarkably stable. From the time they begin their careers in the Senate to their final terms, there is very little change in their voting. To measure the overall change in roll-call behavior for leaders, I calculated the distance between voting scores of the first Congress to the last Congress served. Negative values indicate movement toward absolute zero, or movement away from the party's extreme pole of −1 or +1.

Figure 4.5 shows the career change in voting behaviors of Senate majority leaders. From Kern to Bill Frist (R-TN), movement in leaders' voting was remarkably low. In fact, with the exception of Knowland,[72] voting movement fell within the 0.2 range, described as the norm by Poole and Rosenthal (1997). Assumption of leadership clearly showed no obvious change in the overall roll-call voting behavior of Senate majority leaders—not even during the congresses immediately surrounding leadership selection.

Figure 4.6 shows the distance in voting scores from the Congress immediately before to the first Congress as Senate majority leader. Movement between these congresses is negligible—certainly not approaching Poole and Rosenthal's (1997) 0.2 threshold. It is evident, in addition to overall stability, that assumption of leadership brings with it no sudden change in voting behavior (contra Sullivan, 1975; Van Der Silk & Pernacciaro, 1979). From either perspective, over the course of a senatorial career or immediately with leadership, there is no significant change in the voting behavior of Senate majority leaders.

Still, as apparent in figure 4.4, a prominent trend is the individual voting behavior of Democratic majority leaders. For every Democratic leader who served longer than a single term (Kern excepted), there was a noticeable shift leftward in their voting behavior. For some, like Robinson and Byrd, the drift was almost imperceptible; for others, like Barkley and Mansfield,

Party Constraints 83

FIGURE 4.5. Career ideological change of U.S. Senate majority leaders.

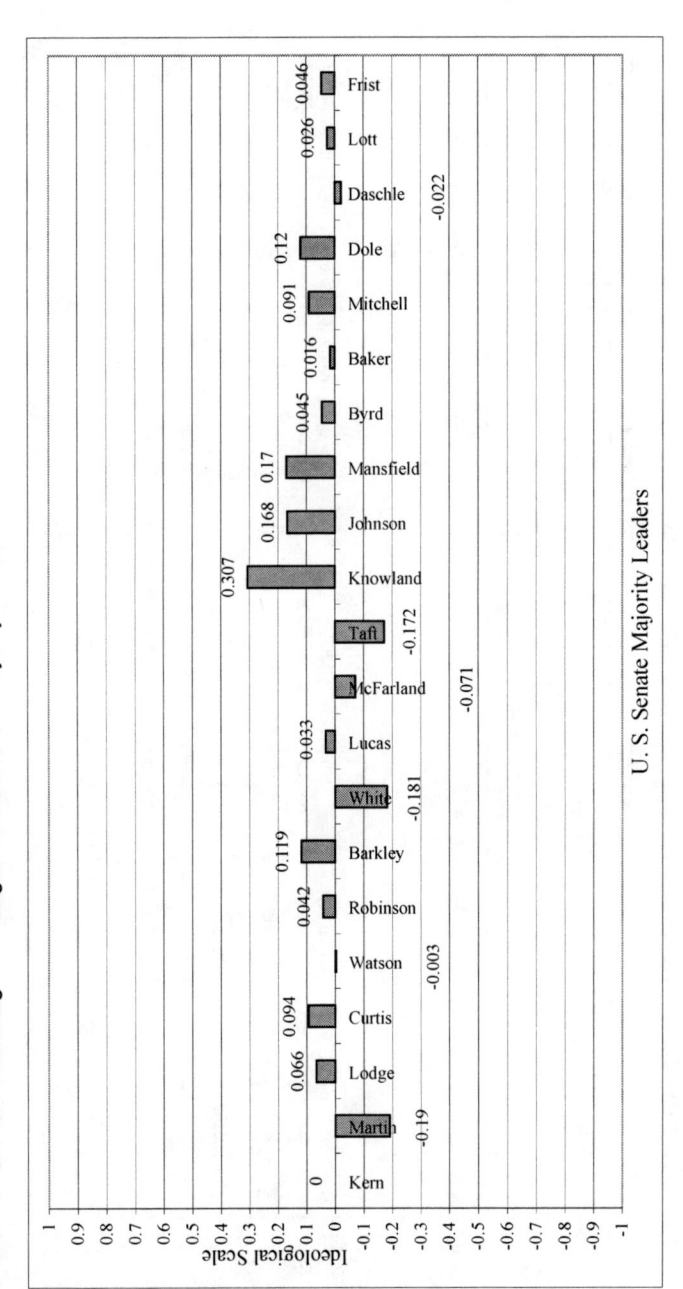

Leader	Value
Frist	0.046
Lott	0.026
Daschle	-0.022
Dole	0.12
Mitchell	0.091
Baker	0.016
Byrd	0.045
Mansfield	0.17
Johnson	0.168
Knowland	0.307
Taft	-0.172
McFarland	-0.071
Lucas	-0.033
White	-0.181
Barkley	0.119
Robinson	0.042
Watson	-0.003
Curtis	0.094
Lodge	0.066
Martin	-0.19
Kern	0

U. S. Senate Majority Leaders

84   Majority Leadership in the U.S. Senate

Figure 4.6. Immediate ideological change of U.S. Senate majority leaders.

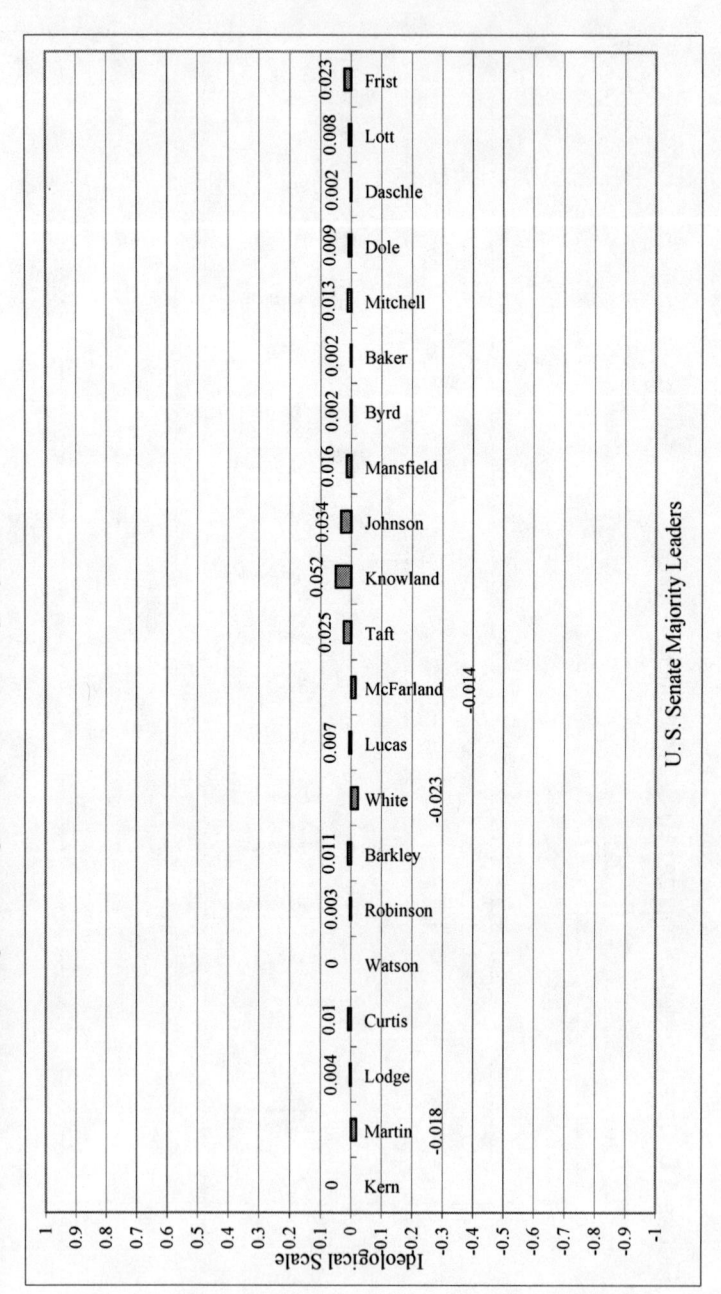

Leader	Value
Frist	0.023
Lott	0.008
Daschle	0.002
Dole	0.009
Mitchell	0.013
Baker	0.002
Byrd	0.002
Mansfield	0.016
Johnson	0.034
Knowland	0.052
Taft	0.025
McFarland	—
Lucas	0.007
White	−0.023
Barkley	0.011
Robinson	0.003
Watson	0
Curtis	0.01
Lodge	0.004
Martin	−0.018
Kern	0

Ideological Scale (−1 to 1)

U. S. Senate Majority Leaders

the movement was more dramatic. Only Barkley's movement countered his party's. Perhaps indicative of his presidential or vice-presidential ambitions, Barkley and his Senate partisans diverged as the latter filled with Southern conservatives. All other movement by leaders mirrored similar directional, if disproportionate, shifts in their party. That this behavior is evident in leaders separated by 20 congresses suggests something about the position of majority leader rather than about a particular era.

Majority Matters

Because this trend is almost universal to multiple-term leaders over the course of nearly a century, it seems this movement is not the result of exogenous contextual forces, that is, New Deal politics, conservative coalition, reform era, Republican revolution, and so forth. Instead, the universality of this phenomenon suggests it is endogenous to partisan forces and the construct of the office.

In all congressional behaviors, but specifically voting, scholars have highlighted the dual effects of state and party, and two things common to all majority leaders are their state and party constituencies. It may be that this progressive tendency of leaders is explained by changes in their constituents' preferences. David Mayhew (1974) is pertinent: even majority leaders would be expected to change with their state in order to be reelected. Maintaining office is their underlying goal; to fulfill all others (e.g., to remain leader), they must be reelected. Therefore, changes in voting behavior may result from changes in state constituency as leaders adjust to reflect a growing polarization in the electorate (Aldrich & Rohde, 2001). On the other hand, movement may reflect the growing polarization within the Senate (Hetherington, 2001), and thus is a response to their party constituencies. In that nearly all movement by multiple-term leaders is reflected by changes (to much lesser degrees) in their party's median and mean,[73] it seems likely that the drift in voting behavior correlates to party composition. I hypothesize that majority leaders become more extreme as their majority changes, specifically, as they lead broader rather than narrower majorities.

The size of congressional majorities has not yet been examined for its effects on the behavior of majority leaders. There is strong literature on coalition formation and sizing, which suggests the larger the coalition, the harder to maintain (Riker, 1962). Yet, beyond the volumes of research drawn from econometrics and formal models, legislative politics offer observations on the effects of large versus narrow majorities. For example, the influx of Northern liberal Democrats in 1958 has been established in lore as a principal cause of congressional reforms, enabling the rise of conditional party government (Rohde, 1991, pp. 7–14). And Caro (2002) wrote empathically of how this "influx" diminished Lyndon Johnson's leadership style. Johnson was much constrained by a larger and more widespread caucus, and he revealed his fear of holding the reins of a potentially runaway majority: "…I have concluded from talking to those men that they are all reasonable men. The purpose of the big new majority will be to be responsible, to be progressive without being radical…"[74] If indeed, as the 1958 example suggests, more partisan members equate to more extreme voting, then this extreme shift of leaders may result from larger majorities.

Data and Method

To examine influences on Senate majority leaders' roll-call voting, I tested a model that reflects dual roles of senator and leader by predicting the voting behavior of Senate majority leaders on the basis of certain party and state variables, the twin pillars of legislative behavior. The dependent variable is the first-dimension DW-NOMINATE scores for Senate majority leaders since Kern in 1913.[75] The unit of analysis is each Congress with a Senate majority leader ($N = 47$, accounting for dual observations when Barkley took over midterm at the death of Robinson and when Knowland did the same at the death of Taft).

Independent variables are drawn from both established literature and new observation. I measured state constituency preference as the Democratic percentage of the two-party presidential vote in the Senate majority leader's home state. I normalized this measure to reflect state deviation from the national Democratic share. Thus, the difference is negative if the state is more Democratic than the total vote and positive if not. For leaders whose terms did not coincide with the four-year presidential election cycle, I used the presidential vote preceding their selection as leader. As a gauge of geographic constituency preferences, Democratic presidential vote share is standard (e.g., Levendusky & Pope, 2004).

To test for party effects, I included a variable that is the ideological median of the Democratic and Republican parties (again, measured by DW-NOMINATE scores).[76] The party median represents the mainstream of the majority leader's party; and while he is the leader, he is no less subject to pressure of his party members. I expected this variable to be highly significant because, for much of the time, the majority leader is the median voter of his party.

I also added another party-oriented variable—margin of majority. This variable is scored on a scale of 22 (Lodge in 1921) to –57 (Robinson and Barkley in 1937) and configured so that it actually measures the Republican margin of majority. The Democratic seat margin is labeled with a negative sign to make it compatible with the dependent variable, which was scored within a range of +1 (perfectly conservative) to –1 (perfectly liberal).

Findings

Table 4.1 presents ordinary least squares (OLS) estimates of the effects of party and constituency on majority leaders' voting behavior.[77] I first applied the model to all Senate majority leaders and then to leaders separated by party.

Model 1 presents the findings for state and party variables absent the measure of party median (since it should be the strongest predictor). Without party median, the size of majority is significant in predicting how Senate majority leaders will vote. For every seat increase in their majority, the leaders' vote scores will slightly increase (or move toward their respective poles of extremity) by 0.015 units ($p = 0.000$). It appears that Democratic majority leaders will become more liberal, and Republican leaders more conservative as greater numbers provide a more secure majority with fewer members of the opposition needed for a cross-party governing coalition.

TABLE 4.1. OLS estimates of leaders' voting behavior.

Independent Variables	Model 1	Model 2	Model 3	Model 4
Party Median	—	1.004*	0.350	0.429
		(0.064)	(0.240)	(0.260)
Democratic Presidential Vote	−0.288	−0.102	0.044	−0.360
	(0.406)	(0.125)	(0.137)	(0.325)
Republican Margin of Majority	0.015*	0.004*	0.002*	0.001
	(0.003)	(0.001)	(0.001)	(0.003)
_cons	0.226	0.066	−0.247*	0.416*
	(0.190)	(.059)	(0.110)	(0.187)
R^2	0.574	0.924	0.197	0.392
	$N = 47$	$N = 47$	$N = 29$	$N = 18$

Note. Robust standard errors, clustered around each leader, are reported in parentheses.
*t test: $p < 0.05$.

The measure of constituency influence is insignificant in predicting the voting behavior of leaders. Although home-state preferences appear irrelevant, the negative sign indicates that any effects would be to deflate (or moderate) the leaders' voting scores. If constituency is a determinant of a representative's (in the generic sense) voting behavior, and common sense if not established research indicates it plays some role (e.g., Miller & Stokes, 1963; Erikson, 1978), then this variable does little to capture the extent of its stimulus.

Model 2 includes the party median variable, and it is perfectly significant ($p = 0.000$). The single best predictor of a leader's voting behavior is his party's median. Figures 4.3 and 4.4 show this to be the case, as leaders are very often the median voter of their party. And, in fact, the standardized coefficient of party median shows an almost one-to-one relationship with leaders' vote scores. That is, for every 1-point increase in party median, leaders' scores will increase by virtually the same (1.004 units).

The effects of constituency influence gain nothing, but it is important to note that the margin of majority variable remains significant. Even with party median—a perfect predictor—added, seat margin still is a significant determinant of majority leader voting behavior.

Assuming that party is not monolithic, that is, Democratic and Republican parties may exert different degrees of influence on their respective leaders, I modeled roll-call voting of majority leaders separately by party. From Model 3, it is evident that for Democratic leaders, party median as an individual predictor is not as strong as for all majority leaders. This is visually evident in figures 4.3 and 4.4, as Democratic leaders typically were further from their party median than their Republican counterparts were from theirs. In fact, Democrats were the outliers among majority leaders, being more than a single standard deviation removed from their party mean.

With regard to constituency influence, measured by percentage of the Democratic presidential vote, there also is no significant effect on Democratic leaders' voting behavior. The positive sign is expected, meaning that increases in Democratic vote share lead to increases in Democratic leaders' voting scores (making them more liberal); however, the effect is far from significant.

In this model, the most significant effect on Democratic leaders' voting behavior is the margin of their majority. For every seat increase, Democratic leaders vote more liberally (albeit by only 0.002 units). Once more, I refer to the visual representation in figure 4.4. Those leaders that drift, slightly but significantly, to the left over the course of their tenure as leader (e.g., Barkley, Johnson, and Mansfield) are those with increasing majorities during their multiple terms.

For Republicans, the picture is less defined. In Model 4, the measure of constituency preference again exhibits no predictive effect on leaders' roll-call voting. The relationship is in the expected direction, in that a more Democratic electorate will result in more moderate voting scores from their senator/leader, but it is insignificant in its effect. Moreover, while size of majority produces significant effects in the overall model and for Democratic leaders specifically, it does not appear to influence Republican leaders.

Interpretations and Implications

The most noteworthy finding of this research is that, in general, Senate majority leaders are located within the midrange of their party. In some instances, the majority leader is the median member of his party. What is important about this observation is its continuity across office holders. The finding is a virtual constant, which suggests that something about the office of majority leader demands centrism.

These findings support centrist expectations of party leadership and derive meaning from classical median-voter theory in that positioning himself in the middle of his partisan coalition allows the leader not only to maximize his vote share (Downs, 1957) toward becoming majority leader but also to mobilize greater support for his party line and even to establish cross-party coalitions while being leader. Being a median voter positions the leader to maintain his center base, to ensure his reelection, but it also has effects for legislating. Truman (1959) early on noted that the legislative party was a group of individuals, like-minded, but individualistic nonetheless. To lead such disparate subjects, the majority leader must consolidate these fragments into a power base. Where else to do this but at the structural median? It is this location that permits the leader to function as a "broker" (Truman, 1959) among competing groups; at the mean and median, the majority leader is situated to build coalitions. He is in a position to communicate to and bargain with incongruent factions, within his party and that of the opposition. Even when parties are cohesive among themselves, as in the recent era of "conditional party government" (Aldrich & Rohde, 2001), they still are comprised of individuals. In fact, Sinclair (1989, 2001a) demonstrated the violation of such Senate norms as reciprocity, seniority, and apprenticeship and the concomitant rise in individual prerogatives even as party cohesion hit its high. The majority leader as median voter situates himself to mediate and communicate with these individuals, his partisans and those in the opposition necessary for ad hoc policy-making coalitions.

While Truman (1959) wrote of the difficulties of maintaining partisan coalitions, Sinclair (2001b) emphasized how the supermajoritarian rules of the Senate require the leader not only to hold together his own party but also to add members of the opposition. At present, ending or preventing a filibuster requires three-fifths of senators to invoke cloture.[78] Given the narrow majorities of the 1980s and 1990s, that benchmark of 60 has been hard to cobble together. Sinclair framed this as the "dilemma" of majority party leadership in the Senate, that is, to gain partisan advantage in a superpartisan institution. The majority leader is first the leader of the majority party, but he also has a responsibility to keep the Senate functioning. He is charged with getting the majority party's policy agenda passed, but for getting bills passed nonetheless. To the extent the Senate stalls in gridlock (Binder, 2003), with the majority pressing for greater advantage and the opposition refusing to yield, the majority leader loses on both counts. To fulfill this "tough role," Sinclair (2001b, p. 70) observed, "the dominant strategy of leaders tends to be one of accommodation." This strategy of accommodation then is best carried out at the middle rather than at the extreme. The leader loses his own if he is either too polarized (in which case, the opposition can split the majority party itself) or too lax (in which case, he fails to carry his base). By positioning in the middle of his party, he not only maximizes his support within his party, but in so doing, he speaks for the mainstream and his actions carry the weight of its membership to the opposition. That most of his members are located with him makes the leader more formidable in pursuing his partisan advantage. And at the same time, he is not too polarizing a figure against which the opposition would balk or otherwise attempt to "divide and conquer" the majority. Finding Senate majority leaders at the middle solves Sinclair's dilemma: being a median voter enables the majority leader to fulfill expectations of party and Senate.

An important caveat should be noted here: middle does not equate to moderate. While the majority leader may be at the mean or median of his party, it does not imply he is close to the middle of the chamber, nor does it indicate his proximity to the other party. And, it does not predict that outcomes or policy will be moderate. These findings minimally signify that the majority leader is where his members are, even if that mean and median have been becoming more extreme, as scholars have witnessed over the past two decades.

This work adds a subtle variation on the leader as middleman in highlighting a perceptible shift of some majority leaders toward the ideological extremity of their party as their tenure as leader progresses, thus supporting the divergence hypothesis. More noticeable in Democratic leaders than in Republican, this trend fluctuates with partisan context. An increasing majority conditions a voting shift toward the ideological extreme. It does so, however, only for Democratic leaders. Findings for Republicans are not statistically significant, though they suggest that Republican leaders are more strongly tied to their party constituency than to state constituency. Fundamentally, this inconsistency is evidence that party is not monolithic; the effects of partisanship are not uniform across leaders. Party matters, but it matters in different ways for Democratic than for Republican majority leaders as leaders have different parties to lead and different strategies to pursue.

The relationship between majority size and the ideological location of majority leaders may be explained in that larger majorities actually make their own caucus more fractured; that is, the larger the coalition, the harder to maintain. As a principle, heterogeneity increases with size. Whereas a smaller majority would allow the leader more leeway to exert control (Rohde, 1991),[79] more partisans constrain the leader as he is pressured to deliver for his caucus, for example, in terms of agenda (Lee, 2008). The majority leader moves to maintain his majority as more partisans make for more partisan voting. It is logical that large increases in majorities come about in landslide elections. Historically, these landslide elections, in which one party spectacularly triumphs over the other, result from a shift in the macropolitical context (Erikson, MacKuen, & Stimson, 2002) within Congress and the electorate. The 1958 election and the ensuing entry of Northern liberal Democrats into the Senate in the 86th Congress is one such example; the 1994 Republican revolution in the 104th House is another. In their wake, the public mood clearly favored one party above the other. Under these conditions, then, it should not be a surprise that the increased majority constrained their majority leader toward more partisan preferences. In real terms, as larger Democratic majorities emerged in 1958 and fluctuated throughout the 1960s and 1970s and more liberal members comprised that larger Democratic majority, leaders such as Johnson and Mansfield, who heretofore had operated closer to the middle, were pulled leftward, constrained by factions within their party. Moreover, as a matter of strategy, the liberal bloc holds more sway over a majority leader because that faction is more intense in their preferences as opposed to moderate members, who by definition are less intense.[80]

Conclusions

The findings presented in this chapter clearly challenge and modify Peabody's (1976) and others' like assumptions that, if not at selection, then as leader, Senate majority leaders "soon become" middlemen within their parties. Instead, Senate majority leaders occupy the median (oftentimes exactly so) early in their careers and at their selection as majority leader, but drift from their party's midpoint as leader. Rather than the convergence theory described by Peabody and Sullivan (1975) (see also Matthews, 1960), it appears that Senate majority leaders follow a pattern of divergence. They begin their senatorial career at or near the mean and median, but throughout their period of party leadership, they drift toward their party's extreme. For Senate majority leaders, then, majority matters. The numerical advantage majority leaders have in the chamber is not a license for power; instead, majority leaders are constrained by the ideological demands of the majority party they lead.

CHAPTER 5

EXTRA-INSTITUTIONAL CONSTRAINTS

PRESIDENTIAL EXPECTATIONS OF SENATE MAJORITY LEADERS

In October 2007 Senate Majority Leader Harry Reid (D-NV) appeared with Minority Leader Mitch McConnell (R-KY) at McConnell's namesake center at the University of Louisville.[81] The two talked about their relationship in the U.S. Senate, and Senator Reid greatly praised the institutional affection of McConnell, adding that the two had a "good relationship," which, given its supermajoritarian rules, Senate politics require of the majority and minority leaders. Reid continued to praise McConnell for being unlike his predecessor, Bill Frist (R-TN). Reid said Frist was a "wonderful human being," but he had no institutional understanding. This vacuity was to be expected, however, because Frist's ascension to majority leader was, according to Reid, the "only time in history where a senator became majority leader because the president wanted him."

Events leading up to Frist's selection were dramatic: Trent Lott (R-MS) began serving as majority leader when Bob Dole (R-KS) resigned in 1996 to run as the Republican nominee for president. Thus, Lott started with a Democratic president, Bill Clinton, but was anticipated to work with George W. Bush after the 2000 elections. While those elections put a Republican in the White House, Republicans and Democrats in the Senate were left with an even 50-50 split, and talk centered on how to organize around this unique structural arrangement. There were two majorities (or none at all) and both Tom Daschle (D-SD) and Trent Lott were to serve as majority leaders.[82] The historical anomaly became all the more bizarre when, within a few months, Jim Jeffords (R-VT) switched his partisan affiliation from Republican to Independent and began organizing with the Democrats, which gave Daschle the majority leader's desk. Equilibrium lasted for a year and a half until the 2002 elections swept in a narrow Republican majority, and Lott was poised to cement sole control of majority leadership. On holiday break after the elections, however, Lott was celebrating the 100th birthday of Democrat-turned-Dixiecrat-turned-Republican Senator Strom Thurmond of South Carolina, as legendary for his early racism as for his later longevity. An off-the-cuff remark made in celebration of Thurmond's political endeavors was viewed by many as evidence of Lott's personal racial biases and reverberated through the media.

Within two weeks, after initial support from the White House, fellow Republicans, and even Minority Leader Daschle, there were calls for Lott's resignation as majority leader, and his one-time supporters began to echo the demand. A week after Lott's remarks, President Bush made a high-profile speech in which he disavowed Lott's comments and then remained silent for the next week while the conventional wisdom formed that with carefully placed leaks the administration, notably Bush advisor Karl Rove, was "orchestrating" a behind-the-scenes coup (Allen & Milbank, 2002; Bumiller, 2002; Kurtz, 2002; Lemann, 2003; Lott, 2005; Martinez, 2003). Rumors had persisted through the 107th Congress that the president did not get along with Lott, either personally or professionally, from as far back as 1990 when Lott pointedly had criticized Bush's father, President George H. W. Bush, for reneging on his antitax pledge (Lemann, 2003). With the roar mounting, Trent Lott resigned his post as majority leader on December 20, 2002.

While President Bush had declined to intervene in advocacy of Lott, he had been working behind the scenes to garner support for a man whom he thought could promote his legislative agenda of "compassionate conservatism." This new brand of Republicanism fit Bill Frist; a doctor by profession, he was still new to the Senate and not a Beltway type. He was one to remake the image of the Republican party both within and without the Senate and was thought especially appropriate to salve Lott's gaffe. Bush had selected his favorite and began lobbying among the "old bulls" in the Senate for their support. Before too long, John Warner (R-VA), Pete Domenici (R-NM), and Ted Stevens (R-AK) had spoken together and separately endorsed Frist as their next leader, and by conference call on December 23, 2002, Bill Frist, M.D., was selected by acclamation as majority leader for the incoming Senate.

So Harry Reid was right in attributing Frist's selection to presidential demands, but he was wrong in claiming that it was unprecedented. In fact, the first Senate majority leader, John W. Kern (D-IN) was selected, after only two years in the Senate, because of his support for President Woodrow Wilson's progressive policies. The president needed a man in the Senate to guide his legislative agenda, and Kern's role in doing so set a path that has continued for Senate majority leaders and presidents since.

THE LOGIC OF UNIFIED GOVERNMENT

Among students of congressional leadership, as among practitioners, an important but understudied factor is interinstitutional relationships. These relationships, as they exist among leaders of the legislative and executive branches, serve to constrain behavior; for example, the behaviors of majority leaders in the Senate are constrained by presidential expectations. These constraints are all the more acute when the leaders are of the same party as the president; then, the president is chief partisan and leaders serve as the president's "lieutenants" (Bond & Fleisher, 1990). Scholars since David Truman (1959) have theorized and evidenced that congressional majorities of the president's party are more successful in securing their preferences because of the resources of unified government. However, emphasizing only legislative *success* on roll-call votes overshadows the *constraints* that unified government imposes on majority leadership within the Senate.

Presidential constraints on Senate majority leadership are twofold: presidential influence may be exercised in the selection of leaders as well as in their function. Because the office of Senate majority leader exists by custom, without a constitutional mandate, its emergence and development were prone to partisan and institutional influences. Scholars have offered competing explanations for the emergence of the office; some (e.g., Rothman, 1966; Gamm & Smith, 2000, 2002a, 2002b, 2004; Smith, 2005; Smith & Gamm, 2005) have looked to developments within the chamber, while others (Munk, 1974) have pointed to extra-congressional developments. Both agree that John W. Kern, elected Democratic caucus chairman in 1913, was the first to be referred to as "Senate majority leader" (Gamm & Smith, 2002b; Munk, 1974).

Setting the Path
Margaret Munk (1974) linked the birth of formal leadership offices in the Senate to the expansive reach of the president. Rather than hypothesizing leadership as a response to internal context, such as party competitiveness, as had been Gerald Gamm and Steven Smith's (2002b) assertion, she posited that external factors, namely growing expectations of the presidency, spurred an innovation in the Senate. During the early part of the 20th century, the nationalization of what once had been local issues grew exponentially. The conquering of the frontier and the concentration of urban areas, both linked by railroads, were at once drawing from and supplying an industrial revolution. With this, the hand of the presidency in legislative matters became less likely to be regarded as intrusive and more likely to be demanded by the electorate and Congress alike. It was "in response to this extra-congressional development that a new

practice—one of *partnership* between president and congressional leaders for the purpose of formulating and adopting legislative programs—developed in the Senate" (Munk, 1974, p. 24).

Thirty years after this research, Gamm and Smith (2000, 2002a, 2002b, 2004; Smith, 2005; Smith & Gamm, 2005) produced a series of studies on the emergence and historical development of the office. Using content analysis of major newspapers of the day, they pinpointed the appearance of "official" leadership positions in the Senate and linked it with periods of strong party competition. They noted that as formal leadership positions emerged, leaders became chief spokesmen for their parties and, in so becoming, provided "policy leadership," affecting not only *how* the Senate conducted business (process and procedure) but also *what* business the Senate conducted (setting agendas and passing legislation). Still, an intrachamber focus neglects the extent that presidents influenced the agendas that Senate majority leaders pushed. This influence, present at the beginning, has overshadowed the development of relationships between presidents and Senate majority leaders since Woodrow Wilson and John W. Kern.

Path Dependence
To understand this trend, this chapter relies on the analytical value of "path dependence." As a theory of explanation, path dependence has found purchase in historical studies as well as in those of the social sciences, primarily economics. Given its disparate uses, path dependence has in its most generalized sense become little more than a "notion" meaning that "history matters" (Pierson, 2000, pp. 251–252). Within political science, Paul Pierson (2000, 2004) has argued the value of path dependence with almost missionary zeal. To explain political phenomena, their causes and consequences, he conceptualized path dependence as a process of "increasing returns" (Pierson, 2000, 2004). Drawn from economics literature, the premise is that as decisions in a social process are perpetuated from the original, the expense of change increases such that deviation from the path is undesirable if not impossible.[83] Or, in the language of returns, the value of remaining the same is greater than the value

of change. The result is development (a large consequence) conditioned by the original position (a relatively small or contingent event) (Pierson, 2000). Relevant to the present analysis, scholars of "new institutionalism"— a methodological return to the assumption that behavior is shaped by the institution in which it is embedded (March & Olsen, 1984)—especially are interested in ways in which initial structures and functions of political institutions set continuing operation and development. In the case of Senate majority leadership, the structure of the office—including its practices as well as its norms and values—guides the behavior of its holders relative to presidential relationships. It so happens that continuity rather than change marks the subsequent development of the office.[84] Thus, not only does the president represent a constraint on the selection or operation of leadership but so too does the path of development constrain Senate majority leadership.

Data and Method

By examining cases of Senate majority leaders and presidents coexisting during unified government (see table 5.1) and one unique case of a Senate majority leader and president in divided government (see table 5.2), this chapter, based on an array of data from leading historians, journalistic accounts, and archival collections, traces president-leader relations since Kern. These cases were chosen on the premise that unified government affects congressional behavior (Ripley, 1969a)[85] and for the heightened appearance of presidential influence that the record provides. These cases gain utility because periods of unified government cover most of the years of the history of the office of the Senate majority leader, yielding a sizeable sample from which to draw (compare tables 5.1 and 5.2) and covering significant eras of Senate majority leadership and legislative activity. The cases are not meant to be directly comparable, nor do they represent a linear timeline of the history of the office. Rather, the theme of presidential influence—whether in selection of Senate majority leaders or in the carrying out of their duties—links these observations. The unique case of Senate Majority Leader Lyndon Johnson (D-TX) and President Dwight

TABLE 5.1. Unified government: U.S. Senate majority leaders and presidents.

Democratic President	Democratic Majority Leader	Republican President	Republican Majority Leader
Woodrow Wilson	John W. Kern (IN)	Warren Harding	Henry Cabot Lodge (MA)
Woodrow Wilson	Thomas S. Martin (VA)	Calvin Coolidge	Henry Cabot Lodge (MA)
Franklin D. Roosevelt	Joseph T. Robinson (AR)	Calvin Coolidge	Charles Curtis (KS)
Franklin D. Roosevelt	Alben W. Barkley (KY)	Herbert Hoover	James E. Watson (IN)
Harry Truman	Alben W. Barkley (KY)	Dwight D. Eisenhower	Robert A. Taft (OH)
Harry Truman	Scott W. Lucas (IL)	Dwight D. Eisenhower	William F. Knowland (CA)
Harry Truman	Ernest W. McFarland (AZ)	Ronald Reagan	Howard H. Baker, Jr. (TN)
John F. Kennedy	Mike Mansfield (MT)	Ronald Reagan	Robert J. Dole (KS)
Lyndon B. Johnson	Mike Mansfield (MT)	George W. Bush	C. Trent Lott (MS)
Jimmy Carter	Robert C. Byrd (WV)	George W. Bush	William H. Frist (TN)
William J. Clinton	George J. Mitchell (ME)		

TABLE 5.2. Divided government: U.S. Senate majority leaders and presidents.

Democratic President	Republican Majority Leader	Republican President	Democratic Majority Leader
Woodrow Wilson	Henry Cabot Lodge (MA)	Dwight D. Eisenhower	Lyndon B. Johnson (TX)
Herbert Hoover	James E. Watson (IN)	Richard Nixon	Mike Mansfield (MT)
Harry Truman	Wallace H. White, Jr. (ME)	Gerald Ford	Mike Mansfield (MT)
William J. Clinton	C. Trent Lott (MS)	Ronald Reagan	Robert C. Byrd (WV)
		George H.W. Bush	George J. Mitchell (ME)
		George W. Bush	Thomas A. Daschle (SD)

Eisenhower is an example of a majority leader and presidential relationship during a period of divided government that merits special attention, for it represents an exception that proves the rule. That is, the power that Johnson exercised as Senate majority leader under divided government makes all the more clear the presidential constraints that hinder Senate majority leadership under unified government. All in all, these cases offer a perspective on interinstitutional constraints on the birth and development of the office of Senate majority leader.

Findings indicate, first, a counterpoint to standard intrachamber explanations of leadership development and, second, an historical partnership between presidents and Senate majority leaders in setting and pushing legislative agendas. This partnership is conspicuous in the Senate because its history of individualism dilutes the effects of majority partisanship (Lawrence, Maltzman, & Smith, 2006) and because of the informality with which the head of the upper chamber emerged. The role of Senate majority leader remains shaped by expectations established in its first years and, thus, suggests a path-dependent evolution of the office. Moreover, the implications for this development are significant for both presidential and legislative theories of leadership. For presidential leadership, a partnership with the leader of the Senate reinforces an individual rather than institutional perspective of the presidency—one that underscores personal bargaining and negotiating skills (Neustadt, 1960) in addition to unilateral action (Howell, 2003)—and highlights enduring contexts that shape traditions of executive authority. For congressional leadership, Senate majority leaders have in the president yet a fourth constituency to represent together with state, party, and the institution. For both, these findings add another complexity to the constitutional tradition of separation of powers and the balance between them.

Early Leaders

John W. Kern (D-IN)

John W. Kern was in no small part selected leader for his ties to the president and his policies (Kern having chaired the platform committee at the Democratic National Convention that nominated Wilson). Probably more than another president would have, Wilson, given his academic background and political-science expertise (e.g., Wilson, 1885), was determined to use the powers of the presidency to affect a progressive legislative program. He found sympathy among certain Senate Democrats who recognized that they needed someone to guide his proposals to fruition. Kern was relatively new to the Senate as was a narrow Democratic majority, the latter having come about in the 1912 election that brought progressive Democrats to challenge Republicans and Southern conservatives. As proponents for change in both party and senatorial affairs, this group of junior Democrats formed a bloc favoring various reorganization efforts. They put forth many proposals, all of which were aimed in some fashion to undermine the seniority system that they felt had shut them out of policymaking.[86] The end goal was the removal of Thomas S. Martin (D-VA) from party leadership; as caucus chairman, he had been a stringent gatekeeper against progressive legislation (Oleszek, 1991).

In his two years in the Senate, Kern had proven himself to be a stalwart on progressive policy, acting for pension reform, workers' rights, and even campaign-finance regulation. It is unclear whether Wilson or the Senate liberals first recommended Kern for the post, but both agreed that he should be the guide for the president's program (Munk, 1974). The progressive tide was so overwhelming that the conservative faction did not field a candidate, with Martin having withdrawn a month before balloting (Oleszek, 1991). Therefore, his colleagues' most visible, if not deadliest, blow to the seniority system came when they irreverently selected first-term Senator John W. Kern majority leader on March 5, 1913.[87]

With Kern at the helm, in 10 days, this bloc of progressives managed to reshuffle committee assignments in the steering committee, and when the dust had settled, the headline in the *Washington Post* read, "Senate is Wilson's: President's Friends In Control Under Reorganization" (March 16, 1913, p. 6).[88] Out of this Senate upheaval came the first Senate majority leader, birthed in the expectation of loyalty to the presidency. There was no talk of separation of powers or checks and balances; rather, these progressive senators bound themselves to a president and his program and chose one of their own to promote it through to passage. "Never before had the president's party in the Senate intentionally elected a floor leader for the primary purpose of implementing an executive-initiated legislative program" (Munk, 1974, p. 31).

As Munk also noted, the relationship between Wilson and Kern was not merely a formal one. Not content simply to present his package to the Senate, Wilson frequently telephoned his congressional leadership and held conferences in the president's room in the Capitol when key legislation was pending. But it was on Kern that he especially depended. Kern discussed with the president not only administration objectives but also how they might be received in the Senate. Kern's biographer told that Kern often walked alone to the White House at night to meet with Wilson, giving instructions to his and the president's staff that "no publicity should ever be given to [my] visits at the other end of the avenue" (Bowers, 1918, p. 363).

Although Kern secured many of Wilson's programs, he was most successful in establishing a precedent for a White House-Senate alliance that has continued through each of his successors, although each leader has played the role in different ways according to the demands of the president as well as his own.

Joseph T. Robinson (D-AR)
Members of the White House staff of Franklin D. Roosevelt were not shy about dabbling in legislative affairs, and for his unprecedented New Deal programs, Roosevelt found in Majority Leader Robinson a willing ally. Robinson had accepted his party's 1928 nomination for vice president and running mate to Alfred E. Smith for president. Munk (1974, p. 32) wrote that Robinson "shelved his Southern conservatism" to become a ready advocate of New Deal legislation. That is misleading, however, since Robinson was never a conservative Southerner.[89] He was always on whatever line may be drawn to distinguish moderate and liberal Democrats; a progressive Southerner, he was an exception among majority leaders—lying beyond his party's ideological mainstream (see chapter 4). From the Emergency Banking Relief Act of 1933 through provisions to end the gold standard

and to create the Tennessee Valley Authority, Robinson worked quickly and feverishly to give the president his "whole-hearted cooperation, day and night" (qtd. in Bacon, 1991, p. 82).[90] His health was tenuous by the end of his first Congress, and after the blur of legislation began to sink in, he privately expressed some doubts about the new laws and the rapidity at which they were enacted (Bacon, 1991). But publicly, he was Roosevelt's faithful advocate, even leading the fight for a bill outlawing a certain tax refund in the face of opposition from his fellow Southerners, most Democrats, and virtually all senior senators. This prompted one writer to muse, "One wonders if Senator Robinson's fidelity to official duty is not carrying him rather far" (qtd. in Bacon, 1991, p. 82).[91]

After two congresses of this tension, in 1936, Roosevelt and Robinson (both without serious primary opposition) were reelected in landslides, and the president proposed his most audacious executive and legislative maneuver—to enlarge the Supreme Court with members of his choosing to ensure a majority favorable to upholding his New Deal programs, which had begun finding their way to the highest adjudication. Immediately, the "court-packing" plan split Democrats in the Senate, but also rather immediately, the Supreme Court capitulated by upholding the Wagner Labor Relations Act of 1935, prompting Robinson to advise his president to withdraw the court-reform proposal (Bacon, 1991; Barkley, 1954; Ritchie, 1991). Roosevelt, however, did not view the plan as moot despite the "switch" in court opinion and pressed harder for Robinson to find the votes. After much persuasion, Roosevelt modified the plan to require retirement for aged justices, and Robinson pushed for the substitute bill in no small part because his own nomination to the court was at stake (Bacon, 1991). Roosevelt felt he had to fill a vacancy with Robinson, who was viewed by most as a conservative but whom Roosevelt knew to be loyal to his progressive cause. So Robinson set to work urging his colleagues to support the modified plan, if not for its merits, then for the sake of old friendships and political favors (Bacon, 1991). On the eve of debate, the count stood at 40 for, 40 against, and 16 undecided. Debate opened on the floor and was in full form with threats of filibuster and rulings on points of order. Donald Bacon wrote that "[Robinson's] face reddened, his body trembled, his arms flailed as he smote the opposition" (1991, p. 91). And after two such intensive days, he returned home and died in his apartment of an apparent heart attack. He had expired in his expected role, majority leader as presidential broker; "he died because he was forced into a battle at a time when he should never attempted such a fight," said Senator Royal Copeland (D-NY) (Bacon, 1991, p. 92).

Alben W. Barkley (D-KY)
Mourning did not hinder Roosevelt or his Senate colleagues. Jockeying to replace Robinson as majority leader began on the funeral train from Washington to Little Rock, and Alben Barkley and Pat Harrison (D-MS), chair of the finance committee, were the frontrunners. Roosevelt intervened in the vacuum by penning a letter to Barkley, assistant leader under Robinson and acting majority leader upon his death, the day after Robinson died. The salutation "My dear Alben" was a signal to many Senate Democrats that Roosevelt had finally stepped over the line by fully endorsing a candidate that would have no choice but to support the president in turn. While such affection for Barkley was overt, Roosevelt also positioned aides behind the scenes to campaign for him (Ritchie, 1991), and on July 21, 1937, Barkley was selected by the last ballot—a proxy vote—38 to 37. "Roosevelt's involvement in the Senate's internal affairs simply confirmed suspicions for those who saw dictatorial tendencies behind his actions, and more deeply entrenched the party's division over the court bill" (Ritchie, 1991, p. 129).

From the outset of his tenure, Barkley carried the mark of Roosevelt, and many colleagues felt he spoke for the administration rather than the Senate. It was probably of little coincidence, then, that on his first day as majority leader, Roosevelt suffered perhaps his greatest legislative defeat—the Senate voted overwhelmingly to recommit the court bill, and by a similar margin, 71 to 19, the Senate overrode a presidential veto on an act to extend farm interest rates.[92] With this and subsequent actions, Barkley as majority leader felt the blame from the president and his New Deal liberals for not passing all of the president's program and from conservatives for adhering to it so closely (Ritchie, 1991).

War came, and Barkley had served more than a full term as majority leader. In 1944 Roosevelt proposed a tax bill to finance the war effort that Congress passed, but only after cutting it to one-fifth what he had originally asked. Barkley strongly urged the president to sign, claiming this was the most he could get in an election year, but Roosevelt held his ground and stunned Barkley by vetoing the measure, making him the first executive ever to veto a revenue bill (Ritchie, 1991). Barkley took it as a personal affront, although he felt constrained by his responsibility as majority leader to support the White House. Sensing the rift between the two was beyond repair, he decided to resign as majority leader because he believed he could no longer fulfill the role of chief supporter of the president. The implications of this decision are stark—he believed his loyalty to the president to surpass that to his party colleagues. He gave up his role as *Senate majority leader* while supporting a *party* position that contradicted that of the *president*. Barkley fulfilled the role of Senate leader in terms of what he could do for the White House and inextricably cemented the expectation of an executive-legislative alliance.

Rumors spread around the Capitol of his plans, so that on the morning he rose to speak, the chamber was filled from gallery to floor. In his speech, he exhorted members to override the president's veto before pledging to resign when the Democratic conference met the following morning. Roosevelt sought to mollify his relationship with his majority leader even as the caucus unanimously reelected Barkley leader: "By his one-vote margin in the 1937 contest when he was first elected leader, the impression was given, and it has been the impression ever since, that he spoke to us for the president. Now that he has been unanimously elected, he speaks for us to the president," proclaimed Senator Elbert Thomas (D-UT) (Ritchie, 1991, p. 147). But once restored, Barkley continued to bridge the gap between the White House and Senate primarily in the form of administrator rather than initiator.

Upon Roosevelt's death, Barkley found himself tied to a new president, but his role soon was altered when the Democrats lost their Senate majority in the 1946 elections. Even as minority leader to President Harry S. Truman, Barkley was no more independent. In fact, his conception of majority leadership was so fixed to the White House that he encouraged the Republican Majority Leader Wallace H. White (R-ME) to cooperate with the Democratic president:

> By and large, no matter what party is in power—no matter who is president—the majority leader of the Senate is expected to be the legislative spokesman of the administration...It is his duty to confer with the president about the wisdom and the propriety of recommendations that he makes to the Congress, the chances of their enactment, sometimes even to suggest to the President that he call members of the Senate down to the White House and explain to them so that they may understand his measures...[93]

THE MODERN MOMENT—LYNDON B. JOHNSON (D-TX)

A decade later, Senate Democrats were in the opposite position, and this case of a majority leader and a president under divided government is an exception that proves the rule. With a Democratic majority in the Senate, there was a Republican in the White House, and for the first time since the emergence of formal leadership, the Democrats who had dominated for decades had a majority but no president. In addition, their leader was Lyndon Johnson, still new to the Senate, who just two years earlier had replaced Ernest McFarland (D-AZ), upon his electoral defeat at the hands of Barry Goldwater (R-AZ), as party leader on the word of Richard Russell (D-GA). At the time, Johnson was the youngest, but not the newest (Kern still holds that distinction), to have been selected party leader. And he quickly proved himself capable of leadership. There has been no shortage of documentation and analysis of the Johnson years in the Senate, and scholars universally agree that during his tenure, he was "master of the Senate" (Goodwin, 1976, p. 114; Caro, 2002). As majority leader, his reputation was one of cajoling, pleading, threatening, pledging, cornering, wrangling, and prodding, and there is little doubt that he changed the office of majority leader by the sheer force of his personality.[94] His time marks a watershed in the evolution of the post; no leader before or since has worn the office like him. In internal dealings with his fellow senators, Johnson was shrewd, calculating, and frequently triumphant.[95]

With regard to his relationship with President Eisenhower, Johnson adopted the philosophy of his predecessors in Senate majority leadership: "Johnson always felt that when a president asked for something like [a foreign policy resolution], he had to have it, because if you turned him down then it looked as though there was genuine division within the United States."[96] His reasoning was less deferential than calculating. He saw the wave of popularity that carried Eisenhower into office and recognized it would be self-defeating for Senate Democrats to challenge him, so Johnson worked at cultivating a relationship with Eisenhower:

> Lyndon Johnson used to could go down and have drinks with Dwight Eisenhower all the time, and it was an essential part of their relationship, just to have a social relationship with President Eisenhower. Johnson was afraid of Eisenhower, he was afraid of his popularity and he was afraid not to [go]—he didn't want to be seen as somebody who was unkind to Eisenhower, for political reasons he didn't...He knew that he was smarter than Eisenhower, quite a lot smarter politically and knew more about Washington and the town here.[97]

So, he led his majority as the loyal opposition: "I think it's the opposition's duty to carefully consider and weigh every recommendation that the Executive makes and support those that can be supported in good conscience and oppose those that can't, and when they are opposed, to oppose them on principle and oppose them in a principled manner."[98] The strategy came from George Reedy, who among other titles was chief of staff of the Democratic policy committee and served as general political strategist for Johnson; it was a study in triangulation:

> Eisenhower had been associated with so many Democratic presidents and had been in on the making of so much foreign policy that was made under Democrats during a period when the Republicans, and particularly the Republicans under [Republican leader Robert A.] Taft, were opposed to that policy, that he and the congressional Republicans were just bound to be at loggerheads and that the Democrats might as well take advantage of it. Now, it made an awful lot of sense, so much sense that when [Johnson]

started calling Democrats in individually and hitting them with it, they just had to buy it. They didn't like it, but they just had to buy it. And it was one of the methods that did achieve a very strong form of unification among the Democrats.[99]

Plus, he read the mood of the public and not only its attraction to Eisenhower but also its weariness of partisan bickering: "[E]very time the Democrats cast a vote against Eisenhower, out in the country people were saying, 'Uh huh, they think it's their business to oppose Eisenhower. They aren't voting against that bill because it's a bad one, they're just against it because they're Democrats.'"[100]

Johnson's support was not unlimited, however, and at times the president and Senate majority leader faced off:

> The two men had to oppose each other...Eisenhower, after all, had certain obligations to the Republican Party and Johnson certainly had obligations to the Democratic Party. And there was a certain point at which Johnson's tactic of supporting Eisenhower against the Republicans was becoming damn embarrassing with an election coming up.[101]

President Eisenhower at times commented on the "cold war of partisan politics" with the Democrats in charge of Congress, leaving Johnson to rebut that Democrats had passed more of Eisenhower's program than the Republicans would have had they controlled Congress.[102] Without speculating on counterfactuals, Senate Democrats under Johnson had done much to advance Eisenhower's proposals; the key to success was the foreign-policy focus that occupied the president and Congress during that decade. "Most of the Eisenhower proposals were in foreign policy fields, where he and the Democrats were much more sympathetic than he and the Republicans."[103]

Johnson, as a Democratic majority leader without a Democratic president, chose to outline his own legislative program. He developed an 11-point agenda covering familiar issues, including Social Security, taxes, school construction, public roads, and immigration, "around which it should be possible to mobilize substantial Democratic support, including

Southern, and with minimum requirements for Republican assistance to assume passage."[104] This series of legislative proposals was focused on domestic politics, an arena in which the Democrats had a comparative advantage as Eisenhower concentrated his agenda on foreign policy. This initiative in turn, most likely, reduced Johnson's constraints as majority leader. In fact, circumstances as much as personality defined Johnson's tenure. If he had been constrained by a Democratic administration with heavy legislative preferences, it is unlikely that he could have been as strong a leader as he was. The context of divided control, in large measure, allowed Johnson to be chief partisan:

> It's one thing to be a Democrat to whom the Republican president comes to make arrangements and accommodations, and another to be told to get a certain bill through. It's one thing to do, as Johnson had done with the Democratic Policy Committee, to run your own Administration and another to receive bills from the Administration and be told to get them through in as nearly a coherent form as possible.[105]

While he did not have the advantage of a president to use the tools of the office to accomplish policy, Johnson also was not constrained by responsibilities to yet another "master." Thus, this case of Senate majority leadership under divided government is exceptional in that Johnson was a majority leader who found power, but that he did so under divided government supports the proposition that leaders under unified government are constrained by presidential demands.

THE POST-JOHNSON ERA—MIKE MANSFIELD (D-MT)

Mike Mansfield became majority leader in January 1961, after nearly a decade as assistant leader to Lyndon Johnson. Johnson was now about to be inaugurated as vice president and his and Mansfield's colleague John F. Kennedy, as president. Mansfield professed reticence at accepting the leader position and did so only after several calls from the president-elect and the vice president-elect (Baker, 1991; Oberdorfer, 2003). There even was a call from Bobby Baker, Johnson's aide de camp, who, until scandal forced him out, worked with Mansfield as secretary for the majority.[106] That staffing arrangement was tangible evidence of presidential influence in the Senate majority leader's office. Once he took the job, Mansfield would not relinquish it until he had set the longevity record for holding the office. His period as leader, 1961 to 1976, would coincide with no fewer than four presidencies—Kennedy, Johnson, Richard Nixon, and Gerald Ford. For half that time, under presidents Kennedy and Johnson, Mansfield operated under unified government.

It has become commonplace to describe Mansfield's performance as a reaction against and departure from Johnson's energetic and dynamic leadership. Mansfield's philosophy of leadership can only be described as humble: "I will be the leader, but responsibility will be diffused. I would like, if possible, to make our efforts cooperative. If there is a decision to be made, I'll make it...but only after consultation, advice, and counsel."[107] Colleagues who served under both Johnson and Mansfield were especially observant of the change: "Mansfield is so far in the other direction from Johnson. Mansfield is more of a gentlemanly man than Johnson ever thought of being, but Johnson got things done."[108] This stylistic difference between the two majority leaders is probably best exemplified in this example from Senator Thruston Morton (D-KY):

> [Johnson] was a tough leader, and I think you have to be tough to run that place. I can remember time after time when then-Senator Johnson would say, "All right, I don't care how late we stay here tonight. We're going to finish this bill."...Now, Senator Mansfield, for whom I have the greatest affection—he started out being too easy. If I went to Senator Mansfield and said, "Mike, this is my anniversary, or my birthday; I hope we can get through early tonight; I've got a dinner party." "Oh sure, I'll accommodate you." Well that's fine, but that doesn't get the job done.[109]

If Mansfield was reserved in managing the floor, he was equally mild behind the scenes. Senator William Proxmire (D-WI) described his service on the Democratic steering committee under Johnson and then under Mansfield: "[Johnson] would give his list and we'd simply ratify it... Mansfield didn't make any effort to influence it. In fact, he felt that it was up to the Steering Committee to do it and he didn't want to have any input in that."[110] In fact, Proxmire further recalled that Mansfield never tried to get him to vote for a particular measure or engage in methods of persuasion to push a bill: "Mansfield felt that wasn't his function."[111]

If Mansfield's style of majority leadership differed from Johnson's, his dependent relationship with presidents resembled that of his predecessors and successors. Mansfield himself exhibited familiar expectations of service to his Democratic president. At the outset of his leadership, Mansfield proclaimed, "It is incumbent on me,...to bring a fusion of views in order to pass responsible legislation. That legislation is going to be the president's program."[112] "My job is to represent the Senate to the president, and the president to the Senate...It's kind of a spot and one of the reasons I didn't want the job."[113] From a man who did not want the job in the first place came a clear understanding of its constraints.

To new Democratic members in 1969, Mansfield explained the new order of divided government by way of describing how he had led Senate Democrats and the policy committee under unified government:

> Whatever functions this committee might have had beyond the routine scheduling of legislation were muted. We...mostly considered bills on the calendar and how best to deal with the Administration's legislative program. On occasion, we exchanged...our sentiments respecting the Administration's policies and other matters. In turn, the sense of these sentiments was communicated by me, in confidence, to President Kennedy and President Johnson. As leader of the nation as well as of the party, the president determined what disposition to make of these Senate Democratic views in the policies of the Administration.[114]

Mansfield's admission that he and the Senate Democratic policy committee had existed to represent presidential policies was made clearer when he contemplated the absence of a Democratic president:

> The question which is on my mind now and has been on my mind for some weeks is the kind of changes which may be in order. We no longer have at the White House an automatically receptive ear to the views of Democratic senators. Conversely, I might add,

we do not have an automatic party concern in seeking to cushion whatever difficulties the new Administration may bring upon itself.[115]

The last sentence signals what was for Mansfield an important duty of his majority leadership—to buffer the president against himself. Instead of finding the prospect of Senate majority leadership under divided government liberating, as did Johnson,[116] Mansfield seemed to flounder and return to the status quo of deference to the president:

> I would open the discussion only by reiterating my personal view that we must put, above all else, the interests of the nation and the president's unique role in safeguarding them as well as the demeanor and effective operation of the Senate as the constitutional institution through which each of us serves those interests. These are the highest priorities. Beyond that, I have no preconceived notions of how we should proceed either in the leadership of the Senate or in this committee, in the light of the changed circumstances. I am open to any and all suggestions with respect to the leadership of the Senate and with respect to the operation of this committee.[117]

As legislative proposals flowed under the initiative of President Kennedy, the White House pressed Mansfield into service frequently; Don Oberdorfer (2003, p. 175) found records of 50 appointments a year with Kennedy from 1961–1963. Activity only intensified under Johnson, and through private meetings (about 63) and telephone calls (more than 200), the president made known his legislative needs (Oberdorfer, 2003, p. 225). Although Johnson was prone to apply "The Treatment" to get his way, he rarely, if ever, took that approach with the laid-back Mansfield. Instead, transcripts of recorded telephone conversations indicate Mansfield was deferential to his former Senate colleague, now president, "saying 'Yes, sir' to Johnson's suggestions..., and even occasionally addressing Johnson as 'boss'" (Oberdorfer, 2003, p. 225). Many interactions dealt with military action in Vietnam, and on this issue, Johnson feigned consultation when decisions regarding, for example, escalation had already been made. Mansfield himself described his association with President Johnson: "All told, I am down [at the White House] four or five times a week. I am invited to sit in with the National Security Council. I get a phone call nearly every day."[118] On the issue of Vietnam, president and Senate majority leader were split; Mansfield, having been an emissary from President Franklin Roosevelt to China, had a personal interest in Asian affairs, but he never was a vocal detractor of the president's policies. But when the White House, in an attempt to pay for its vast domestic agenda, cut some veterans' hospitals, including one in Miles City, Montana, the Senate majority leader pushed back. Mansfield wrote to Johnson reminding him of the cross-cutting pressures of the office:

> I can and do recall the time when you were the senator from Texas and the majority leader. At that time, I could understand and sympathize with your position on matters of this kind which affected your state very directly. But I also recognize your changed situation as president and I can understand and appreciate the scope and demands of your national responsibilities.... As a senator from Montana I can act in no way other than in the best interests of my state. As majority leader,...I have always tried to do what I could to help you in the discharge of your present heavy national responsibilities as president and I will continue to do so to the best of my ability. Were you still in your old shoes, I am sure you would act in the same fashion.[119]

At one point in his tenure, Mansfield clarified his obligation to the president as he saw it:

> Now, if a serious question of difference ever arose, I would consider it my duty to go to the president and discuss it with him, and if we couldn't reach an accommodation, then I would have to consider taking action of some sort as far as the leadership is concerned.... If If the difference were serious enough I would resign from the job. ("Why Kennedy's Program," 1962, p. 67)

Mansfield's pledge is starkly reminiscent of his predecessor Alben Barkley's resignation when he "fell on his sword" in protest of Roosevelt's veto of a tax bill. The majority leader of the Senate retained the shackle of the president that has constrained Senate majority leaders since the beginning.

REPUBLICAN PRESIDENTS AND REPUBLICAN SENATE MAJORITY LEADERS

If the path of development of the Senate majority leader's office seems bound to relationships between Democratic majority leaders and Democratic presidents, recent history seems to confirm these relationships in Republican Senate majority leaders and Republican presidents. Just as there are noticeable partisan differences in the voting behavior of Democratic and Republican Senate majority leaders, as evidenced in the previous chapter, there might be partisan differences in president-leader relations. Indeed, in her survey of executive-legislative interactions between president and majority leader, Munk (1974) observed that Republican leaders have been less inclined than Democrats to form a team relationship with presidents. She attributed this trend not to a fundamental difference between the two parties but to the fact that "the modern period has been devoid of strong, aggressive Republican presidents" (p. 36). Moreover, the Republican party has rarely had majority control of the Senate at the same time it has controlled the White House.

Beginning with the majority leadership of Henry Cabot Lodge (R-MA), Republicans seemed to set their own terms for presidential expectations (Widenor, 1991). President Harding's lack of managerial inclinations and Lodge's foreign-policy interest distanced them both from Senate agenda setting so that a faction of progressives effectively controlled the chamber (Munk, 1974). And Senate Majority Leader Robert A. Taft (R-OH) took advantage of President Eisenhower's legislative passivity to set the balance of legislative power squarely in the Senate (Merry, 1991). Although Taft followed the norm of partnership by, for example, weekly conferences with the White House, the presidential agenda for whose success he was responsible was shaped by his ideological preferences—perhaps a bitter irony given that Eisenhower had defeated him for the Republican presidential nomination (Munk, 1974). Still, it was William F. Knowland

(R-CA) who publicly dissented from some of President Eisenhower's policies (such as Eisenhower's opposition to the Bricker Amendment[120]) and who thus exhibited a leadership independent of the White House. Knowland's independence caused some in the Eisenhower administration who had been conditioned by the tag-team relationship they witnessed with Democratic Senate majority leaders and Democratic presidents, to call for Knowland's resignation (Munk, 1974; Montgomery & Johnson, 1998). Of course, this party division doubtlessly enabled Johnson's strategy, once Democrats had reclaimed a Senate majority, to succeed and mark his tenure as a watershed moment.

Munk (1974) wrote after the terms of President Eisenhower, during that of Richard Nixon, and before Ronald Reagan and George W. Bush. After a generation, the universe of cases has expanded, and her conclusions can be updated.

Howard H. Baker, Jr. (R-TN)

Howard H. Baker, Jr. (R-TN) had served as the leader of Senate Republicans for four years while they were in the minority. With the election of 1980, Republican senators rode Ronald Reagan's coattails to a majority and returned Baker as their leader. And from the beginning, even after Reagan had trounced him in Republican primaries, Baker gave no indication that he was anything other than Reagan's man in the Senate.

For example, all senators with their busy schedules frequently decline invitations to speak at high-school commencements, to have photos taken on the steps of the Capitol with Girl Scout troops, to autograph index cards for someone's collection, among a myriad of requests asked of them. Baker declined many such appeals on the basis of, not his work for the Senate, but his work for President Reagan. His letters of declination read: "...the president's proposals are commanding all of my time; and I, therefore, have to restrict all meetings and outside activity in order to devote full-time to the swift passage of the president's economic program."[121] Baker's excuse was less than hyperbole; elsewhere he remembered, "I dealt with him extensively and almost daily. It wasn't long before I thought I had a pretty good and in-depth feeling for the Reagan personality, which was very special."[122] Unlike relationships between previous Senate majority leaders and presidents, Baker and Reagan learned about each other through politics, as Reagan admittedly "didn't know the players that well."[123] But once acquainted, the relationship quickly became strong and personal; when President Reagan was hospitalized after the assassination attempt, Senate Majority Leader Baker was one of the few for whom Mrs. Reagan made an exception to all visitation.[124]

Like other Senate majority leaders before him, Baker understood his role as majority leader relative to the president. Ruminating on his leadership, Baker offered insight on how future Senate majority leaders should fulfill their duties:

> Work with the president, whoever he or she may be, whenever possible. When I became majority leader after the elections of 1980, I had to decide whether I would try to set a separate agenda for the Senate, with our brand new Republican majority, or try to see how our new president, with a Republican Senate, could work together as a team to enact our programs. I chose the latter course, and I believe history has proved me right.[125]

In fact, he was so attuned to Reagan's program that two years after Baker retired from leadership and from the Senate, Reagan appointed him his chief of staff. He served during the last tumultuous years of Reagan's second term, calming waves from the Iran-Contra affair.

Robert J. Dole (R-KS)
Following Baker's Senate retirement, the race for Republican leader was thrown open, and no fewer than five candidates emerged for only the third balloting for majority leader.[126] Bob Dole was ultimately successful and in a news conference announcing his victory, portrayed the Senate as his top priority followed by the president's program: "Our agenda is to retain the Republican majority in 1986, and at the same time we will support the president's program *when we can*" (Rogers & Shribman, 1984, emphasis added). But he apparently saw a stronger duty to the administration than his remarks implied; he said later that he planned to work closely with

the White House and referred to President Reagan as his "*boss*" (Granat, 1984, emphasis added). And two years later when talk began of his running in 1988 to succeed Reagan, senators and pundits alike questioned his role as majority leader, observing that as leader, he is the "president's man; as candidate, he must also be his own" (Rogers, 1986). Dole was criticized for his loyalty to Reagan, and his candidacy discounted for having settled too closely with Reagan's agenda (Rogers, 1986). Although he initially sought to make his leadership independent from the White House, he was unsuccessful and, in the end, marked for doing what has been expected from majority leaders since the origin of the office—being the president's chief legislative advocate.

William H. Frist, M.D. (R-TN)
The next marker on the path was the transition from Lott to Frist under President George W. Bush. Bush's intervention in the selection of the Senate majority leader may appear unseemly, but it is not unprecedented. His desire for a working partner to conform to his will on a legislative agenda and to accomplish that program has been evidenced by predecessors since Woodrow Wilson similarly handpicked Kern to lead a new "progressive" Democratic program. Roosevelt campaigned for Barkley's ascension to the leader's desk. And the pattern was repeated by President-elect John F. Kennedy, who begged in a series of phone calls for Mike Mansfield to take the helm after Johnson, so the majority leader could press for his civil-rights programs (Oberdorfer, 2003; Valeo, 1999). While President Bush may not have been as overt as Roosevelt's letter to Barkley generations earlier, the outcome and effects were the same: Bill Frist was selected majority leader, and he carried, among scholars and senators themselves, the blessing as well as the stigma of Bush's personal touch (e.g., Cochran & Nather, 2003; Oppenheimer, 2005a).

Bush's support carried a quid pro quo; his intervention in Frist's selection as majority leader suggested he needed Frist to accomplish a signature proposal—overhaul of Medicare. The legislation carried a $300 billion price tag and found opposition on both sides of the aisle. Who better to guide Medicare reform but a surgeon? Trent Lott supposed this legislative strategy explained why Bush didn't offer his support to Lott during the Thurmond affair—"they felt Frist would have been more likely than I to steer the drug bill through the Senate. They would have been right about that. I would not have let this particular prescription drug plan pass through the Senate on my watch" (Lott, 2005, p. 292). That rumor perhaps gains credence with the hard path the Medicare bill took to become law, finally passing on a narrow vote and with the pleadings of Majority Leader Frist to his predecessor Lott (Lott, 2005).

The debt of presidential intervention in Frist's selection was further paid by his service toward securing President Bush's judicial nominations. Perpetually simmering, it seems, in the background of partisan politics are disputes about judicial nominations. The minority party seeks to exercise whatever leverage it can muster by practicing its constitutional dictate to "advise and consent"—emphasis on advise, less on consent. Per the norm in contemporary politics (Binder & Maltzman, 2009), the Senate Democratic minority had bided its time in acquiescing to presidential appointments in the hopes that the election in 2004 would bring a change of party and thus the opportunity for a Democratic president to fill the benches. When Bush was elected to his second term, Democrats continued to stall, hoping Bush's lame-duck status would preserve the seats in hopes of a Democratic presidential victory in 2008. Of course, this strategy, in part, was recompense for the Republican delay of President Clinton's judicial nominees a term earlier. In answer to the lengthy Democratic filibuster of judicial nominations, some Republicans called for Senate Majority Leader Frist to exercise the "nuclear option." A parliamentary weapon, this alternative to the standard cloture vote would remove judicial nominations from the types of motions that may be filibustered. Former Majority Leader Lott described the strategy this way:

> It was simplicity itself: We would ask the presiding officer, as a point of order, what vote was required to approve a judicial nominee. The answer, of course, would be a simple majority. The Democrats would appeal that ruling by the presiding officer of the Senate. After that, however, the motion could be tabled by a majority vote. Bam! We'd have a new precedent that would defeat

filibusters and give nominees what they deserve—a clean vote, with the victory or defeat determined by a simple majority. (Lott, 2005, p. 288)

This way around judicial filibusters would be nuclear in that it would destroy any remaining comity in a Senate known for bitter partisanship. The nuclear option was thwarted by a bipartisan group, dubbed the "Gang of 14," who in a series of late-night meetings arrived at a compromise that would preserve a hallmark of Senate procedure while finally calling for an up-or-down vote on Bush's judicial nominations. In this battle, Senate Majority Leader Frist met with blame mostly from conservative elites. After having promised conservatives that he would secure roll-call votes on Bush's judicial nominees, Frist was roundly criticized for not pushing the nuclear button and for being outmaneuvered not only by Democrats but also by members of his own majority party (Cook, 2005; Nagourney, 2005).[127] The criticism highlights the expectation for the Senate majority leader to acquiesce to and fulfill a presidential agenda.

INTERPRETATIONS AND IMPLICATIONS

The partnership between Senate majority leaders and presidents has meaning in several respects. First, it supports an extra-congressional explanation (e.g., Munk, 1974) for the birth of the office of Senate majority leader. Whereas standard congressional literature (Gamm & Smith 2000, 2002a, 2002b, 2004; Smith 2005; Smith & Gamm, 2005) has pointed to intrabranch influences on the emergence of Senate leadership, this research emphasizes an interinstitutional dimension to the founding and development of the office. Moreover, the evolution of the office has been path dependent—decisions made at the outset between Kern and Wilson established expectations for all that would follow. The interinstitutional contexts in which the office was born shaped the relationship between future presidents and Senate majority leaders in service if not outright selection, thus the path as well as the president constrain majority leaders. Understanding the creation and evolution of the office and its persistence depends on two important features. The first is that the designation of Kern as founding leader was a casual event, especially his relationship with the president, which led to significant and lasting consequences. The second is that once the interbranch relationship was positively established, there were no ready or necessary demands for an alternative. The most recent marker on the path—Bush's involvement in Frist's selection—was not an isolated response to political expedience. Instead, it was part of a recurring pattern of partnership that reinforced interbranch functions.

Second, an alliance between the leader of the Senate and the leader of the executive branch violates standard norms of separation of powers. The president is poised to set and shape the agenda in the upper house of Congress—something the framers would not have envisioned. That the framers created three "separate and coequal" branches of government is the stuff of elementary social studies, and that this separation is circumvented not by the usual checks and balances but by a partnership between the White House and the upper chamber extends the bounds of the "imperial presidency" (Schlesinger, Jr., 1973).

Third, in terms of theories of presidential leadership, this finding suggests an *individual* rather than *institutional* perspective of the presidency, one that emphasizes the power of the individual president rather than the power of his bureaucracy. That presidents are proactive in legislative agenda setting suggests individual personalities can affect policy change at the core as well as at the margins. Furthermore, the president exercises this individual power by persuasion (Neustadt, 1960) rather than by unilateral action (Howell, 2003). The success of the president's legislative program depends on his partnership with the Senate majority leader, thus compelling him to exercise his "power to persuade" (Neustadt, 1960). Lastly, this linkage reveals interbranch constraints on congressional leadership. That is, the behaviors of leaders are limited not only by partisan and institutional constraints *within* the chamber but also by presidential demands *without*. Senate majority leaders, then, have a fourth constituency—together with state, party, and senate—to represent in the president.

CONCLUSIONS

There have been 21 Senate majority leaders, from John Kern to Bill Frist. Kern set the path; Barkley dramatically confirmed it; and Frist followed more than a half-century later. Thus, as path-dependency theorists would tell us, the expectation that birthed the office shaped its development. And remarkably, the trend has continued for Democrats and Republicans alike; across periods of fluctuating partisanship, both weak (as during the mid-century divide in the Democratic party) and strong (as during the contemporary resurgence of party cohesion); even to some extent under divided as well as unified government; and with leaders as varied in their personality styles as Lyndon Johnson and Bill Frist. Moreover, this finding is important for theories of both congressional and presidential leadership. For presidential leadership, an executive-legislative partnership reinforces individual rather than institutional perspectives of the presidency. It is further evidence of what Richard Neustadt (1960) so simply explained years ago—the president is negotiator-in-chief and his powers are largely a function of how well he persuades others to follow his plan. For congressional leadership, it highlights yet another constituency that majority leaders have to balance—not only geographic, not only rank-and-file, not only partisan, but also interinstitutional. So while Senate majority leaders may carry the title "leader" and the demands for delivering policy that come along with it, they are constrained by yet another legislative leader—and one outside the chamber.

CHAPTER 6

EXTRA-INSTITUTIONAL CONSTRAINTS

STATE EXPECTATIONS OF SENATE MAJORITY LEADERS

> It's like having Larry Bird or Michael Jordan suddenly added to your basketball team.... You can play at a higher level.
> —Senator Lamar Alexander (R-TN)
> on his same-state colleague Senator Bill Frist (R-TN)
> being named Senate majority leader (Bivins, 2003)

As one component of David Mayhew's (1974) model of congressional behavior, "credit claiming" is of interest to scholars and pundits for its effects on representation and lawmaking. Distributive politics, or the processes by which members of Congress deliver the goods to claim credit for, is the clichéd "grease in the wheels," helping members build legislative coalitions in the chamber and maintain electoral coalitions in their districts or states. Despite its elemental utility, credit claiming is not a constant. Members vary in their attention to it according to any number of contextual factors, processes of procurement, and of course, outcomes and effects (both institutional and personal). Some of those variations are revealed by examining the role that credit claiming plays in majority leadership of the U.S. Senate.

Competing with the demands and expectations placed on him by his party, by the institution, and by the president, the Senate majority leader is further constrained by his state. After all, the leader is still a senator, elected by voters in his state and charged with representing their interests. His state is his first constituency, in sequence if not always priority. This chapter observes the dual role of leader and senator, emphasizing how expectations for standard member behavior, specifically providing "pork," change when the senator assumes leadership. Once the senator becomes leader, his relationship to his state begins to transform from representative to patron as he seeks to meet the heightened demand for distributive benefits, benefits that might serve as side payments as the majority leader attempts to balance the constraints of multiple constituencies.

This chapter, first, establishes that Senate majority leaders bear an elevated expectation to supply benefits to their geographic constituents and thus confront an added constraint on their leadership. Data on the number and amount of earmarks on appropriations bills before, during, and after majority leadership indicate this transformation in demands and expectations but raise further questions about the specific processes by which leaders participate in distributive politics and the outcomes of their efforts. There follows a review of the relevant literature on distributive politics, with emphasis on a wide array of processes by which federal dollars are allocated as well as consequences for lawmaking and representation. Case studies from the archives of two former Senate majority leaders—Howard H. Baker (R-TN) and George J. Mitchell (D-ME)—evidence some of these theoretical constructs and, above all, illustrate some "hows" and "whys" of "who gets what" (Lasswell, 1936).

GREAT EXPECTATIONS

Among the many activities of members of Congress, credit claiming is elemental. Generating the belief that the member is responsible for desirable outcomes, or at least the pursuit of claims to claim credit for, consumes "much of congressional life" (Mayhew, 1974, p. 53). This pursuit increases in importance for certain members at certain times in their congressional careers, particularly when a senator becomes leader of the majority party in the Senate. His state comes to expect more benefits as he is positioned within the institution to get more benefits. For instance, after Bill Frist assumed the position of majority leader, Tennessee media (e.g., Bivins, 2003) were replete with speculation on how the state would be prioritized for federal dollars now that the second-term senator had jumped in the Senate rankings. And the expectation appears to be justified.

Leadership and Earmarks

There are hard data, sufficient not ample, on federal expenditures to states going back to about 1971. In periodically changing publications, the department of commerce and the bureau of the census have compiled and published raw numbers on federal dollars allocated to individual states, and most show increases in this level of funding at the time a state gains a majority leader. However, raw numbers of dollars distributed state-wide are too broad for meaningful inferences about sources or types of outlays. Increases in funding may reflect a variety of influences: multi-year appropriations with packaged raises; the efforts of the leader's same-state colleague or even of the state's House delegation; inflation; population growth; and numerous other influences. Therefore, to get a picture of particularized benefits awarded to states, I examined earmarks allocated to Senate majority leaders' states before, during, and after leadership.

Earmarks, those line-item additions to appropriations bills, allocate federal funds on a noncompetitive basis and apart from usual budgetary needs and requests of government departments. Thus, they are evidence of attention to particular constituencies by members of Congress. Because they are federal funds distributed outside the normal budgetary process, earmarks, for all the benefits they bring to localized constituencies, have been the bane of national politics, pilloried as government waste. Members of Congress, therefore, have had the difficult task of trying to hide their "porking" efforts from a national audience while broadcasting them to their electoral constituency to reap the benefits of credit claiming. In 2007 the task of researchers and watchdogs was made easier as, after a season of reform, Congress instituted a requirement, beginning with FY2008, that all earmarks be identified by their sponsor.[128] Before this requirement, attributing specific earmarks to specific members of Congress could only be based on circumstantial evidence. Because no government agency collected data on earmarks, enumeration was left to watchdog groups. Therefore, for this research, data on the number and amount of earmarks come from the annual *Pig Book* produced by Citizens Against Government Waste (CAGW), a nonprofit, nonpartisan organization.[129]

The *Pig Book*, begun in FY1991, identifies earmarks contained in each appropriations bill. In the early years, the group sampled the more sensational projects, but beginning in FY1995, it took a more comprehensive approach, cataloging each earmark in each appropriations bill, by state, and by chamber. Thus, I relied on data from fiscal years 1995–2009, a 14-year span that covered the tenures of five Senate majority leaders. From this compilation, I identified earmarks that originated in the Senate, on all 13 appropriations bills, for the fiscal years before, during, and after majority leadership. Admittedly, earmarks originating in the Senate, with two members per state, are not attributable to the efforts of the Senate majority leader.[130] However, such data do give us an overview from which we can draw inferences on the role of the Senate majority leader if his state witnesses an increase in earmarks during his leadership. His same-state colleague, in effect, acts as a constant. Before, during, and after classifications strictly refer to majority leadership, not party leadership. So for example, Tom Daschle's (D-SD) "before" record is prior to his being Senate majority leader, not party leader. Although it is realistic to expect party leadership to confer some advantages in distributive politics, majority leadership might be expected to compound those advantages.

TABLE 6.1. Number and amount of earmarks by U.S. Senate majority leader, 1995–2005.

Senate Majority Leader	Before	During	After
George J. Mitchell (D-ME)			
FY1995	—	11 $20.03M	—
FY1996	—	—	1 $220,000
Robert J. Dole (R-KS)			
FY1995	15 $21.156M	—	—
FY1996	—	7 $34.181M	—
*FY1997	—	10 $20.121M	—
FY1998	—	—	6 $5.679M
C. Trent Lott (R-MS)			
FY1995	8 $13.316M	—	—
FY1996	11 $19.991M	—	—
*FY1997	—	12 $37.07M	—
FY1998	—	21 $810.421M	—
FY1999	—	32 $60.059M	—
FY2000	—	34 $438.342M	—
FY2001	—	75 $605.432M	—
*FY2002	—	72 $606.19M	—
FY2003	—	—	77 $123.709M

(continued on next page)

TABLE 6.1. (*continued*)

Senate Majority Leader	Before	During	After
FY2004	—	—	74 $116.625M
FY2005	—	—	88 $83.259M
Thomas A. Daschle (D-SD)			
FY1995	5 $8.4M	—	—
FY1996	2 $10.5M	—	—
FY1997	3 $11.179M	—	—
FY1998	5 $9.35M	—	—
FY1999	14 $15.597M	—	—
FY2000	12 $31.868M	—	—
FY2001	29 $33.42M	—	—
*FY2002	—	61 $87.027M	—
FY2003	—	55 $72.683M	—
FY2004	—	—	35 $49.736M
FY2005	—	—	32 $31.209M
William H. Frist (R-TN)			
FY1996	3 $6.863M	—	—
FY1997	3 $3.05M	—	—
FY1998	0 $0.000	—	—

(*continued on next page*)

Extra-Institutional Constraints 131

TABLE 6.1. *(continued)*

Senate Majority Leader	Before	During	After
FY1999	2 $600,000	—	—
FY2000	5 $6.05M	—	—
FY2001	10 $15.115M	—	—
FY2002	14 $53.03M	—	—
FY2003	20 $124.773M	—	—
FY2004	—	28 $44.147M	—
FY2005	—	28 $17.15M	—
FY2006	—	27 $59.862M	—
FY2007	—	1 $2.6M	—
FY2008	—	—	15 $9.67M
FY2009	—	—	22 $29.48M

*Less than full year as Senate majority leader.

Table 6.1 shows the number and dollar amount of earmarks per leader. The general trend is that majority leaders get more, in number and dollar amount, as leader than before or after, even as the overall level of earmarking increases over the decade. Perhaps the case of Maine is the starkest. Although data are lacking for Maine in the years before and during Mitchell's time as majority leader, FY1995, his final year as Senate majority leader, and FY1996, the first year after his service as majority leader had ended, offer a sharp comparison. During Mitchell's final year, the Senate earmarked 11 appropriations worth more than $20 million for projects in Maine, but after he left the Senate, only one ($220,000 for blueberry research) was set aside for the state. The outcome for Kansas is equally blatant. In Bob Dole's (R-KS) last full year as leader, Kansas was awarded $34 million in earmarks; after Dole, its take declined to less than $6 million. Trent Lott (R-MS) also shows a dramatic increase in his "porking" potential as leader compared to before and after, from about $20 million to as much as $800 million. However, the enormous provision of federal dollars to Mississippi is an outlier for at least two reasons—first, Mississippi's senior senator Thad Cochran (R) was a member of the Senate appropriations committee during the same period, and second, earmarks worth multihundreds of millions of dollars were defense projects (e.g., in FY1998, $720 million for construction of naval assault ships). Still, the numbers bear telling because while the ship projects could have been sent to major manufacturers in Maine, Connecticut, Virginia, or elsewhere, they were sent to shipbuilders in Pascagoula, Mississippi—Lott's hometown.

After Lott and before and after Daschle, there appeared lower levels of pork-barreling than during their periods as leaders. The only leader who appeared to buck the trend is Bill Frist. Tennessee seemed to get more federal outlays in the fiscal year before he became leader than during his majority leadership. Two factors may account for this unexpected finding. First, appropriations for FY2003 were prepared in Fred Thompson's (R-TN) final year in the Senate. The senior senator had served since 1994 and may have been especially active toward a big payoff in his last year. The two biggest earmarks that year were $40 million for cleanup at the Oak Ridge Nuclear Labs and $65 million for the creation of East Tennessee Technology Park. Second, Frist's activity in distributive politics during his leadership may be obscured by the blossom of earmarks added in conference committees. During his tenure, there developed a general trend of more and more earmarks being added during conference committees as opposed to regular appropriations markups. Presumably as earmarks became more a hallmark of bad government, members of

Congress sought greater cover for their earmarking efforts in the anonymity of conference committees, which are not open to public record. While Tennessee received 27 Senate earmarks in FY2006, fully 60 were added in conference, including $6.2 million for a commuter rail line in Nashville in the final conference report of the transportation appropriation bill that was claimed by Senate Majority Leader Frist (Tackett, 2005). For the obvious reason that both representatives and senators participate in conference, I do not count such earmarks toward leaders' totals. However, for FY2004 and FY2005, more earmarks for Tennessee were added in conference than in previous years. It is likely that instead of becoming less active in distributive politics, Frist simply changed his arena of action. FY2007 is an anomaly in the trend. After years of increase, including seven consecutive years of record-setting dollar amounts for pork, FY2007 offered a dramatic reversal in the number and amount of earmarks (Citizens Against Government Waste, 2007). The drop-off resulted from a culmination of election-year politics in which earmarks became a prime target. In 2006 only two appropriations bills were enacted, the others having been blocked by a consortium of fiscally conservative senators who expressed frustration at the seemingly perpetual growth of earmarks. The House and Senate appropriations committee chairmen, Representative David Obey (D-WI) and Senator Robert Byrd (D-WV), both known as maestros of the earmark process, enforced a moratorium on earmarks for the remainder of FY2007. The result was an overall deflation in the number and amount of earmarks that affected Tennessee in Senate Majority Leader Frist's final year.

These data by themselves, however, reveal neither the means by which Senate majority leaders act in distributive politics nor the ends that result from their efforts. Nor do they elaborate on the variation of benefits for which the Senate majority leader is responsible. There is, nevertheless, a rich body of research that offers some explanations of both processes and outcomes. This research merits exploration before reporting cases that at once illuminate these theories and offer new perspectives on the expectation for Senate majority leaders to deliver goods.

Processes and Outcomes of Distributive Politics

Congressional scholars, since Theodore Lowi's (1964) introduction to disaggregable policies, have produced a broad literature on federal outlays, including the processes of distribution and the outcomes and effects of such goods. The roots of distributive politics can be endogenous or exogenous to Congress. Endogenous influences on distributive politics include committees and parties. A focus on the committee-based organization of Congress emphasizes the operation of committees as preference jurisdictions, in which members are seated on committees (mostly not universally) according to constituency or personal preferences or needs (Carsey & Rundquist, 1999b; Hall, 1987; Hall & Grofman, 1990). Committees then facilitate vote trading or logrolling among members for distributive goods (Evans, 1994, 2004; Shepsle & Weingast, 1995; Weingast & Marshall, 1988; Wilson, 1986).

Congress may be organized by committee, but committees are organized by party, and another view emphasizes the role of parties in the distributive process. Parties shape policy (including distributive goods) to the advantage of their members (Cox & McCubbins, 1993; Rohde, 1991; Sinclair, 1983), and goods are directed to members of the majority party (Carsey & Rundquist, 1999a). Beyond the institutional pillars of committee and party, still other work has highlighted individual rather than group advantages in securing pork-barrel projects. For example, seniority increases a member's prospects in the distribution of benefits (Roberts, 1990).

Outside Congress, the characteristics of House districts (Adler, 2000) appear to be significant in that money flows to those that need it (Hird, 1991), and recipient jurisdictions are key actors as local governments actively seek federal goods (Rich, 1989). However, R. Douglas Arnold (1979, 1990) emphasized the role of the bureaucracy as it supports and enables members in their pursuit of distributive goods. Describing a tandem relationship between the two institutions, he observed the dependence of bureaucracy on Congress for allocated resources and the reliance of Congress on the bureaucracy for implementation of their spending requests.

Still, these methods of procurement do not suggest much by way of outcome or effect. For what purpose or with what effects do committees, parties, or individuals seek distributive benefits? Within Congress, distributive politics operate to secure coalitions. Whether "minimum winning" (Riker, 1962; Riker & Ordeshook, 1973) or "universalistic" (Barry, 1965; Lee & Oppenheimer, 1999; Shepsle & Weingast, 1981; Stein & Bickers, 1995), the legislative coalition results from vote trading or logrolling to accrue more particularized benefits (Ferejohn, 1974) or actual substantive policy (Evans, 1994, 2004). Diana Evans (1994, p. 894) found that distributive projects are used "to help committee leaders to construct supporting coalitions for legislative packages that satisfy the leaders' own goals, including general benefits legislation." Distributive goods, then, are side payments to gain support for national policy, and thus, enable leaders to pursue their policy-making goals (Fenno, 1973).

There is a body of work suggesting that members of Congress may deviate from voting their district's (or state's) preferences as long as they provide pork as recompense. Stephen Ansolabehere and James Snyder (2000), Timothy Groseclose (2001), and Christian Grose (2004) purported a valence theory of position taking. That is, the supply of pork projects, like any other intangible, nonpolicy-related attribution, is a valence advantage (Stokes, 1963) to incumbent legislators. This advantage operates to give incumbents greater leeway to move away from their constituency median in their voting behavior. The relationship is parabolic with greater deviation at the points of fewest and most project allocations (Grose, 2004).

An alternative theory is based on a trust hypothesis (Grose, 2004) from Richard Fenno's (1978) elucidation of the relationship between representative and constituent. As a legislator's career progresses, he may build trust with his constituents by casework, by other forms of service, and by providing distributive benefits. This trust then acts as capital on which he can draw to deviate from voting his constituents' policy preferences. As he gives to voters, he can diverge from some of their preferences.

Furthermore, the relationship between a valence advantage, like pork, and voting is also related to electoral outcomes. Some models (Groseclose,

2001) have predicted a direct and positive relationship between valence advantage and the likelihood of winning reelection: the greater the former, the greater the latter. But others (Grose, 2004; Londreagan & Romer, 1993) have linked such an advantage not directly to winning but to vote share of the incumbent: he secures his vote share as he increases his advantage (i.e., provides more pork).

Robert Stein and Kenneth Bickers (1995) molded the argument to emphasize selection effects—those incumbents who are electorally vulnerable in the first place will pursue distributive benefits for their constituencies (see also Bickers & Stein, 2000). But for his parsimony, Mayhew's (1974) explanation seems most powerful—credit claiming furthers the underlying goal of all congressional action, to get reelected.

Subtle variations in each of these hypotheses and findings do not obscure their common statement, that is, pork serves as a form of payment to an electoral constituency for flexibility in other behaviors. The ramifications of this proposition are startling in that it offers an explanation for how Senate majority leaders attempt to balance state demands against those of multiple constituencies.

Data and Method

For details about how Senate majority leaders attempt to meet expectations, I turned to case studies drawn from research in the archival collections of senators Baker and Mitchell. These archival collections, unlike any other data set, show the "politics" of political interactions. Memos, hand-jotted notes, phone slips, letters, and reports detail interactions with constituents—state, party, senate, and president alike. And an examination of these papers for the years prior to leadership and for those years as leader shows noticeable differences in activities and styles before and after. Archives leave a paper trail of the leader's case and project activities to follow. From these, it becomes apparent which projects kept the leader's attention, why they did so, how he used his influence inside and outside the Senate to advance the causes, and with what outcomes.

The cases of Howard Baker and George Mitchell demonstrate credit-claiming efforts on widely different scales, through very different means, and with stark contrasts in outcomes. Baker succeeded in securing a range of funds for his home area of Scott County, Tennessee, changing the landscape and economic present and future of the region. Mitchell, even though he was majority leader, could not keep Loring Air Force Base off the 1991 Base Realignment and Closing (BRAC) commission list, changing if not devastating the local economy. In both cases, there is an overriding expectation for leaders to provide for home constituents.

HOWARD H. BAKER, JR. (R-TN)

Howard Baker's county of residence was and is now Scott County, in eastern Tennessee on the Kentucky border. His hometown, Huntsville (population 387), serves as the county seat. The area was rural and unprosperous, abundant in scenery but lacking in economic development. When Senator Baker assumed majority leadership in 1980, annual per capita income was $7,830.[131] Industry was sparse, and there were no major highways crisscrossing the county. Demographically, the population declined during the 1960s and 1970s as many exited for opportunities elsewhere. Those who stayed were overwhelmingly White and older, with many residents going back generations. These were the classic eastern Tennessee Republicans that V.O. Key (1949) wrote about. Before and during the Civil War, this area of Tennessee refused to secede and was sympathetic to the North. A strong strand of Republicanism marks the region, and it is this district that sent Baker's father, Howard H. Baker, Sr., to the House for 13 years beginning in 1951, and filled the seat upon his death in 1964 with his second wife, Irene (Annis, 1995). Baker's ties to Scott County were deep, and once he became majority leader, he and Scott County officials together were on the lookout for ways to improve the region.

Straight away, his influence, whether real or perceived, was obvious. A Rural Electrification Administration (REA) loan application had been approved for Scott County in 1980, only to be deferred owing to a budget freeze. Within six months of Baker's assuming the post of majority leader, a $5.9 million loan was reapproved and the money released.

A similar tale describes the expansion of gas utilities: an initial loan from the Federal Housing Administration (FHA) was denied before Baker's stint as majority leader but was granted after formal requests from Baker as majority leader. About the same time, the city of Huntsville began working on water utilities. The Huntsville Utility District Water Project was an exercise in federalism as the national government worked with the state to address water concerns outlined in an extensive engineering report. Baker wrote letters to both state and federal agencies urging cooperation. He arranged a package in which the state of Tennessee provided a "Community Development Block Grant" that was supplemented by a loan from the FHA.

In keeping with his theme of providing and upgrading basic services to this heretofore overlooked and bypassed area, Baker often relied on creative means. In 1983 he was approached by a county group to help "historic Rugby" with various community-restoration projects. Rugby was founded in 1880 by an Englishman as a "community for the practice of agriculture and trade among the younger sons of English gentry, who traditionally had no inheritance upon which to live."[132] The experiment in Victorian living lasted only about 20 years, but in 1966, interested residents began to push for the restoration and historic preservation of the village. The project received an endorsement from the National Park Service and plans for full restoration were detailed in diagrams and reports. Again, Majority Leader Baker broached the matter with then-governor, later junior senator, Lamar Alexander, who, with Baker, helped secure another "Community Development Block Grant" from a state economic-development agency. But Baker's interest was more than historic preservation—he proposed funds to build a water system ostensibly to help the museum complex but whose benefits spread to the broader community. For this, he lobbied both the National Education Association and the Institute of Museum Services, an independent federal grant-making agency, to share the educational and historical benefits of the project. Within a year, Baker had obtained and announced an Economic Development Administration (EDA) grant from the Department of Commerce.

After this strong emphasis on infrastructure, there is an evident shift in his efforts toward economic development of the region. The Helenwood Industrial Project was an attempt to make the now-incorporated city of Helenwood into a corridor for industry, and therefore jobs, by providing acreage and buildings. At 30 acres, the park would be relatively small but was the method du jour for economic growth at the time. In June 1983 Baker wrote to the Tennessee Department of Economic and Commercial Development a three-sentence letter:

> I am writing in behalf of the grant application which Scott County has submitted to the Tennessee Community Development Block Grant Program. These funds will be used to provide side developments for the Helenwood Industrial Corridor. It appears to me that this application has merit, and I hope that you will give it favorable consideration.[133]

The grant was announced two months later. It was followed shortly by a letter from the Scott County executive, Dwight Murphy, who was prolific in his grant applications on a variety of projects (most of these described thus far) and showed no compunction about asking for Majority Leader Baker's help or thanking him for a job well done. He wrote,

> The day the EDA Grant was announced was the happiest day I have experienced since assuming office. For the first time since the new Truck and Trailer Industries started construction, I breathed a sigh of relief. If sewers had not been funded, the Helenwood Industrial Corridor would have been a total flop instead of a major asset to the community...I am fully aware that you went beyond the normal demands of your job to see this grant was funded. I will always be thankful for the extra effort you put forward to make this project a reality...I want to thank you for all you have done for Scott County.[134]

Another project for the city of Huntsville shows Baker's personal touch at lobbying with a "to Lamar, from Howard" letter. The request was again for a Tennessee "Community Development Block Grant" to build a parking lot specifically for handicapped needs around the downtown cluster of Huntsville's public and community-service buildings. In his letter to Governor Alexander ("Lamar"), Baker asked: "[I]n keeping with our recent conversation, I urge you to favorably consider the Huntsville proposal which will ensure the proper delivery of services to the elderly and handicapped. Thank you for your personal attention to this matter."[135] The grant was approved.

The largest and most controversial of his "pork" distribution was that for the Scott County Airport. From 1982 to 1984, Baker was able to funnel $1.48 million in federal aid for an airport managed by his pilot and which he used for visits to the family compound in Huntsville. The funds went for construction of a runway extension, a taxi wing, new approach lights, and a larger airplane parking area, all improvements to make this airport in a rural outpost jet-compatible. What was then the General Accounting Office (GAO)[136] audited the project and reported that Transportation Secretary Drew Lewis had approved it despite its being rated "low priority" by Federal Aviation Administration (FAA) field staff. Regulations were that grants could only have been approved if rated as qualified by the FAA. An article in the *Memphis Commercial Appeal* (Brosnan, 1984) questioned the project, which seemed to epitomize pork-barrel politics. Baker denied the power of his influence, saying he "never talked to Secretary [Drew] Lewis about it" and "never called anyone up on the phone and said, 'I want that grant'" (Brosnan, 1984).

This case study provides some key indicators of significance for a transformation from representative to patron. Within the collection of his papers,[137] of all projects during his tenure as majority leader, most are for Scott County and Huntsville. Moreover, the bulk of such projects are dated from 1982–1984, when Baker served as majority leader. In fact, files show only one project for Scott County before Baker became majority leader, but 12 as leader. And the one preleadership project was a proposal in 1968, shortly after Baker entered the Senate, for a sewage system for Huntsville to ameliorate public-health hazards that occur after heavy rains flood septic tanks and other makeshift sewers. An extensive engineering report sold the benefits and workability of the system, and the financing plan called for a 60-40 split with 60% of the costs covered by an EDA grant and the remainder by the city of Huntsville itself. The bottom line for the federal government was $117,600. The grant was not approved. In short, before becoming majority leader, Baker was not able to accomplish much, if anything, directly for Scott County, but as majority leader, not only did proposals proliferate but they also met with universal success.[138]

In lobbying for pet projects, Baker's methods and scope were restrained. Baker's staff played roles as brokers between county officials and citizens in, first, applying for grants, and, then, navigating the bureaucratic maze to follow up. Baker himself behaved as a "hidden-hand" leader:[139] staff did the bulk of information seeking and providing. They knew contacts in Scott County and in federal agencies and served to link the two. They were brokers, advising in grant writing, shepherding these projects through proper channels, and following up to be sure funds were received. There is little evidence of Baker's forcing or threatening, and his letters have an air of "just bringing to your attention." Because of Baker, Scott County became salient to grant-making agencies, both federal and state. Not all of Baker's influence was devoted to Washington. He asked for Scott County's share from state coffers as well. In this way, being majority leader gave him access to access, which he used to assist his hometown. Baker helped his home constituents with the basics first. Sewage, gas, and water utilities, even telephone lines—what many considered necessities—did not come to Scott County in any measurable way until Baker, as leader, acted. To be sure, projects such as the airport improvements were more luxury than necessity, but the point remains: being leader helped Howard Baker help Scott County.

Today, Scott County is still rural, but its population is growing, mostly between ages 25–54, thanks to a spate of industries now residing along the Helenwood Corridor and a new 100-acre industrial park in Huntsville itself. Per capita income is still lower than both state and national averages, but has increased over the decades.[140] The local chamber of commerce advertises Scott County as a "great place for new businesses" thanks to its industrial complexes and an infrastructure consisting of the Citizens Gas Utility District, Huntsville Utility District Water System, and the Highland Telephone Cooperative, all of which Majority Leader Baker had a hand in modernizing if not creating.

GEORGE J. MITCHELL (D-ME)

At the outset, the office of Senator George Mitchell had a reputation for being lax in general constituency service. Given the choice, Mainers would take their concerns to his same-state colleague Senator William S. Cohen (R). To be fair, Mitchell was disadvantaged from the beginning, when in 1980 he was appointed to take over after the resignation of Senator Edmund Muskie (D), who left a heap of unfinished casework. Concern over handling general constituency service (mail, requests, inquiries, etc.) intensified when Mitchell became majority leader in 1989.

A staffer wrote to Mitchell in April 1990:

> The correspondence section of your Maine office has been trying to cope with the consequences of your becoming majority leader for about fifteen months now…, and I think it is time to re-evaluate what it will take to preserve a responsive presence vis a vis Maine constituent concerns and inquiries.[141]

The concern was regarding "general grumblings" among Maine constituents of "an increase in tardy responses" and "lack of responsiveness" to state voters. There was "a widespread impression that you [Senator Mitchell] are not as accessible as you used to be. The general thrust of the complaints is that now that you are majority leader, you are not as responsive to Maine constituents and their needs."[142] Of course, if the charges of neglect were valid, they had reason to be: before he became majority leader, Mitchell's office handled about 500–700 pieces of mail per week from Maine alone ("Out of state mail was discarded, by and large.").[143] As majority leader, the volume increased to upwards of 2,000 pieces of mail per week, mostly out-of-state, which Mitchell's staff no longer had the luxury to discard or ignore.

Against this backdrop of general dissatisfaction with basic constituency service and casework, a drama was playing out that in the end would show the majority leader as ineffective in big projects as in mail service. In October 1988 the Senate voted on the creation of a BRAC commission, a 12-member body to periodically and independently evaluate and recommend military bases for rearranging or closing in accordance with military and economic needs. The purpose of the commission was to take the task out of the hands of Congress, which would be reluctant to reduce or close military bases, historically a classic source of pork projects, from themselves and their colleagues. BRAC passed the Senate by a vote of 82–7, and Senator George Mitchell was one of the seven who voted against it.

BRAC quickly set to work and on December 24, 1988, submitted to the secretary of defense and made public a proposed list of closings of 86 installations and 54 realignments. The secretary of defense then approved its recommendation on January 5, 1989. After about 45 days for debate, the House and Senate, by majority vote, were to vote the slate up or down, and the list would move to presidential consideration and possibly veto. In early December 1988 speculation was that Loring Air Force Base in Limestone, Maine (Aroostook County), would *not* be on the BRAC list.

A decade earlier, Loring had dodged a planned closure thanks to presidential politics: President Carter's popularity was sinking and he faced a primary challenge, especially in neighboring New Hampshire, from Senator Edward Kennedy (D-MA). To maintain support in Maine and to avoid negative spillover effects in New Hampshire, Vice President Mondale visited the state and met with Senator Muskie; "in the course of his visit he perceived the obvious necessity for immediate and tangible evidence to Maine Democrats of the Administration's commitment to their needs and became an essential and critically important ally in this struggle."[144] In short order, Mondale sided with the Maine delegation against the Pentagon, and Loring was spared. The creation of BRAC was largely a response to the politics surrounding this first attempted closure of Loring.

After its "second chance," neighboring Aroostook County remained economically depressed with Loring AFB as the prime, if not only, source of economic activity. The base was located in northern Maine, on the border with New Brunswick, Canada. Strategically, it was the closest base for European (read, Soviet) operations and relied on about 3,800 military personnel (plus 5,000 dependents) and 1,200 civilian workers. Moreover, counting base-related jobs in the surrounding area, Loring produced "a total secondary impact of approximately 3,000 jobs."[145] A report prepared at the request of state officials suggested that if Loring were to be closed, between 6,000 and 9,000 civilian jobs, $237 million in personal income, and $518 million in annual retail service sales would be lost (Day, 1988).

After the early December memo, which presented positive projections for Loring, the winds shifted quickly. Within two weeks, fears were abundant that Loring was a target. Bob Carolla, Senator Mitchell's staffer specially assigned to this project, urged the majority-leader-in-waiting to begin presidential lobbying: "...it is important that you personally raise the Loring AFB/Base-Closing issue with President-elect Bush."[146] Senator Mitchell would be assuming leadership of the Senate at the same time George H. W. Bush (a summer resident at Kennebunkport, Maine) assumed the White House.

On January 5, 1989, the secretary of defense, Casper Weinberger, approved the recommendations of BRAC, and Loring was officially spared. Two Maine installations, Brunswick Naval Air Station as well as Loring AFB, had been considered by BRAC, but the plan to realign and merge Brunswick NAS and Loring AFB was blocked by naval officials who did not want to lose another naval air station. Loring remained untouched, but it had less to do with majority leader politics than military bureaucratic politics. The next day Carolla prepared a memo for Mitchell on "outlook/interests" regarding the commission. The memo is telling, for it *begins* with an itemization of the "Leadership Perspective," which is three full pages, and *ends* with "Maine Perspective," barely a paragraph. The effects of the closing on Maine as well as possible strategies for responses to and on behalf of his state were deferred while he considered party effects. For example, the memo noted that New Jersey and Senator Frank Lautenberg (D) would be hardest hit and recommended that Mitchell should seek "to coordinate a response" among all affected members.[147]

The implications of this memo are unsurprising in light of Mitchell's perspective on being majority leader, in which he ranked national and party concerns ahead of state interests. Perhaps this arrangement of priorities explains why he, even as majority leader, was ultimately unable to save Loring AFB.

After the 1988 round of BRAC, Congress in 1990 changed the process by charging the defense department with drawing up an initial list of bases to be considered by the commission. And in 1991 a new round of BRAC proceedings began. This time Loring AFB made the list of bases to be closed. Among other reasons, the air force cited the lack of nuclear capabilities at Loring as well as the present lack of need for a base so far north (the fall of the Soviet Union had brought a quick end to the Cold War just a year earlier). Air-force officials chose not to heavily consider local economic impact in their determination, and it was on this front that Majority Leader Mitchell, and the rest of the Maine delegation, including Cohen, a member of the Senate armed services committee, argued for Loring's preservation during a four-month window of hearings and testimony before BRAC submitted its final report to the president.

During this time, Mitchell and his staff grasped at any thread to rescue Loring, even contending that since Loring was the closest base to Canada, it might be strategically useful to guard against the separatists in Quebec who had been making noises around this time. While "a separate Quebec is obviously no threat militarily to the US..., the separatists are strongly socialistic. An independent Quebec might nullify current free trade agreements between the US and Canada/Quebec and seek other foreign routes."[148] But chiefly, Mitchell's activities were more regular, including individual meetings with and lobbying of commissioners. Talking points of his meetings with Alexander Trowbridge[149] and Arthur Levitt[150] claimed that closing Loring would result in "greater costs to the Federal Government: i.e., unemployment compensation, welfare benefits, defaults of guaranteed mortgages."[151] In May 1991 Mitchell, following other members of the Maine delegation, testified before the BRAC commission, and again his theme was one of the loss of population, jobs, and earnings, echoing Senator Muskie's testimony during the 1979 threatened closure: "[Aroostook County]…was a wilderness when the Department of Defense decided to build Loring…and it will be a wilderness when Loring leaves, leaving behind it the wreckage of people, mostly small business people, who have staked their lives there."[152] This heavy emphasis on economic effects drew criticism from a leading state newspaper. The *Bangor Daily News* editorialized, after the testimony, that relying on such reasoning was, in essence, too little, too late, and too much like the arguments that other congressmen had used, unsuccessfully, to defend a dozen other bases.[153] There was dissatisfaction that lobbying on grounds other than that which the BRAC was charged with considering was bound to be ineffective.

Criticism mounted not just within the state but also within the Senate. Senator Al D'Amato (R-NY), in his testimony on behalf of saving Plattsburgh Air Force Base in his state, charged that "Commissioner Callaway is biased toward Loring AFB and that the commission has faced pressure from the majority leader."[154] Other New York leaders repeated the refrain, calling it "the Mitchell thing." And the *Plattsburgh Press-Republican* carried articles referring to the "heavy-handed lobbying tactics" by "Senator Mitchell and his political cronies."[155] For his part, Mitchell did not deny his political strategy in this or the earlier round, saying "Maine officials should make no apology for using political pressure to save Loring and…that he would use the full clout of his new position as Senate majority leader to reverse a Loring shutdown decision" (Day, 1988).

During the final deliberations of the commission, Majority Leader Mitchell made another push for Loring with phone calls to select members, including Chairman Jim Courter, who in a "tip sheet" drawn by Mitchell's staff was judged to be a swing vote generally "sympathetic in raising Loring's arguments."[156] In one call, Mitchell denied any plans to change the BRAC process after the current round, or to block future rounds, in deference to the "independence and integrity of the process" and cautioned, "the commission's work should reinforce that posture."[157]

On July 1, 1991, the final report of BRAC was submitted to the president, and Mitchell shifted his efforts to the White House. He argued that the commission's final recommendation was at once procedurally misguided (failing to consider neither explicit—"economic impact"—nor implicit criteria—"quality of life") and substantively unfair (closing the second-largest air force base and the one closest to Europe). Mitchell repeated similar points in meetings with National Security Advisor Brent Scowcroft and even offered to provide political cover for the White House to remand BRAC recommendations. Bases in California and Texas, along with Loring, were three strategic air command (SAC) bases considered by the panel, and Mitchell offered to join with the California and Texas delegations to oppose the closure of all, which provide "a more neutral option for the president to consider."[158] In any event, Mitchell made clear to both President Bush and Scowcroft that "the unfairness of what has taken place could produce a congressional backlash against any future base closures."[159]

The president approved, as did Congress, the slate put forth by BRAC in 1991, and Loring AFB officially and finally closed in September 1994, a few months before Mitchell left office. Once Loring's fate was sealed, Mitchell and his staff worked in the appropriations process to try to secure funding for redeveloping the base and providing grants for cleanup and other rebuilding projects. They finally settled on a comprehensive plan to turn the base into a research and development facility under the Environmental Protection Agency and sponsored by the department of energy. An undated request to the energy subcommittee of the Senate appropriations committee asked for $10 million for the "A" priority project. It described the potential impact as "part of key anchor/nucleus for Loring AFB redevelopment."[160] The effort was cautious because the "committee may be wary of precedent of this nature for base closures," and specifically, "Chairman Bennett Johnston has faced AFB closure in Louisiana."[161] In the end, the environs of Loring received a "Rural No-Cost Economic Development Conveyance" in 1997, and parts of nearly 4,000 acres have been deeded from the air force to the U.S. Fish and Wildlife Service for preservation and to the Aroostook band of Micmacs tribe for housing. Currently, the former Loring AFB is now Loring Commerce Centre, boasting 19 businesses that provide 1,000 jobs—miles to go before filling the vacuum of the military-industrial complex.[162]

Interpretations and Implications

There is no single case to illustrate any single theory of distributive politics. The narratives of Baker and Mitchell, instead, reveal factors both endogenous and exogenous in the means and ends of distributing benefits to their constituents. These cases show, in their distinctiveness, the extent to which pork barreling attempts, and their outcomes thereof, will vary according to constituency needs and the personality of Senate majority leaders.

Scope

The scope of both Baker's and Mitchell's projects are widely divergent, serving constituents at both ends of Fenno's concentric model (1978). Howard Baker showed service to a personal constituency;[163] residents of Scott County were friends and family who had supported Baker's political career from its infancy and that of his father before him. The projects were small (in the tens and hundreds of thousands of dollars, not multi-millions) and in character, and seemed to resemble former Senate Majority Leader Lyndon Johnson's (D-TX) efforts to provide for the Texas hill country (Caro, 2002). Rural Scott County had much in common with the once-impoverished environs around Johnson City, Texas, and Johnson paid particular attention to meeting basic needs of electricity, water, and infrastructure—the types of projects Baker successfully garnered for his personal constituency.

Unlike that of Baker, Mitchell's case involves a large-scale benefit which would affect his entire geographic constituency and arguably the most significant type of distributive project. Unique among particularistic goods are those related to military expenditures and projects because they are laden with not only substantive but also symbolic value. Military bases provide a consolidated constituency for members of Congress to cultivate and thus are an easy target for federal dollars. Not to prioritize them makes a symbolic statement against patriotism and materially injures the surrounding economy, which depends on providing goods and services to military families as well as the large contingent of civilian jobs tied to the military complex. In short, members of Congress have a particular responsibility to bases, especially to fend off attempts at closure. This political reality explains why Congress created a BRAC commission in 1988 as a process to insulate its members from making the tough decisions on which bases to consolidate or close. However limited the points of decision for legislators may be, their influence is not limited. In fact, the most important influence on base-closing outcomes appears to be the role of the state's congressional delegation in the process (Whicker & Giannatasio, 1997).

Processes
In both small- or large-scale projects, Baker and Mitchell depended on the largesse of bureaucratic agencies. Organizational theorists (e.g., Allison, 1971; Arnold, 1979, 1990; Wildavsky, 1964) have observed the mutual and interactive interests with bureaucracies and legislatures. Models of bureaucratic politics suggest that agencies will be responsive when their budget is on the line for appropriation, earmarks, or oversight. Following the pattern outlined by Arnold (1979), Baker persuaded bureaucratic agencies to direct dollars to Scott County; outlays were secured from funds already appropriated rather than earmarked.[164] The money was already spent; Baker just lobbied decision makers privately for its allocation.

Because of the scope of the project, Mitchell lobbied not at the margins but the principals themselves, and not privately (or not only privately) but publicly. Through open letters in media, open testimony before the commission, personal phone calls with committee members, and personal meetings with the president, Mitchell was active at every stage for the preservation of Loring.

Legislators' influence may have been minimized by the creation of BRAC, but it hardly is minimal. Of the 152 initially recommended by the department of defense in 1991 for closure or realignment, the committee accepted only 27.[165] Because of the pressure of the states' congressional delegations, 125 were spared[166] in some measure at least (Whicker & Giannatasio, 1997), and although Mitchell may have prolonged Loring's closure, he did not prevent it.

Outcomes

Not only do the scale and processes of the two cases differ but also do the results. Baker was universally successful in his pursuits for Scott County; Mitchell was not for Loring. For his patronage, Baker earned the grateful praise of locals and enjoyed popularity throughout the state until he resigned from the Senate in 1984.

One unintended consequence of Mitchell's personal and public intervention is that it personally linked him to the outcome. Having staked his reputation on the line, he was unable to escape blame when the decision was made to close the base. While decision making may be in the hands of an independent commission, legislators are no less responsible in the minds of their electorate for keeping or losing bases. There exists a direct relationship between base closings and electoral outcomes—closures decrease vote margins (Rocca, 2003)—as perhaps Mitchell anticipated.

Still, his case can be framed by opposing interpretations. The first is that which I have presented here—closure constitutes a failure by a Senate majority leader to provide or keep distributive federal goods for his constituency. The other is that although Mitchell was ultimately unsuccessful in keeping Loring open, he perhaps could be credited for preventing it from being closed sooner. The base did survive an earlier attempt at the start of Mitchell's leadership, during the 1988 round of BRAC, its second threatened closure in as many decades. Its history of attempted closures perhaps suggests inevitability[167]—Loring was marked.

But that the base's final closure came when its senator was at the helm as Senate majority leader is significant. Mitchell was able to convince neither the commission nor the administration (from president to national security advisor) to spare the base, even with the threat of coercion by congressional curbs on future BRAC rounds or of congressional gridlock as a backlash. Perhaps he would have been helped by an administration of the same party, or perhaps his case would have found more sympathy had he not opposed the initial creation of the commission. In any case, the outcome was politically damaging to Mitchell, and it was economically debilitating to Loring and its environs. The failure of the most influential member of the Senate to save such a fundamental distributive benefit as a military base overshadowed the remainder of Mitchell's leadership. He was due for a reelection campaign the fall that Loring AFB finally shut its doors but bowed out in March amid speculation of a fortified Republican operation to defeat him.

Conclusions

Above all, the evidence presented here, both as data on the number and amount of earmarks and as case studies about the processes of distributive politics, emphasizes state constraints on Senate majority leadership, specifically the expectation that majority leaders will use their elevated position to deliver benefits to their home constituents. This expectation and leaders' responses thereto find meaning in Mayhew's (1974) concept of credit claiming, a congressional behavior that varies according to representational and legislative, or in the present research, leadership contexts.

The pursuit of distributive benefits suggests an effort to meet state expectations that come with Senate majority leadership. Although success is not guaranteed, the theory that benefits increase for states that have a Senate majority leader indicates leadership is advantageous to securing benefits. The logic of distributive politics (e.g., Grose, 2004) affirms that benefits serve as a side payment to permit flexibility of action. In patronage, perhaps Senate majority leaders have found at least one strategy in the attempt to balance multiple constituencies of state, party, senate, and president.

CHAPTER 7

CONCLUSIONS

[W]e have no really adequate model of party leadership as it exists in Congress, and...none can be constructed because we lack simple descriptions of many of the basic working parts of the system. (Huitt, 1961, p. 334)

The preceding pages have been an attempt to ameliorate Ralph Huitt's lament a generation ago that had gone unheeded with regard to Senate majority leadership. This work provides the first comprehensive description of how a senator becomes majority leader, what a Senate majority leader does, and how a Senate majority leader's multiple constituencies act as constraints.

CONSTRAINED BY MULTIPLE CONSTITUENCIES

"The job of majority leader has a lot of headaches and few compensations," wrote Senate Majority Leader Mike Mansfield (D-MT) to one of his state constituents.[168] Unique among congressional leaders, Senate majority leaders are positioned to balance multiple, and often competing, roles. First elected senator by voters from a state, the focus of senatorial behavior is blurred by majority leadership that introduces not only party, but majority-party demands on the senator-turned-leader. The Senate majority leader is expected to advance majority-party fortunes in a supermajoritarian institution. However, the demand for partisan leadership is at once countered by expectations to preserve institutional loyalty, which traditionally is based on egalitarian and individualistic ideals. Further complicating the balance are demands expressed by extrainstitutional actors—the president of the United States as well as voters of his home state. Even as presidential involvement in legislative innovation and operation has increased through time, the president has required a "man in the Senate" to guide agendas and push objectives. The emergence of the office was birthed in this expectation and after nearly a century and 21 Senate majority leaders, the expectation remains. These multiple constituencies, then, represent multiple constraints.

Senate
The job description for Senate majority leader entails duties vast and varied. The tasks take the leader from the well of the Senate to the world stage as he represents the upper legislative chamber. These duties thus invoke an unsteady balance of institutional and partisan obligations on Senate majority leadership. As the head of the Senate, the majority leader, first, organizes the chamber by, among other aspects, negotiating committee ratios, and as head of his party, the Senate majority leader makes committee assignments (often rubber-stamping recommendations of his party's steering committee). Moreover, although he may not set the Senate's agenda, especially if the president is of the same party, the majority leader is responsible for managing it within the chamber. The majority leader schedules and calls for votes, but only after he, ever aware of the threat of filibuster, mobilizes members of his own party and coaxes support from the opposition. The leader has few informal powers, and even fewer formal ones, to cajole or threaten members into submission, as professionalized party machinery (like policy committees), rather than the Senate leader's office, provides inducements to senatorial behavior. His

sole institutional power is the "right of first recognition," which gives him primacy on the floor in an otherwise egalitarian chamber. Skilled parliamentarians and manipulative leaders like Lyndon Johnson (D-TX) and Robert Byrd (D-WV) made full use of this advantage to further their goals in the Senate, but otherwise this procedural rule, which requires tactical talent to employ, gives leaders little with which to bargain.

In recent years, the institution has been changed by demands of transparency and the watchful eye of publicity. Having been opened by the proliferation of media, the legislative process now rewards skills of public outreach. With these changes, the office of Senate majority leader also has changed. Institutional leadership demands a spokesman, and press conferences and the proliferation of political talk shows ensure that a portion of each day in the life of a Senate majority leader is spent in front of cameras. There, he represents the Senate in bicameral and interbranch struggles and shapes his party line while refuting that of the opposition. To create strategies for the best possible presentation, the office of Senate majority leader employs a press secretary and staff charged with sustaining a message of institutional loyalty while elevating party preferences.

The institutional demands on Senate majority leadership are at their purest when the majority leader, as head of the Senate, assumes a very visible role in the Washington scene. The leader is just as likely to find himself on society pages as he is editorial pages. From dinner parties to diplomatic audiences, the majority leader is the face of the Senate, and thus constrained by its institutional requirements, tempered by partisan expectations.

Party
There are clear patterns to becoming leader and fulfilling the duties outlined in the previous sections. The road to majority leadership depends, among other criteria, on partisans who consider prior leadership experience in their selection decision. In earlier years, promotion rather than contest was the norm, and the path to the office of majority leader was through the whip's chair. Now, other leadership posts are proving grounds to test the would-be leader's partisan mettle. Both George Mitchell (D-ME) and Bill

Frist (R-TN) made a launching pad from their respective partisan campaign committees. But prior experience, however valuable, is not a prerequisite. Bob Dole (R-KS) was selected to replace Howard Baker (R-TN) without having any leadership experience, although he had served nearly three terms in the Senate. Seniority seems an obvious proxy for leadership experience, but an explicit test for seniority was overruled at the outset with the selection of John W. Kern (D-IN) as first majority leader. He had served only two years in the chamber; later, Lyndon Johnson and Bill Frist also made quick jumps to become Senate majority leader.

Other factors in the partisan selection of majority leader include regional balance and the trickle-down effects of leadership on committee chairmanships. With the declining salience of racial issues, and thus region, as a factional divide in the Democratic party, regional considerations have played a lesser role in selection. Still, the trickle-down effects on committee chairs introduce other transitivities to the selection calculus. Because the leader is prohibited by party rules from serving as chairman of committees, a senator's ascension to the leader's desk often leaves open committee chairs in its wake. The options for filling these vacancies, structured by seniority or party-mandated term limits, can ease or inhibit a senator's move to majority leadership.

As media have grown in number and importance, a foremost consideration in selection is the ability of a senator to speak for his party. Media have become more and more important as they have become at once tools for the party to sell its message and discount that of the opposition. Because oratory does not translate well into sound bites, Robert Byrd was twice challenged for his post (unprecedented and as of yet unrepeated) amid criticisms of his lack of media acumen; he ultimately was unable to meet growing expectations and resigned from the post (also unprecedented except for Alben Barkley's (D-KY) temporary resignation). Byrd's successor, George Mitchell, campaigned to replace him on the basis of his television-friendly persona.

Of the criteria for becoming leader, none is more pervasive for partisans than ideology. David Truman (1959) set the scholarly standard by suggesting that leaders were median voters of their party. His was structural-functional reasoning; that is, leaders must bring together disparate views and the best place to reach all factions is in the middle. His logic echoed Anthony Downs' (1957) modeling of party ideologies: parties move to the middle to capture the greatest amount of support. Subsequent scholars had accepted and repeated Truman's assertion; but only a few had explicitly tested it. William Sullivan (1975) and Jack Van Der Slik and Samuel Pernacciaro (1979) found the opposite: party leaders or aspirants to party-leadership positions were overwhelmingly, if not uniformly, located not at the median of their party but at the extreme. However, these studies were flawed in design. Both lumped all leadership positions into the analysis without distinguishing other leadership posts, such as whip, from majority leader. Inasmuch as the whip undertakes different tasks from the leader, expectations should be for differing behavior. Moreover, both studies were time-bound to an era that was an historical oddity in which cross-party coalitions were the norm rather than the exception; thus, party cohesion was unnaturally low.

The present research at once enlarges and focuses the scope of study by following the roll-call voting of all U.S. Senate majority leaders, since the emergence of the office, over the entire course of their careers, both before and as leader. The voting behavior of future leaders in their Senate years leading up to their selection suggests they are at or very near the middle of their party.[169] On the assumption that being leader might induce behavior different from anticipatory positioning, this inquiry, then, continues the trend-line from premajority leadership through the tenures of majority leaders to observe changes, if there be any, in voting. While previous studies had found would-be leaders in the extreme wing of their party, they are contradictory in their findings for leadership behavior. Sullivan (1975) noted that once a senator had become leader, he moderated his voting behavior toward the center of his party. Again, the roots of this finding are in Truman (1959) and repeated in Robert Peabody (1976): if leaders are not "middlemen" at selection, they soon become so. Theirs is a hypothesis of convergence; that is, leaders begin their Senate careers outside the mainstream but move toward the middle as a function of leadership. On the other hand, Van Der Slik and Pernacciaro (1979), who found that aspirants to leadership are extreme, also found that the voting behavior of leaders is extreme as they move out of leadership. However, as noted before, these studies, aside from producing contradictory findings, are handicapped by designs that over-generalize across positions of leadership and are time-bound cross-sectionally.

Rather, this research presents full career trend lines of all Senate majority leaders to show that just as leaders are at the median of their party before leadership, they remain at the median as leader. However, this longitudinal portrait reveals a variation on an otherwise obdurate trend, persisting over periods of interparty polarization and intraparty cohesion, eras of committee and party government, and unified and divided government: leaders, while remaining within a standard deviation of the center, have a tendency to drift slightly toward their party's extreme. Multivariate analyses based on party and state variables indicate that this movement in leaders' voting behaviors is conditioned by the size of their majority. Enlarged majorities pull the leader toward his party's extreme as more partisans make for more partisan voting. As the leader's majority increases, his movement has the effect of helping to maintain his own partisan coalition.

President

Although the trends described in the previous section are evidence that the leader is constrained by his party inside the chamber, other evidence reveals that the majority leader is also subject to an external partisan constraint—the presidency under unified government. Margaret Munk (1974) hypothesized that the office of Senate majority leader was conceived in expectations for a more active presidency in the legislative process. The majority leader was to be the president's man in the Senate; indeed, that was how the first majority leader, John Kern, found his job. Chosen explicitly for his sympathies to President Wilson's progressive program, Kern spent his political capital trying to sell the president's agenda to the Senate. If there has been an expectation for Senate majority leaders that has continued through the development and evolution of the office, it is this: the Senate majority leader is the president's broker.

Conclusions

The observations of Kern and Wilson in 1913 are just as relevant to the 21st-century relationship between Senate Majority Leader Bill Frist and President George W. Bush. If anything, the replication of a presidential hand in the selection of the Senate majority leader, together with the passage of time, has made the expectation more intractable. The majority leader, then, is constrained by the chief partisan in the White House in addition to fellow partisans in the Senate and charged with the not-always-easy task of reconciling the two.

State

Fundamentally, the Senate majority leader is still a senator elected to serve the interests of his state. However, as the leader assumes more and different constituencies, the representative relationship between senator-leader and home state might not be as substantive as before leadership. Evidence drawn from archival research into the collected papers of former Senate majority leaders suggests a shift to patronage, as the leader uses his status in and out of the chamber to provide distributive benefits to his first electoral constituency. This expression of patronage, first, was elaborated by an examination of earmarks to appropriations bills. States with majority leaders evidence a marked increase in both number and dollar amount of earmarks. That finding was further supported by two case studies—one of successful patronage, Howard Baker, and one not, George Mitchell.

Howard Baker, by virtue of being Senate majority leader, brought basics, such as sewer, gas, and water utilities, to an impoverished area, lobbying both state and federal agencies for grants and loans. In so doing, he was able to change fundamentally the economic base of his hometown of Huntsville, Tennessee, and its environs in Scott County. In contrast, George Mitchell had just assumed the role of majority leader when the first round of the Base Realignment and Closing commission targeted Loring Air Force Base in Maine for closure, and he quickly began a preemptive campaign to keep the base off the list. He was successful then, but two years later in a subsequent round of base closings, Loring made the cut list. Despite Mitchell's lobbying of BRAC commissioners and the White House, Loring was not spared. The closure meant loss of jobs, income, and related services for both military and civilian personnel in this isolated area that was literally built around and for the maintenance of the base. That Majority Leader Mitchell was unable to save a military base, conventionally a big draw for distributive benefits, was inexcusable to many Mainers. It is unlikely that the Loring closure alone affected Mitchell's plans to forego reelection in favor of retirement, but it surely contributed to his decision.

These trends and examples demonstrate how the behaviors of Senate majority leaders are conditioned by constituent expectations, and constituents expect their senator-turned-leader to showcase his status by providing a little extra pork.

Constrained by the Development of the Office

Even as the aforementioned constituencies create constraints on Senate majority leadership, leaders also are limited by expectations grounded in the emergence and path-dependent evolution of the office. The theory of path dependence means more than the perpetuation of precedent. A path-dependent development of a political institution means that as organizational and functional decisions are made, others are foreclosed. The abandonment of certain structural and operational choices does not forever cement the status quo, but it does establish costs for reversal and change. These costs make continuity of present conditions, even if themselves restrictive, easier than change. To be sure, there have been innovations in the office of Senate majority leader since its emergence—like the emphasis on media relations. Just as technology has introduced new demands on the Senate majority leader, others, like those expressed by the president, persist. The story of Senate majority leadership is more one of continuity than change.

All in all, this effort has highlighted constraints on the office of Senate majority leader. The ambiguities surrounding the office allow multiple constituencies, with different and often competing demands, to shape the functions of Senate majority leadership. Lacking a charter, the office of Senate majority leader has been shaped by the expressed expectations of state, party, senate, and president. These multiple constituencies, together with the original conditions of the office, have constrained the development and operation of Senate majority leadership. The present effort has not dissolved these ambiguities, nor lessened the constraints, but in recognizing them, it has clarified enduring functions of Senate majority leadership and variations among Senate majority leaders.

Appendix A

U.S. Senate Majority Leaders, 1913–2007

Senator	Senator	Senate Majority Leader	President
John W. Kern (D-IN)	1911–1917	1913–1917	Wilson
Thomas S. Martin (D-VA)	1895–1919	1917–1919	Wilson
Henry Cabot Lodge (R-MA)	1893–1924	1920–1924	Wilson, Harding, Coolidge
Charles Curtis (R-KS)	1907–1913, 1915–1929	1924–1929	Coolidge
James E. Watson (R-IN)	1916–1933	1929–1933	Hoover
Joseph T. Robinson (D-AR)	1913–1937	1933–1937	Roosevelt
Alben W. Barkley (D-KY)	1927–1949, 1955–1956	1937–1947	Roosevelt
Wallace H. White, Jr. (R-ME)	1931–1949	1947–1949	Truman
Scott W. Lucas (D-IL)	1939–1951	1949–1951	Truman
Ernest W. McFarland (D-AZ)	1941–1953	1951–1953	Truman
Robert A. Taft (R-OH)	1939–1953	1953	Eisenhower
William F. Knowland (R-CA)	1945–1959	1953–1955	Eisenhower
Lyndon B. Johnson (D-TX)	1959–1961	1955–1961	Eisenhower
Michael J. Mansfield (D-MT)	1953–1977	1961–1977	Kennedy, Johnson, Nixon, Ford

(*continued on next page*)

Appendix A *(continued)*

Senator	Senator	Senate Majority Leader	President
Robert C. Byrd (D-WV)	1959–present	1977–1980, 1987–1988	Carter, Reagan
Howard H. Baker (R-TN)	1967–1985	1981–1985	Reagan
Robert J. Dole (R-KS)	1969–1996	1985–1987, 1995–1996	Reagan
George J. Mitchell (D-ME)	1980–1995	1989–1995	George H. W. Bush, Clinton
C. Trent Lott (R-MS)	1989–2007	1996–2001	Clinton, George W. Bush
Thomas A. Daschle (D-SD)	1987–2005	2001–2003	George W. Bush
William H. Frist (R-TN)	1995–2007	2003–2007	George W. Bush

Sources. Floyd Riddick (1988) and the *Biographical Directory of the U.S. Congress* (http://bioguide.congress.gov).
Note. $N = 21$.

Appendix B

A Note on Sources

Howard H. Baker, Jr., Papers, Hoskins Library, University of Tennessee, Knoxville, February and March 2004, http://bakercenter.utk.edu/main/department.php?dep=100

The Baker papers are the foundation of the Howard H. Baker, Jr., Center for Public Policy. Although the collection had been opened for almost a decade, it was still new to researchers. Files are divided into various subgroups (legislative, political, administrative, public relations and press, and personal were pertinent to my research). I examined principally: Senate Leadership; Senators File; Congressional Record Clippings and Reprints of Baker's Remarks, 1967–1984; Political File, 1966–1984; Agencies, Boards, Commissions, and Departments File, 1973–1984; Appointments and Schedules; Project File, 1968–1984; Personal Correspondence File, 1977–1984; and Staff Correspondence Files, 1977–1983.

Lyndon B. Johnson Presidential Library, University of Texas, Austin, April 2004 and April 2005, http://www.lbjlibrary.org/

The Johnson collection is part of the national archives and therefore the most extensive and most professionally attended of all the collections. My interest was almost exclusively in the Senate Papers, 1949–1961. Within that division, several files proved pertinent: Legislative Files, 1949–1960; Papers of the Democratic Leader, 1951–1960; Subject Files, 1958–1961; Case and Project Files (further classified by departmental, military, rivers and harbors, veterans, and positions). However, the LBJA Subject Files also proved valuable: "[i]n 1958 the Johnson Senate staff created the Lyndon Baines Johnson Archives (LBJA) as part of its plan to institute a records management program. The staff screened Lyndon B. Johnson's noncurrent House and Senate files, scheduled portions for disposal, and placed many items of permanent value in LBJA. From 1958 to 1963 the staff continued to file documents in LBJA, and a few items were added during Johnson's presidency" (http://www.lbjlib.utexas.edu/johnson/archives.hom/holdings/pre-pres.asp). The Johnson Library also maintains an extensive collection of oral histories. A link to a helpful guide of available oral-history interviews is available on the Web site. Many oral histories themselves are available online; others are available via loan from the library.

George J. Mitchell Papers, Bowdoin College Library, Brunswick, Maine, June 2004, http://library.bowdoin.edu/arch/mitchell/

The Mitchell collection was the most recently opened, and many files were still restricted. However, the library staff quickly passed my request to view particular folders to Senator Mitchell, who just as quickly opened them to my research. The exceptions were U.S. Senate: Constituent Service files, consisting of folders from each of Mitchell's field offices; for privacy reasons, Senator Mitchell wished to limit these records to those constituents named within. My focus centered on the U.S. Senate: Majority Leadership Records, 1986–1994, including administration files, press and media activities, and domestic affairs. But other sections were relevant as well: U.S. Senate: Office Administration Records, Subject Files, 1980–1994; U.S. Senate: Legislative Records, Maine Defense Bases and Industries, Loring Air Force Base, 1987–1994; U.S. Senate: Personal Activities, Political Files, 1980–1994. At his retirement, Senator Mitchell's staff catalogued and shipped his files to his alma mater, so the collection lacks the direction of a professional archivist.

Mike Mansfield Library, University of Montana, Missoula, July 2004, http://www.lib.umt.edu/dept/arch/mss065.htm

Because of his extraordinary tenure of service, both as senator and as Senate majority leader, Mansfield's collection surpassed in bulk Johnson's nonpresidential papers. Most researchers examine the Mansfield collection for its insight into Asian affairs beginning with the Vietnam War and continuing through his service as ambassador to Japan. The Senate: Leadership series was central to my research, although I also examined the following series as well: Senate: Montana; House/Senate: Personal; Senate: Intergovernmental Correspondence; House/Senate: Speeches; and Senate: Federal Agencies. Mansfield's papers were originally prepared and processed by his Senate staff but benefited from professional archiving once they reached the Mansfield Library. However, the collection suffers from preservation problems with many documents and clippings that are fragile beyond use.

The Miller Center of Public Affairs, University of Virginia, http://millercenter.org/academic/oralhistory

The Miller Center, a public-policy institute that sponsors nonpartisan academic and policy research and analysis, has developed a presidential oral-history project. Specifically devoted to presidencies since Jimmy Carter, the project is a trove of interviews of key figures in presidential administrations. This wide net covers a variety of individuals in all branches and bureaucracies of government and, for purposes of my research, provided a way to tap into views on executive-legislative relations, specifically with regard to individual presidents and Senate majority leaders. Additionally, many transcripts of oral histories from other presidential libraries are linked here, so the scope of coverage predates the Carter years.

NOTES

1. MMA, Collection 65, Series XIX, Box 589, Folder 16, letter to Chris Stevens, June 20, 1962.
2. See appendix A for a listing of the 21 Senate majority leaders from 1913–2007.
3. To be sure, some congressional scholars have recognized the uniqueness of the U.S. Senate (e.g., Baker, 1980, 1989; Fenno, 1982).
4. Indeed, Cox and McCubbins (2003) credited her with reframing scholarship on leadership in Congress.
5. Evans and Oleszek (1999) applied their contextual framework to explain legislative outcomes (the Telecommunications Act of 1996 and the Kennedy-Kassebaum Health Insurance Portability and Accountability Act of 1996) more than to establish a theory of congressional leadership.
6. "Discretion and constraints" represent opposite states or conditions of freedom of action. The present inquiry focuses on Senate majority leaders' relatively unfettered maneuverability without threat of sanction from one or more of his principal constituencies—state, party, senate, and president. A leader is subject to other kinds of discretion and constraints, from cognitive to political to moral. I have concentrated on those affected by his constituencies.
7. MMA, MSS 65, XIX: House/Senate: Personal, 1943–1977, Box 589, Folder 11, interview with L. M. Berniere—second in a series, n. d.
8. The right of first recognition is perhaps the only formal, procedural power in the arsenal of the Senate majority leader. On the floor, among multiple requests for recognition, the presiding officer will recognize the Senate majority leader first, enabling him to offer amendments, substitutions, or generally control the floor at the expense of the minority (Watkins & Riddick, 1964).
9. For the full account of this encounter, see Valeo (1999, p. 215). And, for an alternate perspective, see Oberdorfer (2003, p. 339).
10. HHBA, MS 2000, Box 43, Folder 21, "My duties and responsibilities as a member of Congress," 1983.
11. MMA, MSS 65, XII: Miscellaneous, Box 92, Folder 13, letter to Mr. and Mrs. Robert A. Fagan, April 6, 1962.
12. MMA, MSS 65, XVIII: Intergovernmental correspondence, Box 29, Folder 5, letter to Mrs. W. C. Moore, March 16, 1963.

13. GJMA, M202.6.4.6.1, Box 813, "1991 Memos," June 25, 1991.
14. LBJL, Senate papers, Box 517, Folder: 1954 General files (Democratic leader), memorandum on being Democratic leader versus senator, n. d.
15. LBJL, Senate papers, Subject files 1960, Folder: Senate, U.S.—Leadership (1of 2), "Senator Lyndon B. Johnson/Democrat, Texas," *The Log* (XLIII:1), Champion Paper and Fiber Co., Hamilton, OH, January 1960.
16. Ibid.
17. LBJL, Senate papers, Box 419, Folder: Reedy: Memos, 1956 (1 of 3), memorandum on leadership, n. d.
18. LBJL, Senate papers, Box 420, Folder: Reedy: Memos, March 1957, memorandum on Johnson's leadership style, n. d.
19. See *Congressional Record*, 1960, p. 12444.
20. Transcript, letter (June 2, 1982) attached to George Reedy oral history interview IV, May 21, 1982, by Michael Gillette, LBJ Library. Online: http://www.lbjlib.utexas.edu/johnson/archives.hom/oralhistory.hom/Reedy/reedy%20web%204.pdf (July 24, 2009).
21. See appendix B for details on sources. See also Kelly (2005) for the utility of archival data to political-science research.
22. Grants from the Department of Political Science, Vanderbilt University, and the Lyndon B. Johnson Foundation made this possible.
23. Many of these oral histories are available for loan or copy at the aforementioned libraries or available online through The Miller Center for Public Affairs at the University of Virginia (http://millercenter.org/academic/oralhistory/index) (July 24, 2009).
24. http://www.cagw.org (July 24, 2009).
25. Some psychological conceptualizations view leadership as a personality trait or skill (Chaplin, 1985, p. 253). Still other definitions focus on behavioral aspects, gauging leadership as success in guiding or directing the conduct of others (Ibid.). Even some political definitions speak of "persuasion," "inspiration," or "making them [followers] believe that a proposed course of action is the correct one" (Robertson, 1993, pp. 274–276).
26. See also Reber (1995, p. 411). Among political scientists, Lasswell and Kaplan (1950, pp. 152–161), Paige (1977), and Burns (1979) are notable for efforts to clarify an elusive but common topic.
27. Note Fenno's (1973) discussion of the multiple goals of members of Congress in comparison to Mayhew's (1974) assumption of reelection as a single goal.
28. See Cooper and Brady (1981) for a likeminded study of contextual effects on House leadership styles.

Notes

29. Given Frist's medical background, this is a particularly salient topic with him. For several years, he has made annual trips (sometimes by surprise to avoid publicity) to perform surgeries and treat AIDS victims in impoverished Africa.
30. Byrd (1995) apparently disagreed with the date at which the president pro tempore was relieved of appointment obligations.
31. Establishing a precedent of unanimity that exists to this day, the incumbent caucus chair, Thomas Martin (D-VA), withdrew, so Kern was elected by acclamation.
32. For a detailed discussion of collective action principles and propositions, see Mancur Olson (1971).
33. However, under party rules, the Republican majority now applies term limits, which supersede the seniority rule, to its committee chairs.
34. No senator may serve longer than six years as chairman or ranking member of a committee (*Rules*, 2004).
35. Johnson would get more senior senators to request a particular assignment in order to deny a request he did not favor.
36. The constraints placed on Senate majority leaders by presidents are discussed in depth in chapter 5.
37. The Democratic leader was also chair of the entire conference as well as the steering committee.
38. Perhaps this decentralization was a backlash to Johnson's request that as vice president he retain the chair of the DPC. In response, Senate Democrats voted unanimously to gain the right to confirm or reject nominations to the DPC by the Democratic leader (Caro, 2002).
39. Daschle campaigned for majority leader, but by the time his service began, Democrats were in the minority.
40. The 60-vote threshold was implemented in 1975. Prior to that, Rule XXII, originally adopted in 1917 (after Kern's service as majority leader), established a two-thirds vote to end debate.
41. HHBA, MS-2000, Box 2, Folder 22: Memo/Letters to Republican senators, 1981, "I have directed the Secretary for the Majority..." January 21, 1981.
42. GJMA, M202.6.2.1.4, Box 105, "Index of Legislative Memorandum 1980," n. d.
43. The case of Byrd's resignation and the importance of media relations are discussed in greater detail as a criterion for leadership selection in chapter 3.
44. Barbara Sinclair (1995) and Douglas Harris (1998) both marked "the rise of the public speakership." The same demands, such as the contemporary nature of mass media, are no less forgiving of Senate majority leaders.

45. More on presidential constraints is discussed in chapter 5.
46. This distinction is drawn and explicated by Edward Carmines and James Stimson (1989).
47. Former secretary of the Senate Francis Valeo wrote, "After he began to appear with some regularity on these programs, interrogators learned that it was necessary in interviewing Mansfield to have on hand two or three times the usual number of prepared questions or risk running out of profundity before running out of time" (1999, p. 22).
48. For a brief statement on the varieties of media experiences, see Roger Davidson and Walter Oleszek (2004, p. 181).
49. Mansfield was a regular in Georgetown salons probably as much for his wife's enjoyment as any obligation to his job (Oberdorfer, 2003).
50. HHBA, MS-2000, Boxes 50–56.
51. Lawton Chiles (D-FL) challenged Senate Majority Leader Robert Byrd (D-WV) in 1984, and Bennett Johnston (D-LA) challenged Byrd in 1986.
52. Trent Lott (R-MS) resigned December 20, 2002. Bill Frist (R-TN) was selected December 23, 2002.
53. In early 2005 speculation began on who would fill the role after Bill Frist, who had pledged retirement in 2006. Reports trickled out that Assistant Leader Mitch McConnell (R-KY), in a campaign headed by fellow Republican Robert Bennett (R-UT), had already secured 40 votes—more than enough to win (Gehrke, 2005).
54. His death was associated with his responsibilities as majority leader. He died of a sudden heart attack one night after lengthy debate on the Senate floor over President Roosevelt's legislation to enlarge the size of the Supreme Court.
55. John W. Kern (D-IN), the first Senate majority leader, was also the first to be turned out of the Senate while leader. However, this loss was before the ratification of the 17th Amendment, so he was evicted by his state legislature and not by popular election.
56. Charles Curtis (R-KS) bypassed more senior members upon his selection in 1924, thereby breaking the seniority rule for the Republican party.
57. Daschle, in fact, began polling his chances the very day Mitchell announced his retirement (Hook, 1994).
58. This strategy of "going public" was originally formulated by Kernell (1986) to describe presidential tactics in dealing with Congress.
59. Mansfield's replies of "yip" or "nope" demanded producers of *Meet the Press* to have a reservoir of questions for him at least double that for other guests (Valeo, 1999; Oberdorfer, 2003).

60. Portions of this chapter appear in "A Man for All Seasons: Partisan Constraints on U.S. Senate Majority Leaders," *Party Politics*, in press, and are reprinted here with permission.
61. Republican caucus rules, however, prevent the party leader (and whips) from serving as chair or ranking member on a committee while in leadership (*Rules*, 1990).
62. Keith Poole and Howard Rosenthal found that spatial movement, or the movement of legislators' voting scores within a spatial domain, had been in decline since around the Civil War (p. 74). And since the 1950s, change in voting scores from Congress to Congress amounted to roughly 0.2 units, or 1% the diameter of the space (1997, p. 74).
63. Aage Clausen and Clyde Wilcox (1987), however, in their examination of the policy positioning of leader-aspirants, did not find evidence of party positioning in anticipation of leadership selection.
64. In Aldrich's party model, the party selects a leader whose constituency preferences do not conflict with the party, and thus, the leader is free to maximize party policy without shirking his constituency. In other words, parties choose leaders from safe seats. In the same vein, Eric Heberlig, Marc Hetherington, and Bruce Larson (2006) showed that party leaders are increasingly more ideologically extreme than their party caucuses. They attributed this selection of "extremists" to their success in fundraising by demonstrating, first, that ideologues tend to be electorally safe in their respective districts which frees them for fundraising, and, second, that campaign contributions increase the likelihood of leadership selection. Whether this pattern is applicable to the Senate, where electorates are not so homogeneous, is a testable proposition.
65. King and Zeckhauser (2002) did note, however, that the more senior in rank the figure, the more extreme his position within the party—for example, the Senate majority leader would have a voting score more extreme than his party's whip.
66. In a more nuanced study of party positioning among leaders and aspirants in both House and Senate, Clausen and Wilcox (1987) examined party positions by issue domain rather than pure ideological placement. Their "partisanship theory" found leaders located with the median of their party, which they interpreted as a reconsideration of the "middleman theory" of Peabody (1976). However, it should be noted that their theory had less predictive power for the Senate than the House. Likewise, Bernard Grofman, William Koetzle, and Anthony J. McGann (2002) found party leaders were located away from the median toward the mode of their parties. Their study, and thus their finding of extremism, however, was concentrated in the House.

67. Such movement can be immediate or progressive.
68. To further complicate expectations, Brian Posler and Carl Rhodes (1997) found evidence of both trends, differentiated by party. Democrats in signaling leadership intentions tended to move away from the opposition party in their preselection careers; Republican would-be leaders, however, aligned with the median party member. It should be noted, however, that although the breadth of this study is impressive, covering House leaders from 1875–1987, it is limited to the House alone.
69. Note that some leaders serve as minority leader or another leadership position before becoming majority leader. However, I have looked at the Senate majority leader independently. While there is doubtless a high correlation between occupying lower party leadership positions and becoming majority leader, I make no presumption that the ascendance to majority leader is only a promotion, or a natural progression. In many instances, these selections are contested; indeed, even with an incumbent majority leader, the selections at the beginning of each Congress are more than perfunctory, with one or more senators challenging the leader.
70. In creating their spatial model of ideological placement of legislators, Poole and Rosenthal (1997, p. 25) hypothesized that the position of a legislator is constant over time and that any shifts that do occur reflect simple linear movement, empirically measured by DW-NOMINATE scores. These scores, since their creation, have become a standard measure among scholars of legislative behavior, even in a comparative perspective (Poole & Rosenthal, 2001).
71. For a more complete picture of central tendency, I included party means and medians, but for graphical simplification, I included standard-deviation markers around the mean only. For this as well as the following statistical analysis, results did not change with measures of mean or median.
72. Knowland's substantial movement from centrist to partisan Republican may be explained by his presidential ambitions. Thinking President Eisenhower and, by association, Vice President Nixon to be moderate Republicans, Knowland believed that to capture the party nomination from Nixon required him to run to Nixon's right. Hence, he exhibited a marked transformation from the likes of Eisenhower to the mold of Robert A. Taft (R-OH) (Montgomery & Johnson, 1998).
73. Barkley is the only leader whose shift diverged rather than paralleled his party's track during his tenure.
74. LBJL, Senate papers, Subject files, Box 117, Folder: Senate, United States—Leadership, "Notes taken at Senator Johnson's Press Conference," November 19, 1958.

75. Following an anonymous reviewer's recommendation, I created a dependent variable that was each leader's distance from his party median rather than his absolute score. There was no change in results.
76. Tests using party means did not alter the results.
77. These were computed using Stata 8.0 software.
78. Rules were changed in 1975 to move the threshold from two-thirds to three-fifths. See Sarah Binder and Steven Smith (1997) for a discussion of politics of the filibuster.
79. David Rohde described this behavior as "conditional party government" in the postreform U.S. House: "As homogeneity of preferences increased, party leadership became more vigorous and party cohesion in voting increased" (1991, p. 39).
80. Thanks to an anonymous reviewer for adding to this reasoning.
81. Harry Reid and Mitch McConnell, "Senate Leadership," University of Louisville, C-SPAN, October 15, 2007. Online: http://www.cspanarchives.org/library/index.php?main_page=product_video_info&products_id=201547-1 (June 20, 2009).
82. For details on this unique structural arrangement, see Daschle (2003, pp. 36–40).
83. Among these expenses are fixed costs, learning effects, and coordination effects (Pierson, 2000, p. 254). Each is applicable to the office of Senate majority leader.
84. Guy Peters, Jon Pierre, and Desmond King (2005) criticized path dependence for its inability to explain both continuity and change.
85. Granted, David Mayhew (1991) found that neither divided nor unified government makes much difference in either congressional oversight of the executive branch or the "standard kind of important legislation" (p. 4). However, for our purposes, neither measure is apropos to the behavior of Senate majority leaders whose duties do not include investigation but do include agenda setting no matter the importance of the presidents' proposals. Therefore, given what we know about the job description of the Senate majority leader (see chapter 2), it is reasonable to conclude that whether or not the president is of the same party affects how the leader does his job.
86. This era was a precursor to the legendary election of 1958, which ushered in an era of reform over two subsequent decades.
87. The bloc had wired Kern asking for his cooperation in their plans to make him leader. He never replied outright, but he began gathering votes so that his selection when the caucus convened was a foregone conclusion.

88. For a full discussion of the politics surrounding Kern's ascension, see Walter Oleszek (1991).
89. His DW-NOMINATE scores consistently located him to the left of his party's mean. See chapter 4.
90. JTRA, Series 9, Subseries 1, Box 206, Folder 6, letter to W. C. Dawson, April 1, 1933, quoted in Bacon (1991, p. 82).
91. JTRA, Series 9, Subseries 1, Box 206, Folder 6, "Mark Sullivan's Letter," unidentified newspaper clipping, July 1935, quoted in Bacon (1991, p. 83).
92. Barkley originally had voted for the act but on the vote to override made the following statement: "...[H]aving myself, when the bill passed the Senate originally voted in favor of it, in view of the additional reasons given by the president in his message,...I feel that, notwithstanding my former attitude and position on the matter, I am justified in voting to sustain the veto of the president" (*Congressional Record*, 1937, p. 7363).
93. MMA, Collection 65, Series XXII, Box 13, Folder 6, "The Majority Leader of the Senate," by George B. Galloway, Library of Congress: Legislative reference service, February 2, 1959, quoting Alben W. Barkley, *Lectures on The Process of Government*, University of Kentucky, 1949: 46–47.
94. See Robert Caro (2002), Paul Conkin (1986), Robert Dallek (1991), Rowland Evans and Robert Novak (1966), Doris Kearns Goodwin (1976), and Randall Woods (2006).
95. Johnson's tactics are legendary: "The Treatment could last ten minutes or four hours. It came, enveloping its target, at the LBJ Ranch swimming pool, in one of LBJ's offices, in the Senate cloakroom, on the floor of the Senate itself—wherever Johnson might find a fellow Senator within his reach... It ran the gamut of human emotions. Its velocity was breathtaking...He moved in close, his face a scant millimeter from his target, his eyes widening and narrowing, his eyebrows rising and falling. From his pockets poured clippings, memos, statistics. Mimicry, humor, and the genius of analogy made The Treatment an almost hypnotic experience and rendered the target stunned and helpless" (Evans & Novak, 1966, p. 104).
96. Transcript, George Reedy oral history interview X, October 14, 1983, by Michael L. Gillette, p. 6, LBJ Library. Online: http://www.lbjlib.utexas.edu/johnson/archives.hom/oralhistory.hom/Reedy/reedy%20web%2010.pdf (June 9, 2009).
97. Transcript, Harry C. McPherson, Jr., oral history interview VII, September 19, 1985, by Michael L. Gillette, p. 9, LBJ Library. Online: http://www.lbjlib.utexas.edu/johnson/archives.hom/oralhistory.hom/mcpherson/mcpher07.pdf (June 7, 2009).

98. LBJ statements, Box 18, "What Congress Will Do Next Year" in *U.S. News and World Report*, interview with LBJ, September 30, 1955.
99. Transcript, George Reedy oral history interview VI, May 23, 1983, Michael L. Gillette, p. 6, LBJ Library. Online: http://www.lbjlib.utexas.edu/johnson/archives.hom/oralhistory.hom/Reedy/reedy%20web%206.pdf (June 9, 2009).
100. Ibid.
101. Transcript, George Reedy oral history interview VIII, August 16, 1983, Michael L. Gillette, pp. 44–45, LBJ Library. Online: http://www.lbjlib.utexas.edu/johnson/archives.hom/oralhistory.hom/Reedy/reedy%20web%208.pdf (June 9, 2009).
102. Ibid.
103. Ibid.
104. LBJA Subject, Box 117, Senate, U.S.-Leadership LBJ (1 of 2), "Congressional Program," memo, October 26, 1955.
105. Transcript, Harry C. McPherson, Jr., oral history interview I, December 5, 1968, T. H. Baker, p. 1 (tape 2 of 2), LBJ Library. Online: http://www.lbjlib.utexas.edu/johnson/archives.hom/oralhistory.hom/mcpherson/mcpher01.pdf (June 7, 2009).
106. MMA, Collection 65, Series XXII, Box 103, Folder 1, "Conversation between Bobby Baker in Miami, Fla. and Senator Mansfield, Wash. D.C." (transcript), November 14, 1960.
107. MMA, Collection 65, Series XIX, Box 589, Folder 11, "Second in a series—Senate Majority Leader Mike Mansfield of Montana," by L. M. Berniere.
108. Barry Goldwater interview, Miller Center, University of Virginia, Lyndon B. Johnson presidential oral history project, June 26, 1971. Online: http://web2.millercenter.org/lbj/oralhistory/goldwater_barry_1971_0626.pdf (June 10, 2009).
109. Thruston Morton Interview, Miller Center, University of Virginia, Lyndon B. Johnson presidential oral history project, February 26, 1969. Online: http://web2.millercenter.org/lbj/oralhistory/morton_thruston_1969_0226.pdf (June 10, 2009).
110. William Proxmire interview, Miller Center, University of Virginia, Lyndon B. Johnson presidential oral history project, February 4, 1986. Online: http://web2.millercenter.org/lbj/oralhistory/proxmire_william_1986_0204.pdf (June 10, 2009).
111. Ibid.
112. Ibid.

113. MMA, Collection 65, Series XIX, Box 588, Folder 23, "New York Writers Report 'Startling Results' Obtained by Mike Mansfield as Senate Leader," *Great Falls Tribune*, August 14, 1961.
114. MMA, Collection 65, Series XXII, Box 89, Folder 11, "Statement of Senator Mike Mansfield to the Democratic Policy Committee," February 4, 1969.
115. Ibid.
116. It does not deny the weight of governmental structure to recognize the role of personality in Johnson's leadership style.
117. Ibid.
118. MMA, Collection 65, Series XIX, Box 588, Folder 23, "'No Split,' Mike Asserts," *Billings Gazette,* April 18, 1965.
119. MMA, Collection 65, Series XIX, Box 603, Folder 12, letter from Mansfield to President Johnson, January 22, 1965.
120. As part of a wave of postwar noninterventionism, the Bricker Amendment was an attempt to amend the constitution to limit ratification of certain treaties and executive agreements. The amendment was opposed by President Eisenhower and failed to pass the Senate by a single vote. Even though he dissented from the president, Senate Majority Leader Knowland left the leader's desk and stood in the rear of the chamber to give a speech denouncing the president's position on the Bricker Amendment, thereby demonstrating a tacit understanding of the expectation that he should be a vessel for presidential preferences.
121. HHBA, MS-2000, Box 53, Folder 28, March 1981 appointments, letter to Larry R. Smith, March 6, 1981.
122. Howard Baker interview, Miller Center, University of Virginia, Ronald Reagan presidential oral history project, August 24, 2004. Online: http://web1.millercenter.org/poh/transcripts/ohp_2004_0824_baker.pdf (June 20, 2009).
123. Max Friedersdorf interview, Miller Center, University of Virginia, Ronald Reagan presidential oral history project, October 24, 2002. Online: http://web1.millercenter.org/poh/transcripts/ohp_2002_1024_friedersdorf.pdf (June 20, 2009).
124. Ibid.
125. Howard Baker, The leader's lecture series, July 14, 1998. Online: http://www.Senate.gov/artandhistory/history/common/generic/Leaders_Lecture_Series_Baker.htm (June 20, 2009).
126. Barkley won with his one-vote margin nearly 50 years earlier, and McFarland won in 1950 by a wide margin.

127. He was forced into a compromise to invoke cloture on three of the five pending nominations. The arrangement by seven Democrats and seven Republicans seemed to some Republican partisans as submission by the majority to the minority.
128. The Honest Leadership and Open Government Act of 2007 (see http://frwebgate.access.gpo.gov/cgi-bin/getdoc.cgi?dbname=110_cong_public_laws&docid=f:publ081.110.pdf) (July 30, 2009).
129. http://www.cagw.org/site/PageServer?pagename=reports_pigbook2009 (July 30, 2009).
130. Although outside the timeline of this research, it is interesting to note that in FY2009, out of 111 total earmarks originating in the Senate, Senator John Ensign (D-NV) sponsored only one, compared to 58 sponsored by Senate Majority Leader Harry Reid (D-NV). The remaining earmarks were jointly sponsored, which muddies direct attribution.
131. U.S. Census Bureau, "Per Capita Income," Table C3, http://www.census.gov/hhes/www/income/histinc/county/county3.html (July 30, 2009).
132. HHBA, MS-2000, Box 58, Folders 5 & 6, "Washington News Update," May 1984.
133. HHBA, MS-2000, Box 58, Folder 3, letter to The Honorable John Parish, June 30, 1983.
134. HHBA, MS-2000, Box 58, Folder 3, letter from Dwight E. Murphy, October 7, 1983.
135. HHBA, MS-2000, Box 58, Folder 7, letter to The Honorable Lamar Alexander, March 29, 1983.
136. As of July 7, 2004, GAO stands for Government Accountability Office.
137. Granted, such a collection may be incomplete; but even so, such collected papers show what was important to him and his staff.
138. None were outright denied, although two allocations (for fire equipment and another for airport improvements) were not pursued by either Baker or Scott County advocates. A third, for a rural housing project, was introduced too late and forfeited when Baker left office.
139. See Fred Greenstein (1982). Baker, like President Eisenhower, in whom the style was perfected, disguised moves that might appear inconsistent with his public affability. He avoided public controversies whenever possible and relied on staff and other subordinates to take controversial actions.
140. See http://www.scott.tn.us/?q=node/5 (July 30, 2009).
141. GJMA, M202.6.6.1, Box 430, "Memorandum '90," April 13, 1990.
142. Ibid.
143. Ibid.

144. GJMA, M202.6.2.14.2, Box 549, memo re: "Loring AFB/Historical Background," December 14, 1988.
145. GJMA, M202.6.2.14.2, Box 549, memo re: "Loring Air Force Base: Economic Data," October 29, 1988.
146. GJMA, M202.6.2.14.2, Box 549, memo re: "Loring/Base-Closings: Severin Beliveau Suggestion and Other Maine Concerns," December 14, 1988.
147. GJMA, M202.6.2.14.2, Box 549, memo re: "Base-Closings: Outlook/Interests," January 6, 1989.
148. GJMA, M202.6.2.14.2, Box 550, email from Claude Berube to Bob Carolla, April 23, 1991.
149. Trowbridge was secretary of commerce from 1967–1968 and former president of the National Association of Manufacturers.
150. Levitt owned *Roll Call* newspaper and was past chair of the American stock exchange.
151. GJMA, M202.6.2.14.2, Box 550, memo re: "Loring AFB: Meeting with Alexander Trowbridge," May 16, 1991.
152. GJMA, M202.6.2.14.2, Box 550, "Statement of Senator Mitchell, Loring AFB Closure," May 22, 1991.
153. GJMA, M202.6.2.14.2, Box 550, letter to the Editor, *Bangor Daily News*, May 28, 1991.
154. GJMA, M202.6.2.14.2, Box 550, memo re: "Loring AFB: Update," June 20, 1991.
155. Ibid.
156. GJMA, M202.6.2.14.2, Box 551, memo re: "Loring AFB: Final Deliberations," June 26, 1991.
157. GJMA, M202.6.2.14.2, Box 551, memo re: "Loring AFB: Phone Calls before Thursday, June 4, 1991.
158. GJMA, M202.6.2.14.2, Box 550, memo re: "Scowcroft Meeting," July 7, 1991.
159. Ibid.
160. GJMA, M202.6.2.14.2, Box 554, request to energy subcommittee, n. d.
161. Ibid.
162. For details on Loring redevelopment, see www.loring.org (July 30, 2009).
163. Scott County projects did not exhaust Baker's pursuit of resources to distribute among his constituents. Some were much larger in scope and less successful in realization. To wit: his advocacy of a project to build a breeder reactor near the Clinch River. Through several congresses and against three reluctant presidential administrations, Baker kept hopes alive

for this multimillion-dollar project in Tennessee. Eventually, he quietly acknowledged defeat (Annis, 1995).

164. Indeed, Baker's method of direct contact with bureaucratic agents evolved into a practice that members and lobbyists 25 years later refer to as "phonemarking" (Solomon & Birnbaum, 2007). As the political climate became more unfavorable for earmarking, but the demands and rewards no less, leaders used their resources to bypass the congressional appropriations process. For example, just days after he became majority leader in January 2007, Senator Harry Reid (D-NV) contacted Energy Secretary Samuel Bodman and lobbied the department to fund a geothermal-energy project which would benefit the electricity needs of Reid's home state (Solomon & Birnbaum, 2007).

165. Department of Defense, Base Realignment and Closure report, March 1991, http://www.defenselink.mil/brac/docs/1991dod.pdf (July 30, 2009). See also "Prior Rounds: BRAC Installations by Year," http://www.oea.gov/oeaweb.nsf/BRAC+by+Year?OpenForm (July 30, 2009).

166. One of those bases spared was Ellsworth Air Force Base in Rapid City, South Dakota. Thirteen years later, South Dakota's senior senator, and former Senate majority leader, was engaged in a tight electoral battle with challenger John Thune (R), who was backed by the White House. A central issue was the protection of Ellsworth from an upcoming round of BRAC (Hulse, 2004). Daschle already had secured millions of dollars in appropriations for the base (see table 6.1) and promised his clout as party leader would keep the base open. Thune also pledged to preserve the base, counting on his close ties to the White House as collateral. This recent exchange is further evidence of the expectation of congressional influence on base closings, not only by voters but also by legislators themselves: both Daschle and Thune expected that they, in different ways, could act to preserve Ellsworth. Thune was elected and four months later, Ellsworth appeared on the initial list of closures put out by the defense department. Straight away, Thune was challenged by media and even by his one-time opponent to make good on his promise, and immediately he forged a lobbying partnership with his same-state colleague Tim Johnson (D) (Schmitt, 2005; Stolberg, 2005). Like George Mitchell earlier, they, with the rest of the congressional delegation, made media appearances, gave testimony, and lobbied the commission and even the administration. This round, as before, spared Ellsworth on the final list.

167. Despite perceived inevitability, there is precedent for a majority leader successfully preserving a large-scale project. Mike Mansfield (D-MT), as

Senate majority leader 30 years earlier, successfully lobbied the veterans' administration and the Johnson White House to keep open the Miles City VA Hospital in Miles City, Montana, 1 of 14 targeted for closure across the country. Even when President Johnson "sought to placate Mansfield by proposing to pump more federal dollars into other projects in the Miles City area to compensate for the hospital closing, [t]he majority leader flatly refused" (Oberdorfer, 2003, p. 257). Mansfield, who recognized the political symbolism involved, threatened to pass a bill taking away Johnson's authority to close any hospitals (Oberdorfer, 2003). The Miles City VA Hospital remains open to this day. Like that of Mansfield, Mitchell's case represents major action on a major distributive project.

168. MMA, Collection 65, Series XIX, Box 589, Folder 16, letter to Chris Stevens, June 20, 1962.
169. Prior to majority leadership, these would-be leaders were within one standard deviation of their party's ideological mean as measured by DW-NOMINATE scores (www.voteview.com, July 31, 2009).

REFERENCES

Abramowitz, A. I., Alexander, B., & Gunning, M. (2006). Incumbency, redistricting, and the decline of competition in U.S. House elections. *Journal of Politics, 68*(1), 75–88.

Abramowitz, A. I., & Segal, J. A. (1992). *Senate elections*. Ann Arbor: University of Michigan Press.

Adler, E. S. (2000). Constituency characteristics and the "guardian" model of appropriations subcommittees, 1959–1998. *American Journal of Political Science, 44*(1), 104–114.

Aldrich, J. H. (1995). A model of a legislature with two parties and a committee system. In K. Shepsle & B. R. Weingast (Eds.), *Positive theories of congressional institutions*. Ann Arbor: University of Michigan Press.

Aldrich, J. H., & Rohde, D. W. (2001). The logic of conditional party government: Revisiting the electoral connection. In L. C. Dodd & B. I. Oppenheimer (Eds.), *Congress reconsidered* (7th ed.). Washington, DC: CQ Press.

Allen, M., & Milbank, D. (2002, December 17). Bush won't resist leadership change. *The Washington Post*, p. A01.

Allison, G. (1971). *Essence of decision: Explaining the Cuban missile crisis*. Boston: Little, Brown.

American Political Science Association. (1950). Toward a more responsible two-party system: A report of the committee on political parties [special issue]. *American Political Science Review, 44*(3, Pt. 2, Suppl.).

Annis, J. L. (1995). *Howard Baker: Conciliator in an age of crisis*. Lanham, MD: Madison Books.

Ansolabehere, S. D., & Snyder, Jr., J. M. (2000). Valence politics and equilibrium in spatial election models. *Public Choice, 103*(3–4), 327–336.

Arnold, R. D. (1979). *Congress and the bureaucracy: A theory of influence.* New Haven, CT: Yale University Press.

Arnold, R. D. (1990). *The logic of congressional action.* New Haven, CT: Yale University Press.

Bachrach, P., & Baratz, M. (1962). The two faces of power. *American Political Science Review, 56*(4), 947–952.

Bacon, D. C. (1991). Joseph Taylor Robinson: The good soldier. In R. A. Baker & R. H. Davidson (Eds.), *First among equals: Outstanding Senate leaders of the twentieth century.* Washington, DC: CQ Press.

Baker, R. A., & Davidson, R. H. (Eds.). (1991). *First among equals: Outstanding Senate leaders of the twentieth century.* Washington, DC: CQ Press.

Baker, R. K. (1980). *Friend and foe in the U.S. Senate.* New York: Free Press.

Baker, R. K. (1989). *House and Senate.* New York: W. W. Norton.

Baker, R. K. (1991). Mike Mansfield and the birth of the modern Senate. In R. A. Baker & R. H. Davidson (Eds.), *First among equals: Outstanding Senate leaders of the twentieth century.* Washington, DC: CQ Press.

Barkley, A. W. (1954). *That reminds me.* Garden City, NY: Doubleday.

Baron, D. P., & Ferejohn, J. A. (1989). Bargaining in legislatures. *American Political Science Review, 83*(4), 1181–1206.

Barry, B. (1965). *Political argument.* New York: Humanities Press.

Baumer, D. C. (1992). Senate Democratic leadership in the 101st Congress. In A. D. Hertzke & R. M. Peters (Eds.), *The atomistic Congress: An interpretation of congressional change.* Armonk, NY: M.E. Sharpe.

Bickers, K. N., & Stein, R. M. (2000). The congressional pork barrel in a Republican era. *Journal of Politics, 62*(4), 1070–1086.

Binder, S. A. (2003). *Stalemate: Causes and consequences of gridlock.* Washington, DC: Brookings Institution Press.

Binder, S. A., & Maltzman, F. (2009). *The struggle to shape the federal judiciary.* Washington, DC: Brookings Institution Press.

Binder, S. A., & Smith, S. S. (1997). *Politics or principle? Filibustering in the United States Senate.* Washington, DC: Brookings Institution Press.

Bishop, B. (2008). *The big sort: Why the clustering of like-minded America is tearing us apart.* Boston: Houghton Mifflin.

Bivins, L. (2003, January 19). A Senate leader is a friend in high places. *The Tennessean.*

Black, G. S. (1972). A theory of political ambition: Career choices and the role of structural incentives. *American Political Science Review, 66*(1), 144–59.

Bobic, M. P. (1996). *Revealing leadership through roll call analysis: Howard Baker's effectiveness in the United States Senate, 1977–1982.* Unpublished doctoral dissertation, University of Tennessee, Knoxville.

Bolton, A. (2005, April 14). GOP fears it's losing Frist v. Reid. *The Hill,* p. 1.

Bond, J. R., & Fleisher, R. (1990). *The president in the legislative arena.* Chicago: University of Chicago Press.

Bone, H. A. (1956). An introduction to the Senate policy committees. *American Political Science Review, 50*(2), 339–359.

Bone, H. A. (1958). *Party committees and national politics.* Seattle: University of Washington Press.

Bowers, C. G. (1918). *The life of John W. Kern.* Indianapolis, IN: Hollendeck Press.

Brace, P. (1984). Progressive ambition in the House: A probabilistic approach. *Journal of Politics, 46*(2), 556–571.

Brady, D. W., & McCubbins, M. D. (Eds.). (2002). *Party, process, and political change in Congress: New perspectives on the history of Congress* (Vol. 1). Palo Alto, CA: Stanford University Press.

Brady, D. W., & McCubbins, M. D. (Eds.). (2007). *Party, process, and political change in Congress: Further new perspectives on the history of Congress* (Vol. 2). Palo Alto, CA: Stanford University Press.

Brosnan, J. W. (1984, April 26). Baker denies political push for federal aid to airport. *Memphis Commercial Appeal*.

Brown, L. P., & Peabody, R. L. (1992). Patterns of succession in House Democratic leadership: Foley, Gephardt, and Gray, 1989. In R. L. Peabody & N. W. Polsby (Eds.), *New perspectives on the House of Representatives* (4th ed.). Baltimore: Johns Hopkins University Press.

Bumiller, E. (2002, December 21). With signals and maneuvers, Bush orchestrates an ouster. *The New York Times*, p. A1.

Burns, J. M. (1979). *Leadership*. New York: Harper & Row.

Byrd, R. C. (1995). President Pro Tempore of the Senate. In D. C. Bacon, R. H. Davidson, & M. Keller (Eds.), *The encyclopedia of the United States Congress*. New York: Simon and Schuster.

Byrd, R. C. (2005). *Child of the Appalachian coalfields*. Morgantown: West Virginia University Press.

Campbell, S. (1993, March 7). Mitchell begins building his re-election organization. *Maine State Times*.

Canon, D. T. (1989). The institutionalization of leadership in the U.S. Congress. *Legislative Studies Quarterly, XIV*(3), 415–443.

Carmines, E. G., & Stimson, J. A. (1989). *Issue evolution: Race and the transformation of American politics*. Princeton, NJ: Princeton University Press.

Caro, R. A. (1990). *Means of ascent*. New York: Alfred A. Knopf.

Caro, R. A. (2002). *Master of the Senate*. New York: Alfred A. Knopf.

Carsey, T. M., & Rundquist, B. (1999a). Party and committee in distributive politics: Evidence from defense spending. *Journal of Politics, 61*(4), 1156–1169.

Carsey, T. M., & Rundquist, B. (1999b). The reciprocal relationship between state defense interest and committee representation. *Public Choice, 99*(3–4), 455–463.

Chaplin, J. P. (1985). *Dictionary of psychology.* New York: Laurel.

Cheney, R. B., & Cheney, L. V. (1996). *Kings of the Hill: How nine powerful men changed the course of American history.* New York: Simon & Schuster.

Citizens Against Government Waste. (2007). *2007 congressional pig book summary.* Online: http://www.cagw.org (July 30, 2009).

Clausen, A. R., & Wilcox, C. (1987). Policy partisanship in legislative leadership recruitment and behavior. *Legislative Studies Quarterly, XII*(2), 243–263.

Cloud, D. S. (1996, February 17). Lott has pole position in "race" for leader. *Congressional Quarterly Weekly Report,* p. 385.

Cochran, J., & Nather, D. (2003, January 4). Fast-moving events challenge Frist's debut at Senate helm. *Congressional Quarterly Weekly Report,* p. 16.

Cohadas, N., & Tate, D. (1984, December 15). Senate Democrats re-elect Byrd as leader. *Congressional Quarterly Weekly Report,* p. 3087.

Congressional Record. (1937). 75th Congress, 1st session, p. 7363.

Congressional Record. (1960). 86th Congress, 2nd session, p. 12444.

Conkin, P. K. (1986). *Big daddy from the Pedernales: Lyndon Baines Johnson.* Boston: Twayne Publishers.

Cook, C. (2005, May 28). The Cook report—Frist, Reid lost when gang of 14 took over. *National Journal.*

Cooper, J., & Brady, D. W. (1981). Institutional context and leadership style: The House from Cannon to Rayburn. *American Political Science Review, 75*(2), 411–425.

Cox, G. W., & McCubbins, M. D. (1993). *Legislative leviathan*. Berkeley: University of California Press.

Cox, G. W., & McCubbins, M. D. (2003). A precis on legislative leadership. *Extensions* (Fall), 6–10.

Cox, G. W., & McCubbins, M. D. (2005). *Setting the agenda: Responsible party government in the U.S. House of Representatives*. New York: Cambridge University Press.

Dahl, R. A. (1961). *Who governs?* New Haven, CT: Yale University Press.

Dallek, R. D. (1991). *Lone star rising: Lyndon Johnson and his times, 1908–1960*. New York: Oxford University Press.

Daschle, T. A. (2003). *Like no other time: The 107th Congress and the two years that changed America forever*. New York: Crown Publishers.

Davidson, R. H. (1985). Senate leaders: Janitors for an untidy chamber. In L. C. Dodd & B. I. Oppenheimer (Eds.), *Congress reconsidered* (3rd ed.). Washington, DC: CQ Press.

Davidson, R. H., Hammond, S. W., & Smock, R. W. (Eds.). (1998). *Masters of the House*. Boulder, CO: Westview Press.

Davidson, R. H., & Oleszek, W. J. (2004). *Congress and its members* (9th ed.). Washington, DC: CQ Press.

Day, J. S. (1988, December 17). Presidential politics helped Loring in 1979: 1988 threat of closure may be direct result of earlier ploy. *Bangor Daily News*.

Deering, C. J., & Smith, S. S. (1997). *Committees in Congress* (3rd ed.). Washington, DC: CQ Press.

Doherty, C. J. (1994, November 26). Leadership: Daschle, Dodd fight to stand out in Senate Democrats' race. *Congressional Quarterly Weekly Report*, p. 3393.

Doherty, C. J., & Langdon, S. (1996, May 18). Lott vs. Cochran: A contest of leadership styles. *Congressional Quarterly Weekly Report*, p. 1361.

Downs, A. (1957). *An economic theory of democracy*. New York: Harper and Brothers.

Elving, R. D. (1988, November 19). No safe bets in Senate majority leader's race. *Congressional Quarterly Weekly Report*, p. 3357.

Erikson, R. S. (1978). Constituency opinion and congressional behavior: A reexamination of the Miller-Stokes representation data. *American Journal of Political Science, 22*(3), 511–535.

Erikson, R. S., MacKuen, M., & Stimson, J. A. (2002). *The macro polity*. New York: Cambridge University Press.

Evans, C. L., & Lipinski, D. (2005). Obstruction and leadership in the U.S. Senate. In L. C. Dodd & B. I. Oppenheimer (Eds.), *Congress reconsidered* (8th ed.). Washington, DC: CQ Press.

Evans, C. L., & Oleszek, W. (1999). The strategic context of congressional party leadership. *Congress and the Presidency, 26*(1), 1–20.

Evans, D. (1994). Policy and pork: The use of pork barrel projects to build policy coalitions in the House of Representatives. *American Journal of Political Science, 38*(4), 894–917.

Evans, D. (2004). *Greasing the wheels: Using pork barrel projects to build majority coalitions in Congress*. New York: Cambridge University Press.

Evans, R., & Novak, R. (1966). *Lyndon B. Johnson: The exercise of power*. New York: The New American Library.

Fenno, Jr., R. F. (1973). *Congressmen in committees*. Boston: Little, Brown.

Fenno, Jr., R. F. (1978). *Homestyle: House members in their districts*. New York: Longman.

Fenno, Jr., R. F. (1982). *The United States Senate: A bicameral perspective*. Washington, DC: American Enterprise Institute for Public Policy Research.

Fenno, Jr., R. F. (1996). *Senators on the campaign trail: The politics of representation*. Norman: University of Oklahoma Press.

Ferejohn, J. (1974). *Pork barrel politics: Rivers and harbors legislation, 1947–1968*. Palo Alto, CA: Stanford University Press.

Freeden, M. (2003). *Ideology: A very short introduction*. Oxford, England: Oxford University Press.

Frisch, S. A., & Kelly, S. Q. (2006). Committee assignment politics in the U.S. Senate: Democratic leaders and Democratic committee assignments, 1953–1994. *Congress & the Presidency, 33*(1), 1–23.

Gamm, G., & Smith, S. S. (2000). Last among equals: The Senate's presiding officer. In B. Loomis (Ed.), *Esteemed colleagues: Civility and deliberation in the U.S. Senate*. Washington, DC: Brookings Institution Press.

Gamm, G., & Smith, S. S. (2002a). Party leadership and the development of the modern Senate. In D. W. Brady & M. D. McCubbins (Eds.), *Party, process, and political change in Congress: New perspectives on the history of Congress*. Palo Alto, CA: Stanford University Press.

Gamm, G., & Smith, S. S. (2002b). Emergence of Senate party leadership. In B. I. Oppenheimer (Ed.), *U.S. Senate exceptionalism*. Columbus: Ohio State University Press.

Gamm, G., & Smith, S. S. (2004). Steering the Senate: The consolidation of Senate party leadership, 1879–1913. Paper presented at the annual meeting of the Midwest Political Science Association, Chicago, IL.

Gann, D. (2003, May 11). The price of power. *The New York Times Magazine*, p. 48ff.

Gehrke, R. (2005, July 3). Bennett lays groundwork for next majority leader. *The Salt Lake Tribune*.

Goodwin, D. K. (1976). *Lyndon Johnson and the American dream*. New York: St. Martin's Griffin.

Gould, L. L. (2005). *The most exclusive club: A history of the modern United States Senate*. New York: Basic Books.

References

Graham, K. (Ed.). (2002). *Katherine Graham's Washington*. New York: Vintage Books.

Granat, D. (1984, December 1). Senate Republicans choose officers: Dole elected majority leader; Simpson wins GOP whip job. *Congressional Quarterly Weekly Report*, p. 3020.

Green, M. N. (2004). To kill the king: Leadership challenges to the speaker of the House, 1962–2000. Paper presented at the annual meeting of the Midwest Political Science Association, Chicago, IL.

Green, M. N. (2006). McCormack versus Udall: Explaining intraparty challenges to the speaker of the House. *American Politics Research*, *34*(1), 3–21.

Green, M. N. (2007). Presidents and personal goals: The speaker of the House as nonmajoritarian leader. *Congress & the Presidency*, *34*(2), 1–22.

Green, M. N. (2008). The 2006 race for Democratic majority leader: Money, policy, and personal loyalty. *PS: Political Science and Politics*, *41*(January), 63–67.

Green, M. N., & Harris, D. B. (2007). Goal salience and the 2006 race for House majority leader. *Political Research Quarterly*, *60*(4), 618–630.

Greenstein, F. I. (1982). *The hidden-hand presidency: Eisenhower as leader*. New York: Basic Books.

Grofman, B., Koetzle, W., & McGann, A. J. (2002). Congressional leadership, 1965–96: A new look at the extremism versus centrality debate. *Legislative Studies Quarterly*, *XXVII*(1), 87–105.

Grose, C. R. (2004). Valence advantages, "pork" projects, and position-taking in congressional elections. Unpublished manuscript.

Groseclose, T. (2001). A model of candidate location when one candidate has a valance advantage. *American Journal of Political Science*, *45*(4), 862–886.

Hager, G., & Hook, J. (1994). Choosing a new leader. *Congressional Quarterly Weekly Report*, p. 1489.

Hall, R. L. (1987). Participation and purpose in committee decision making. *American Political Science Review, 81*(1), 105–128.

Hall, R. L., & Grofman, B. (1990). The committee assignment process and the conditional nature of committee bias. *American Political Science Review, 84*(4), 1149–1166.

Harris, D. B. (1998). The rise of the public speakership. *Political Science Quarterly, 113*(2), 193–212.

Harris, D.B. (2006). Legislative parties and leadership choice: Confrontation or accommodation in the 1989 Gingrich-Madigan whip race. *American Politics Research, 34*(2), 189–222.

Harris, D. B., & Nelson, G. (2008). Middlemen no more? Emergent patterns in congressional leadership selection. *PS: Political Science and Politics, 41*(January), 49–55.

Hatfield, M. O. (1997). *Vice presidents of the United States, 1789–1993.* 104th Congress, 2nd session, S. Doc. 104–126. Washington, DC: U.S. Government Printing Office.

Haynes, G. H. (1938). *The Senate of the United States: Its history and practice.* Boston: Houghton Mifflin.

Heberlig, E. S., Hetherington, M. J., & Larson, B. A. (2006). The price of leadership: Campaign money and the polarization of Congress. *Journal of Politics, 68*(4), 989–1002.

Helms, J. (2005). *Here's where I stand: A memoir.* New York: Random House.

Herrick, R., & Moore, M. K. (1993). Political ambition's effect on legislative behavior: Schlesinger's typology reconsidered and revisited. *Journal of Politics, 55*(3), 765–776.

Hetherington, M. J. (2001). Resurgent mass partisanship: The role of elite polarization. *American Political Science Review, 95*(3), 619–631.

Hibbing, J. R., & Theiss-Morse, E. (1995). *Congress as public enemy: Public attitudes toward American political institutions.* New York: Cambridge University Press.

Hibbing, J. R. (1986). Ambition in the House: Behavioral consequences of higher office goals among U.S. representatives. *American Journal of Political Science, 30*(3), 651–665.

Hinckley, B. (1970). Congressional leadership selection and support: A comparative analysis. *Journal of Politics, 32*(2), 268–287.

Hird, J. A. (1991). The political economy of pork: Project selection at the U.S. Army Corps of Engineers. *American Political Science Review, 85*(2), 429–456.

Hook, J. (1987, August 22). Parliamentarians: Procedure and pyrotechnics. *Congressional Quarterly Weekly Report*, p. 1951.

Hook, J. (1988, April 16). The Byrd years: Surviving in a media age through details and diligence. *Congressional Quarterly Weekly Report*, p. 976.

Howell, W. G. (2003). *Power without persuasion: The politics of direct presidential action*. Princeton, NJ: Princeton University Press.

Huitt, R. K. (1961). Democratic party leadership in the Senate. *American Political Science Review, 55*(2), 333–344.

Hulse, C. (2004, April 24). Congressional memo: A longtime courtesy loses in the closely split Senate. *The New York Times*.

Jacobson, G. (2009). *The politics of congressional elections* (7th ed.). New York: Pearson Longman.

Kahneman, D., & Tversky, A. (Eds.). (2000). *Choices, values, and frames*. New York: Cambridge University Press.

Kalb, D. (1996, May 25). Mississippi already a winner. *Congressional Quarterly Weekly Report*, p. 1438.

Kelly, S. Q. (1995a). Democratic leadership in the modern Senate: The emerging roles of the Democratic Policy Committee. *Congress & the Presidency, 22*(2), 113–139.

Kelly, S. Q. (1995b). Generational change and the selection of the Senate Democratic leader in the 104th Congress. Paper presented at the annual meeting of the Southern Political Science Association, Tampa, FL.

Kelly, S. Q. (2005). Using archival sources in legislative research: Choosing the road less traveled. *Extension of Remarks, 28*(2). Online: http://www.apsanet.org/%7Elss/Newsletter/july05/EOR-July-2005.pdf (August 10, 2009).

Kernell, S. M. (2006). *Going public: New strategies of presidential leadership* (4th ed.). Washington, DC: CQ Press.

Key, V. O. (1949). *Southern politics in state and nation.* New York: A. A. Knopf.

King, D. C., & Zeckhauser, R. J. (2002). *Punching and counter-punching in the U.S. Congress: Why party leaders tend to be extremists.* Paper presented at the Conference of Leadership 2002: Bridging the Gap between Theory and Practice, The Center for Public Leadership, Cambridge, MA.

Kolodny, R. (1998). *Pursuing majorities: Congressional campaign committees in American politics.* Norman: University of Oklahoma Press.

Krehbiel, K. (1998). *Pivotal politics: A theory of U.S. lawmaking.* Chicago: University of Chicago Press.

Kurtz, H. (2002, December 21). Loose lips zipped: White House denies it sprang a leak about the leader. *The Washington Post,* p. C01.

Lasswell, H. D. (1936). *Politics: Who gets what, when, how.* New York: McGraw-Hill.

Lasswell, H. D., & Kaplan, A. (1950). *Power and society: A framework for political inquiry.* New Haven, CT: Yale University Press.

Lawrence, E. D., Maltzman, F., & Smith, S. S. (2006). Who wins? Party effects in legislative voting. *Legislative Studies Quarterly, XXXI*(1), 33–70.

Lee, F. E. (2008). Agreeing to disagree: Agenda content and Senate partisanship, 1981–2004. *Legislative Studies Quarterly, XXXIII*(2), 199–222.

Lee, F. E., & Oppenheimer, B. I. (1999). *Sizing up the Senate: The unequal consequences of equal representation.* Chicago: University of Chicago Press.

References

Lemann, N. (2003, May 12). The controller. *The New Yorker*, p. 68.

Levendusky, M. S., & Pope, J. C. (2004). *Incorporating constituency: Modeling legislative politics with constituency, party and personal factors*. Paper presented at the annual meeting of the American Political Science Association, Chicago, IL.

Londreagan, J., & Romer, T. (1993). Polarization, incumbency, and the personal vote. In W. A. Barnett, M. Hinich, & N. Schofield (Eds.). *Political economy: Institutions, competition, and representation*. New York: Cambridge University Press.

Lott, T. (2005). *Herding cats: A life in politics*. New York: Regan Books.

Lowi, T. (1964). *The end of liberalism: The second republic of the United States*. New York: W. W. Norton.

Mackaman, F. H. (1980). *Understanding congressional leadership: A conference report*. Pekin, IL: The Dirksen Center.

March, J. G., & Olsen, J. P. (1984). The new institutionalism: Organizational factors in political life. *American Political Science Review, 78*(3), 734–749.

Martinez, G. (2003, January 4). Race issue kept gaining momentum for Lott. *Congressional Quarterly Weekly Report*, p. 24.

Matthews, D. R. (1960). *U.S. senators and their world*. Chapel Hill: University of North Carolina Press.

Mayhew, D. R. (1974). *Congress: The electoral connection*. New Haven, CT: Yale University Press.

Mayhew, D. R. (1991). *Divided we govern: Party control, lawmaking, and investigations, 1946–1990*. New Haven, CT: Yale University Press.

McMillan, Jr., J. E. (2004). *Ernest W. McFarland*. Prescott, AZ: Sharlot Hall Museum Press.

McRae, Jr., D. (1958). *Dimensions of congressional voting*. Berkeley: University of California Press.

Merry, R. W. (1991). Robert A. Taft: A study in the accumulation of legislative power. In R. A. Baker & R. H. Davidson (Eds.), *First among equals: Outstanding Senate leaders of the twentieth century*. Washington, DC: CQ Press.

Miller, W. E., & Stokes, D. E. (1963). Constituency influence in Congress. *American Political Science Review, 57*(1), 45–56.

Montgomery, G. B., & Johnson, J. W. (1998). *One step from the White House: The rise and fall of Senator William F. Knowland*. Berkeley: University of California Press.

Munk, M. (1974). Origin and development of the party floor leadership in the United States Senate. *Capitol Studies, 2*(Winter), 23–41.

Nagourney, A. (2005, May 25). Compromise in the Senate: The context; A compromise with overtones for 2008. *The New York Times*.

Nelson, G. (1977). Partisan patterns of House leadership change, 1789–1977. *American Political Science Review, 71*(3), 918–939.

Neustadt, R. E. (1960). *Presidential power and the modern presidents*. New York: Free Press.

Oberdorfer, D. (2003). *Senator Mansfield: The extraordinary life of a great American statesman and diplomat*. Washington, DC: Smithsonian Books.

O'Brien, T. L. (2005, January 30). Can Angelina Jolie really save the world? *The New York Times*, p. C1.

Oleszek, W. J. (1991). John Worth Kern: Portrait of a floor leader. In R. A. Baker & R. H. Davidson (Eds.), *First among equals: Outstanding Senate leaders of the twentieth century*. Washington, DC: CQ Press.

Oleszek, W. J. (2007). *Congressional procedures and the policy process* (7th ed.). Washington, DC: CQ Press.

Olson, M. (1971). *The logic of collective action: Public goods and the theory of groups*. Cambridge, MA: Harvard University Press.

Oppenheimer, B. I. (Ed.). (2002). *U.S. Senate exceptionalism*. Columbus: Ohio State University Press.

Oppenheimer, B. I. (2005a). Delayed Republican revolution? Testing the limits of institutional constraints on the Senate majority party. *Extensions* (Spring), 10–15.

Oppenheimer, B. I. (2005b). Deep red and blue congressional districts: The causes and consequences of declining party competitiveness. In L. C. Dodd & B. I. Oppenheimer (Eds.), *Congress reconsidered* (8th ed.). Washington, DC: CQ Press.

Oppenheimer, B. I., & Peabody, R. L. (1977). How the race for House majority leader was won—by one vote. *Washington Monthly*, November, 47–56.

Ornstein, N., Peabody, R., & Rohde, D. (1977). The changing Senate: From the 1950s to the 1970s. In L. C. Dodd & B. I. Oppenheimer (Eds.), *Congress reconsidered* (1st ed.). New York: Praeger Publishers.

Ornstein, N., Peabody, R., & Rohde, D. (1997). The U.S. Senate: Toward the twenty-first century. In L. C. Dodd & B. I. Oppenheimer (Eds.), *Congress reconsidered* (6th ed.). Washington, DC: CQ Press.

Ota, A. K. (2004, November 20). Senate GOP gives its leader a powerful new tool. *Congressional Quarterly Weekly Report*, p. 2733.

Paige, G. (1977). *The scientific study of leadership*. New York: Free Press.

Patterson, S. C. (1963). Legislative leadership and political ideology. *Public Opinion Quarterly, 27*(3), 399–410.

Peabody, R. L. (1967). Party leadership change in the United States House of Representatives. *American Political Science Review, 61*(3), 675–693.

Peabody, R. L. (1976). *Leadership in Congress: Stability, succession, and change*. Boston: Little, Brown.

Peters, B., Pierre, J., & King, D. S. (2005). The politics of path dependency: Political conflict in historical institutionalism. *Journal of Politics, 67*(4), 1275–1300.

Peters, R. (1995). *The speaker: Leadership in the U.S. House of Representatives.* Washington, DC: CQ Press.

Peters, R. (1997). *The American speakership: The office in historical perspective.* Baltimore: Johns Hopkins University Press.

Petersen, R. E. (2009, June 25). *Senate policy committees.* Congressional research service. Online: http://www.Senate.gov/CRSReports/crspublish.cfm?pid='0E%2C*P%2C%5B%3A%23%40%20%20%0A (August 10, 2009).

Pierson, P. (2000). Path dependence, increasing returns, and the study of politics. *American Political Science Review, 94*(2), 251–267.

Pierson, P. (2004). *Politics in time: History, institutions, and social analysis.* Princeton, NJ: Princeton University Press.

Polsby, N. W. (1970). The institutionalism of the U.S. House of Representatives. *American Political Science Review, 62*(1), 144–168.

Poole, K., & Rosenthal, H. (1997). *Congress: A political-economic history of roll call voting.* New York: Oxford University Press.

Poole, K., & Rosenthal, H. (2001). D-NOMINATE after 10 years: An update to Congress: A political-economic history of roll call voting. *Legislative Studies Quarterly, XXVI*(1), 5–29.

Posler, B. D., & Rhodes, C. M. (1997). Pre-leadership signaling in the U.S. House. *Legislative Studies Quarterly, XXII*(3), 351–368.

Preston, M. (2005, June 15). Frist eyes message overhaul. *Roll Call.*

Ragin, C. C. (1987). *The comparative method: Moving beyond qualitative and quantitative strategies.* Berkeley: University of California Press.

Raiffa, H. (1982). *The art and science of negotiation.* Cambridge, MA: Belknap Press.

Reber, A. S. (1995). *Dictionary of psychology.* London: Penguin.

Rich, M. J. (1989). Distributive politics and the allocation of federal grants. *American Political Science Review, 83*(1), 193–213.

Riddick, F. M. (1988). *Majority and minority leaders of the Senate: History and development of the offices of the floor leaders.* Washington, DC: U.S. Government Printing Office.

Riker, W. H. (1962). *The theory of political coalitions.* New Haven, CT: Yale University Press.

Riker, W. H. (1993). *Agenda formation.* Ann Arbor: University of Michigan Press.

Riker, W. H., & Ordeshook, P. C. (1973). *An introduction to positive political theory.* Englewood Cliffs, NJ: Prentice-Hall.

Ripley, R. B. (1969a). *Majority party leadership in Congress.* Boston: Little, Brown.

Ripley, R. B. (1969b). *Power in the Senate.* New York: St. Martin's Press.

Ritchie, D. A. (1991). Alben W. Barkley: The president's man. In R. A. Baker, & R. H. Davidson (Eds.), *First among equals: Outstanding Senate leaders of the twentieth century.* Washington, DC: CQ Press.

Roberts, B. E. (1990). A dead senator tells no lies: Seniority and the distribution of federal benefits. *American Journal of Political Science, 34*(1), 31–58.

Robertson, D. (1993). *Dictionary of politics.* London: Penguin.

Rocca, M. S. (2003). Military base closures and the 1996 congressional elections. *Legislative Studies Quarterly, XXVIII*(4), 529–550.

Rogers, D. (1984, November 20). Politics '84—Majority leader race: Stakes are high in Senate battle. *The Wall Street Journal,* p. 1.

Rogers, D. (1986, August 15). Running hard: Dole's leadership role in Senate helps shape his bid for presidency. *The Wall Street Journal,* p. 1.

Rogers, D., & Shribman, D. (1984, November 29). Dole's election as Senate majority leader is seen as GOP move toward moderation. *The Wall Street Journal,* p. 1.

Rohde, D. W. (1979). Risk-bearing and progressive ambition: The case of members of the United States House of Representatives. *American Journal of Political Science, 23*(1), 1–26.

Rohde, D. W. (1991). *Parties and leaders in the postreform House.* Chicago: University of Chicago Press.

Rothman, D. J. (1966). *Politics and power: The United States Senate, 1869–1901.* Cambridge, MA: Harvard University Press.

Rules of the Senate Republican Conference. (1990, September 24). Washington, DC: U.S. Government Printing Office.

Rules of the Senate Republican Conference. (2004, November 17). Online: http://src.Senate.gov (July 15, 2005).

Russett, C. E. (1966). *The concept of equilibrium in American social thought.* New Haven, CT: Yale University Press.

Schattschneider, E. E. (1942). *Party government.* New York: Farrar and Rinehart.

Schlesinger, Jr., A. M. (1973). *The imperial presidency.* Boston: Houghton Mifflin.

Schlesinger, J. (1966). *Ambition and politics: Political careers in the United States.* Chicago: Rand McNally.

Schmitt, E. (2005, May 14). Military base closings: The overview; Pentagon seeks to shut dozens of bases across nation. *The New York Times.*

Senate is Wilson's, president's friends in control under reorganization. (1913, March 6). *The Washington Post,* p. 6.

Shepsle, K. A., & Weingast, B. R. (1981). Political preferences for the pork barrel: A generalization. *American Journal of Political Science, 25*(1), 96–111.

Shepsle, K. A., & Weingast, B. R. (1995). Positive theories of congressional institutions. In K. A. Shepsle & B. R. Weingast (Eds.), *Positive theories of congressional institutions.* Ann Arbor: University of Michigan Press.

References

Sinclair, B. (1983). *Majority leadership in the U.S. House of Representatives*. Baltimore: Johns Hopkins University Press.

Sinclair, B. (1989). *The transformation of the U.S. Senate*. Baltimore: Johns Hopkins University Press.

Sinclair, B. (1995). *Legislators, leaders, and lawmaking*. Baltimore: Johns Hopkins University Press.

Sinclair, B. (2001a). The new world of U.S. senators. In L. C. Dodd & B. I. Oppenheimer (Eds.), *Congress reconsidered* (7th ed.). Washington, DC: CQ Press.

Sinclair, B. (2001b). The Senate leadership: Passing bills and pursuing partisan advantage in a nonmajoritarian chamber. In C. C. Campbell & N. C. Rae (Eds.), *The contentious Senate: Partisanship, ideology, and the myth of cool judgment*. Lanham, MD: Rowman and Littlefield.

Sinclair, B. (2005). The new world of U.S. senators. In L. C. Dodd & B. I. Oppenheimer (Eds.), *Congress reconsidered* (8th ed.). Washington, DC: CQ Press.

Smith, L. (2005, February 4). Much ado about nothing. *Newsday*, A14.

Smith, S. S. (2005). Parties and leadership in the Senate. In S. Binder & P. Quirk (Eds.), *The legislative branch and American democracy*. New York: Oxford University Press.

Smith, S. S., & Gamm, G. (2005). The dynamics of party government in Congress. In L. C. Dodd & B. I. Oppenheimer (Eds.), *Congress reconsidered* (8th ed.). Washington, DC: CQ Press.

Solomon, J., & Birnbaum, J. H. (May 24, 2007). In the Democratic Congress, pork still gets served. *The Washington Post*, p. A01.

Stein, R. M., & Bickers, K. N. (1995). *Perpetuating the pork barrel: Policy subsystems and American democracy*. New York: Cambridge University Press.

Stewart, J. G. (1971). Two strategies of leadership: Johnson and Mansfield. In N. Polsby (Ed.), *Congressional behavior*. New York: Random House.

Stokes, D. E. (1963). Spatial models of party competition. *American Political Science Review, 57*(2), 368–377.

Stolberg, S. G. (2005, May 26). Threat to base sends Senate on maneuvers. *The New York Times.*

Strahan, R. (2002). Leadership and institutional change in the nineteenth-century House. In D. W. Brady & M. D. McCubbins (Eds.), *Party, process and political change in Congress.* Stanford, CA: Stanford University Press.

Stratton, P., & Hayes, N. (1998). *A student's dictionary of psychology* (3rd ed.). London: Arnold.

Sullivan, W. E. (1975). Criteria for selecting party leadership in Congress: An empirical test. *American Politics Quarterly, 3*(1), 25–44.

Tackett, J. R. (2005, November 21). Senate funding vote puts train on track. *The City Paper,* p. 1.

Taylor, A. (2001, May 12). Senate's agenda to rest on rulings of referee schooled by Democrats. *Congressional Quarterly Weekly Report,* p. 1063.

Truman, D. B. (1959). *The congressional party: A case study.* New York: Wiley.

Valeo, F. R. (1999). *Mike Mansfield, majority leader: A different kind of Senate, 1961–1976.* New York: M.E. Sharpe.

Van Der Slik, J. R., & Pernacciaro, S. J. (1979). Office ambitions and voting behavior in the U.S. Senate: A longitudinal study. *American Politics Quarterly, 7*(2), 198–224.

Watkins, C. L., & Riddick, F. M. (1964). *Senate procedure: Precedents and practices.* Washington, DC: U.S. Government Printing Office.

Weingast, B. R., & Marshall, W. (1988). The industrial organization of Congress. *Journal of Political Economy, 96*(1), 132–163.

Welborn, D. M. (1993). *Republican party leadership in the Senate: 1977–1985.* Paper presented at the annual meeting of the Southern Political Science Association, Savannah, GA.

Whicker, M. L., & Giannatasio, N. A. (1997). The politics of military base closing: A new theory of influence. *Public Administration Quarterly, 21*(2), 176–208.

White, W. S. (1957). *Citadel: The story of the U.S. Senate.* New York: Harper.

Why Kennedy's program is in trouble with Congress. (1962, September 19). *U.S. News and World Report*, p. 67.

Widenor, W. C. (1991). Henry Cabot Lodge: The Senate parliamentarian. In R. A. Baker & R. H. Davidson (Eds.), *First among equals: Outstanding Senate leaders of the twentieth century.* Washington, DC: CQ Press.

Wildavsky, A. (1964). *The politics of the budgetary process.* Boston: Little, Brown.

Wilson, R. K. (1986). An empirical test of preferences for the political pork barrel: District level appropriations for river and harbor legislation, 1889–1913. *American Journal of Political Science, 30*(4), 729–754.

Wilson, W. (1885). *Congressional government.* New York: Houghton Mifflin.

Woods, R. B. (2006). *LBJ: Architect of American ambition.* New York: Free Press.

INDEX

Page numbers in italics refer to figures and tables.

Aldrich, John, 73, 173n64
Aldrich, Nelson, 28, 33
Alexander, Lamar, 125, 138, 140, 179n135
appropriations bills, 20, 126–128, 133, 159
archives, 20, 136
    Baker, Howard H. Jr., 126, 136, 169n10, 171n41, 172n50, 178n121, 179nn132–135
    Johnson, Lyndon B., 170nn14–18, 174n74, 176nn96–97, 177nn99–105
    Mansfield, Mike, 169n1, 169n7, 169nn11–12, 176n93, 177nn106–107, 178nn113–115, 178nn118–119, 181n168
    Mitchell, George J., 126, 136, 170n13, 171n42, 179n141, 180nn144–148, 180nn151–161
Arnold, R. Douglas, 134, 149

Bachrach, Peter, 11
Bacon, Donald, 105
balance, 2, 10–18, 23, 62–63, 102, 116, 123, 126, 136, 151, 153–154, 156
balancing constraints, 2, 10–17, 26, 36, 47, 97, 113, 126, 136, 151, 153–154, 158, 160

Baker, Howard H, Jr., 8, 15, 19, 24, 31, 39–41, 45, 52, *54*, 57, *59*, 64, *72*, *78–79*, *83–84*, *101*, 117–118, 126, 136–142, 148–150, 156, 159, 178n122, 178n125, 179nn138–139, 180n163, 181n164
Baker, Howard H., Sr., 137
Baker, Richard, 8
Baker, Robert, 111, 177n106
balloting, 51–52, 56–58, 61, 63, *65*, 103, 118
Baratz, Morton, 11
Barkley, Alben, 52, *54–55*, *59–61*, 65, *76*, *78*, 80–87, 89, *101*, 106–107, 115, 119, 123, 156, *163*, 174n73, 176nn92–93, 178n126
Base Realignment and Closure (BRAC), 41, 137, 143–150, 159, 181nn165–166
Bickers, Kenneth, 136
Bird, Larry, 125
Brady, D. W., 170n28
Brown, Gordon, 26
Bryan, William Jennings, 33
Burns, J. M., 170n26
Bush, George H. W., 97, *101*, 144, 147
Bush, George W., 39, 44, 96–97, *101*, 117, 199, 120–122, 159

Byrd, Robert, 32, 35, 41–43, 52–*54*, 56–57, *59*, 65–68, 75–*76*, 78, *81–84*, *101*, 133, 155–156, 171n30, 171n43, 172n51
   style as spokesman, 43, 65–66

Campbell, Ben Nighthorse, 63
Canon, David, 58
Carmines, Edward, 172n46
Caro, Robert, 86, 176n94
Carolla, Bob, 144, 180n148
Chafee, John, 57
checks and balances, 103, 122
Chiles, Lawton, *65–66*, 172n51
Citizens Against Government Waste, 20, 128
Clausen, Aage, 173n63, 173n66
Clinton, William J., 96, *101*, 120
coalitions, 13, 27, 29, 35, 37, 47, 56, 63, 74, 80, 85–87, 90, 92, 125, 135, 157–158
Cochran, Thad, *54–55*, 62, 68, 132
Cohen, William S., 142, 145
committee assignments, 30–31, 64, 68, 103, 154, 171n35
committee chairmanships, 28, 60, 63–64, 156, 171n34
committee chairs, 6, 28, 30–31, 35–36, 52, 56–57, *59*–68, 102, 106, 174, 171n33, 171nn37–38, 173n61
Community Development Block Grant, 138–139
congressional
   behavior, 34, 72, 85, 100, 125, 151
   delegations, 46, 149, 181n166
   elections, 30, 67, 95, 170n27, 175n86

congressional (*continued*)
   leadership, 3–5, 8–9, 17, 29, 97, 102, 104, 122–123, 153, 169n5
   leadership selection, 4–6
   majorities, 86, 98
   parties, 13–14
   reforms, 10, 49, 86
Congressional Record, 170n19, 176n92
Conkin, Paul, 176n94
Conservative Coalition, 63, 80, 85
constituencies, 2–3, 9–12, 14–19, 21–22, 24, 37, 43, 47, 61, 71–72, 85–89, 92, 102, 122–123, 126–128, 134–137, 141–142, 148, 150–151, 153–154, 159–161, 169n6, 173n64, 180n163
constraints on senate majority leaders
   party, 13, 23, 49–69, 71–93, 122
   president, 23, 29, 95–123
   senate, 25–46, 122
   state, 125–151
contested selection of Senate majority leader
   contested selection of candidates, 50–*54*, 57, 66, 68
   ideological comparison of candidates, 19, 23, 53, *55*, 58, 61–62, 64, 67–69
   role of ideology, 2, 23, 29, 31–32, 41, 53–58, 62–63, 67–69
Coolidge, Calvin, *101*
Cooper, J., 170n28
Copeland, Royal, 106
Courter, Jim, 146
Cox, Gary, 7, 169n4
Curtis, Charles, *59*, 75–*76*, *78–79*, 80, *83*, *101*, 172n56

Dahl, Robert, 10–11
Dallek, Robert, 176n94
D'Amato, Al, 146
Daschle, Thomas A., 8, 12, 35–36,
  41, 43, 50, 52, *54–55*, *59*, 61,
  63, *76*, *78*, *81*, *83–84*, 96, *101*,
  128, *130*, 132, 171n39, 172n57,
  175n82, 181n166
Davidson, Roger, 8, 172n48
Democratic
  caucus, 28–29, 31, 52, 56, 98
  committee assignments, 30, 60
  leaders, 29–31, 35–36, 50, *54*,
    57, 60, 62, 67, 75, 80–*81*, 87,
    89, 92, 98, *101*, 110, 116–117,
    170n14, 171nn37–38
  leaders vote, 75–*76*, *78*, 80, 82,
    88, 89
  leadership, 8, 18, 29–31, 33, 60,
    80
  Party, 29, *54*, 56, 63, 80, 87, 89,
    103, 110, 123, 156
  Policy Committee, 34–36, 39,
    50, 52, 60, 63, 109, 111, 113,
    178n114
  presidents, 96, *101*, 108–110, 113,
    116–117, 120
  Senatorial Campaign Committee,
    67
  senators, 41, 52–54, 57, 60, 67,
    96, 103, 105–106, 108–110,
    113, 120, 171n38
Democrats, 27–28, 30–32, 35–36,
  40–41, 44, *54*, 60, 62–63, 67,
  80, 86, 89, 105, 107–111, 116,
  120–121, 123, 171n39, 174n68,
  179n127
Dirksen Congressional Center, 4
Dirksen, Everett McKinley, 56

distributive benefits, 3, 12, 20, 24,
  126, 135–136, 150–151, 159–160
distributive politics, 125–126, 128,
  132–136, 148, 151
divided government, 3, 11, 113–114,
  158
  Senate majority leaders and
    presidents, 14, 42, 100–102,
    108, 111
Dodd, Christopher J., *54–55*, 61, 63
Dole, Robert, 32, 41, *54–55*, 57,
  59, 61, 64, 67–68, *76*, *78*–80,
  83–84, 96, *101*, 118–119, *129*,
  132, 156
Domenici, Pete, *54–55*, 57, 64, 67, 97
Dorgan, Byron, 36
Dove, Robert B., 32
Downs, Anthony, 73–74, 157
DW-NOMINATE scores, 19, 53,
  55, 62, 75–*76*, *78–79*, *81*, 86–87,
  174n70, 176n89

earmarks, 12, 20, 24, 126–133, 149,
  151, 159, 179n130, 181n164
  number and amount of earmarks
    by Senate majority leader, *129*
Eisenhower Dwight, D., *101*–102,
  109–111, 116–117, *163*, 174n72,
  178n120, 179n139
elections, 2, 4–6, 12–14, 23, 30,
  34–35, 41, 49–69, 71–72, 74,
  77–*78*, 82, 92–93, 96–98, 100,
  103, 107, 117–122, 133, 136,
  151, 155–158, 170n27, 171n43,
  172n55, 173nn63–64, 174n69,
  175nn86–87
Energy Subcommittee of Senate
  Appropriations Committee, 147,
  180n160

Evans, Diana, 135
Evans, Lawrence, 9, 169n5
Evans, Rowland, 176n94

factors in leadership selection
   effects on committee
     chairmanships, 63–64
   ideology, 2, 23, 29, 31–32, 41,
     53–58, 62–63, 67–69, 71
   prior leadership or seniority, 23,
     58–62, 155–156
   region, 23, 62–64, 156
   spokesman, 64–68, 156
Federal Aviation Administration
   (FAA), 140
Federal Housing Administration
   (FHA), 138
Fenno, Richard, 22, 135, 148, 170n27
floor leader, 37–39
Ford, Gerald, 67, *101*, 112, *163*
Friedersdorf, Max, 178n123
Frisch, Scott, 31
Frist, Bill, 11, 26, 39–41, 43–46,
   59–61, 76, 78–79, 82–84, 95,
   79, *101*, 119–121, 123, 125, 127,
   130, 132–133, 156, 159, 171n29,
   172n53
   selection as Senate majority
     leader, 51, 96–97, 119–120,
     122, 172n52
Frumin, Alan S., 32

Gamm, Gerald, 5, 28, 98–99
Gang of 14, 121
Gates, Bill, 26
General Accounting Office (GAO),
   140, 179n136
Gillette, Michael L., 170n20,
   176nn96–97, 177n99, 177n101

Gingrich, Newt, 68
"going public", 38, 44, 172n58
Goldwater, Barry, 108, 177n108
Goodwin, Doris Kearns, 176n94
Gorman, Arthur Pue, 28–29, 33
Gould, Lewis, 33, 38
Green, Matthew, 9
Greenstein, Fred, 179n139
Grofman, Bernard, 173n66
Grose, Christian, 135
Groseclose, Timothy 135

Harding, Warren G., *101*, 116
Harris, Douglas, 42, 171n44
Harrison, Pat, 52, *54–55*, 106
Hayden, Carl, 56, 62
Heberlig, Eric, 173n64
Heinz, John, 57
Hetherington, Marc, 173n64
Hoover, Herbert, *101*
House of Representatives, 13, 37–38,
   41, 46, 61–62, 64, 92, 127, 134,
   137, 143, 175n79
   leaders, 7, 14, 20, 27, 33–34, 42,
     49–50, 64, 68, 71
   leadership, 3, 9, 50
   leadership studies, 4–6, 8–9,
     17–18, 50, 170n28, 173n66,
     174n68
House and Senate Appropriations
   Committee chairmen, 133
Huitt, Ralph, 8, 10, 18, 153
Humphrey, Hubert H., 56–57,
   65

ideology, 19, 31, 53–58, 62, 68,
   71–93, 156
Inouye, Daniel, 52, *54–55*, 57–58,
   67

job description of Senate majority leadership, 25–47
Johnson, Lyndon B., 8, 14–15, 50, *59*, 117, 119, 171n38, 177nn108–110, 178n119
　archives, 31
　leadership, 29, 35, 40, 45, 61, 89, 93, 100–102, 108–111, 113, 148, 156, 170n15
　leadership style, 8, 16, 31, 38, 43, 75–76, 78, *81*, *83–84*, 86, 112, 114, 123, 155, 170n18, 171n35, 174n74, 176n95, 178n116
　library, 19
　presidency, *101*, 112–115, 181n167
　presidential library, 19
Johnston, J. Bennett, 52, *54–55*, 57–58, *65*–67, 147, 172n51
Jordan, Michael, 125
judicial nominations, 39, 44, 120–121

Kaplan, A., 170n26
Kelly, Sean, 5, 31, 50, 170n21
Kennedy, Edward M., 56, *63*, 143, 169n5
Kennedy, John F., *101*, 111–115, 119
Kern, John W., 1, 29, 32–34, 37, 40, 59–60, *76*, *78*, 80–*84*, 86, 97–104, 108, 119, 121–123, 156, 158–159, 171n31, 171n40, 172n55, 175n87, 176n88
Kernell, S. M., 172n58
Kerr, Bob, 56, 62
Key, V. O., 137
King, David, 73
King, Desmond, 175n84

Knowland, William F., *59*, 75–*76*, 77–*79*, 82–*84*, 86, *101*, 116–117, *163*, 174n72, 178n120
Koetzle, William, 173n66

Larson, Bruce, 173n64
Lasswell, H. D., 170n26
Lautenberg, Frank, 144
lawmaking, 6–7, 105, 125–126
leadership ladders, 4, 58
leadership selection processes, 6, 23, 49–69
leadership styles, 2, 6–8, 20, 22, 31, 34, 43, 57, 66–67, 86, 113, 136, 170n18, 170n28, 178n116, 179n39
Levitt, Arthur, 145, 180n150
Lewis, Drew, 140
Lobbying, 55, 97, 139, 141, 144–146, 159, 181n164, 181n166
Lodge, Henry Cabot, *59*, 65, 75–80, *83–84*, 87, *101*, 116
Loring Air Force Base, 137, 143–147, 149–151, 159–160, 180nn144–147, 180nn151–152, 180nn154–157, 180n162
Lott, C. Trent, 32, 40, 43, 45, 51, *54*, *55*, *59*, 61–62, 68, *76*–80, *83–84*, 96–97, *101*, 119–121, *129*, 132, 172n52
Lowi, Theodore, 134
Lucas, Scott, *54*, 56–57, *59*, *76*, *78*, *81*, *83–84*, *101*, *163*
Lugar, Richard, *54–55*, 57, 64, 67–68

Machiavelli, 10
Mack, Connie, 61
majority, size of, 2, 13, 23, 29, 86–89, 92, 158

Mansfield, Mike, 15, 76, 78, *81*,
  83–84, 111–116
Martin, Thomas S., 29, *59–60*,
  76, 78, *81*, *83–84*, *101*, 103,
  171n31
Mayhew, David, 85, 125, 136, 151,
  170n27, 175n85
McClure, James D., *54–55*, 57, 64,
  67
McConnell, Mitch, 51, 95, 172n53,
  175n81
McCubbins, Matthew, 7, 169n4
McFarland, Ernest W., 52, *54–57*,
  59, 61–62, 76, 78, *81*, *83–84*, *101*,
  108, 178n126
McGann, Anthony, 173n66
McMahon, Brien, 63
McPherson, Harry C., Jr., 176n97,
  177n105
McRae, Duncan, 73
Memphis Commercial Appeal, 140
Miller Center, 167, 170n23, 177n108,
  178n122
minority, 8, 13–14, 28, 35, 38–39,
  44, 49, 56, 120, 169n8, 171n39,
  179n127
minority leaders, 4, 6, 17, 29, 32, 34,
  37–38, 41, 44, 46, 50, 54, *59*, 73,
  95–96, 107, 117, 174n69
Mitchell, George J., 8, 15, 19,
  24, 30–31, 35–36, 39–41, 52,
  54–55, 57–61, 67, 76, 78, *81*,
  83–84, *101*, 126, *129*, 131,
  136–137, 142–151, 155–156,
  159–160, 172n57, 180n152,
  181nn166–167
Mkapa, Benjamin, 26
Mondale, Walter F., 143
Morton, Thruston, 112, 177n109

Munk, Margaret, 59–60, 98, 104,
  116–117, 158
Muskie, Edmund, 142–143, 145

Nelson, Garrison, 4
Neustadt, Richard, 10, 123
Nixon, Richard, *101*, 112, 117, *163*,
  174n72
nominations, judicial, 39, 44,
  120–121
Novak, Robert, 133n94

Oberdorfer, Don, 114, 169n9
Obey, David, 133
Oleszek, Walter, 9, 169n5, 172n48,
  176n88
Olson, Mancur, 171n32
O'Mahoney, Joseph C., 52, *54–55*,
  56, 63
Oppenheimer, Bruce, 4
Ornstein, Norman, 8

Paige, G., 170n26
party caucuses, 11, 13, 23, 26–28,
  173n64
party government, 7, 14, 19, 27–30,
  34–37, 39, 44, 52, 58, 86, 90, 158,
  175n179
path dependence, 2, 99–100, 160,
  175n84
Patterson, Samuel, 73
Peabody, Robert, 4–5, 8, 49–50, 58,
  74, 77, 93, 157, 173n66
Pernacciaro, Samuel, 73–74, 157
Peters, Guy, 175n84
Pierre, Jon, 175n84
Pierson, Paul, 99
Pig Book, 128
Plattsburgh Press-Republican, 146

Index

policy leadership, 5, 65, 99
political action committees (PACs), 41
Poole, Keith, 82, 173n62, 174n70
pork, 12, 126, 128, 132–136, 140, 143, 148, 160
"position-taking", 39
Posler, Brian, 174n68
presidency, 10, 98, 102–103, 122–123, 158
president
   influence, 14, 33, 39, 60, 95–123, 154
president pro tempore, 27, 171n30
presidential
   administrations, 9, 19, 60, 96, 104, 106, 108, 111, 113–114, 117–118, 143, 150, 173n163, 180n163, 181n166
   campaigns, 44, 68
   constraints, 2–3, 11, 14, 17, 23, 29, 34, 42, 54, 72, 95–123, 136, 151, 154, 158, 161, 169n6, 171n36, 172n45, 175n85, 178n120, 178n22
   expectations, 95–123, 154, 159, 178n122
   veto, 14, 72, 106
Presidential Oral History Project, 177nn108–112, 178nn122–124
president-leader relations, 100, 116
press, 43, 45, 52, 66, 68, 146, 155, 172n59, 174n74
Proxmire, William, 112–113, 177nn110–112

race, 4–5, 41, 49, 52–53, 55–57, 61–62, 66–67, 77, 118
Reagan, Nancy, 118

Reagan, Ronald, *101*, 117–119, 178nn122–123
Reedy, George, 109, 170n20, 176n96, 177n99–103
reforms, 6, 10, 18, 33, 49, 85, 86, 103, 199, 128, 175n79, 175n86
Reid, Harry, 36, 63, 95, 97, 175n81, 179n130, 181n164
Republican
   leaders, 30, 35–36, 41, 50, 53, 67–68, 75, 77, 80, 87, 89, 92, 116, 118
   leadership, 30, *54*
   majority, 36, 44, 96, 118, 171n33
   majority leaders, 41, 53, 77, *79*, 92, *101*, 108, 116–121
   Party, 36, *54*, 56–57, 62–63, *76–80*, 87, 96–97, 110, 172n56
   Policy Committee, 34, 36, 43, *59*
   presidents, 116–121
   revolution, 68, 85, 92
   Senate, 30, 32, 45, 57, 60, 64, 77, 109, 117
   senators, 57, 61, 64, 68, 80, 96, 117, 171n41
Rhodes, Carl, 174n68
Ripley, Randall, 10
Robinson, Joseph T., 52, 54, *59*–60, *76–78*, *80–84*, *86*–87, *101*, 104–106
Rohde, David, 6–8, 175n79
Roosevelt, Franklin D., 54, 60, *101*, 104–107, 115, 119, 172n54
Rosenthal, Howard, 82, 173n62, 174n70
Rove, Karl, 96
Russell, Richard, 56, 61–62, 108

Sachs, Jeffrey, 26
Sasser, James, 61, 63
Scowcroft, Brent, 147, 180n158
Secretary of Defense, 143–144
selection of Senate majority leaders
   committee chairmanships, 63–64
   contested selections, 23, 50–57, 66, 68, 71, 174n69
   factors in
     ideology, 2, 23, 29, 31–32, 41, 53–58, 62–63, 67–69, 71
     prior leadership or seniority, 23, 58–62, 155–156
     region, 23, 62–64, 156
     spokesman, 64–68, 156
   processes, 6, 50, 53, 58
Senate
   Appropriations Committee, 12, 30, 58, *65*–66, 132–133, 147
   Armed Services Committee, 30, 145
   careers, 55–56, 62, 71–73, 75, 80, 82, 93, 127, 135, 148, 157–158, 174n68
   Democratic Communications Center, 44
   Democratic leadership, 18, 27–31, 33, 35–36, 44, 50, 57, *59*, 60–61, 67, *76*, *78*, 80–82, 86–87, 89, 98, *101*, 107, 110, 171nn37–38, 174n68
   Democrats, 31, 103, 106, 108–110, 113, 171n38
   exceptionalism, 4
   floor, 37–39
   majority leaders
     office, 27–29, 160–161
     modern, 5, 108–109

Senate (*continued*)
   papers, 19, 33, 39, 136, 140, 159, 170nn14–18, 174n74, 179n137
   Policy Committees, 34–37, 39, 154
   procedure, 5, 47, 52–53, 99, 121
   Republican Conference, 30, 45, 62
   Republicans, 28, 30, 32, 41, 44, 56–57, 62, 64, 67, 89, 92, 96, 116–117
   Rules Committee, 37
Senate majority leader
   contested selection of candidates, 23, 50–57, 66, 68, 71, 174n69
   factors in selection
     ideology, 2, 23, 29, 31–32, 41, 53–58, 62–63, 67–69, 71
     prior leadership or seniority, 23, 58–62, 155–156
     region, 23, 62–64, 156
     spokesman, 64–68, 156
   ideological comparison of candidates for contested selections, *55*
   ideological placement of Senate majority leaders, *79*, *81*
   job description
     agenda-setting, 32–37
     campaigning and fundraising, 40–41
     managing the floor, 37–39
     mobilizing the majority, 39–40
     networking, 45–46
     organizing the chamber, 29–32
     speaking for the party, 42–45
   median voting scores at first Congress, *55*
   number and amount of earmarks by Senate majority leader, *125*

Senate majority leader (*continued*)
  placement at selection, 75
  prior leadership positions, 63
  relationship with president, 14, 23, 34, 95–123, 159
  representation of state, 3, 12, 15–16, 24, 125–151, 159–160
  right of first recognition, 11, 155, 169n8
  selection
    committee chairmanships, 63–64
    contested selections, 23, 50–57, 66, 68, 71, 174n69
    factors in
      ideology, 2, 23, 29, 31–32, 41, 53–58, 62–63, 67–69, 71
      prior leadership or seniority, 23, 58–62, 155–156
      region, 23, 62–64, 156
      spokesman, 64–68, 156
    processes, 6, 50, 53, 58
Senate majority leadership theories, 6–8, 73, 90, 98–99, 102, 123, 126, 135, 160, 169n5, 173n66
Senatorial behavior, 2, 4, 6, 9, 13, 17–19, 21–23, 37, 57, 69, 71–75, 77, 82, 85–89, 97, 100, 116, 122, 125–126, 135–136, 151, 154, 157–158, 160
Senatorial Campaign Committees, 40, *59*–60, 67, 156
Senators
  dual roles of, 21, 24, 86, 126
  seniority, 30–31, 58–62, 64, 90, 103, 134, 156, 171n33, 172n56
separation of powers, 103, 122
Simpson, Alan, 62

Sinclair, Barbara, 5–8, 31, 58, 73, 90–91, 171n44
size of majority, 2, 13, 23, 29, 86–87, 89, 92, 158
Smith, Alfred, 104
Smith, Larry 178n121
Smith, Steven S., 5, 28, 98–99, 175n78
speaker of the House, 9, 14, 17, 27, 42, 50, 64, 68, 71
state expectations of Senate majority leaders, 125–151
Stein, Robert, 136
Stevens, Chris, 169n1, 182n168
Stevens, Ted, *54–55*, 57, 64, 67, 97
Stimson, James, 172n46
Stone, Sharon, 26
Strahan, Randall, 9
Sullivan, William, 74, 93, 157

Taft, Robert A., 35, 42, *59*, 75–79, *83*, *84*, 86, *101*, 109, 116, *163*, 174n72
Thomas, Elbert, 101
Thompson, Fred, 132
Thune, John, 41, 181n166
Thurmond, Strom, 96, 120
Trowbridge, Alexander, 145, 180n149, 180n151
Truman, David, 72, 74, 90, 98, 156–157
Truman, Harry S., *101*, 107, *163*

Unanimous Consent Agreement (UCA), 38
unified government Senate majority leaders and presidents, 97–102

valence advantage, 135–136
Valeo, Francis, 169n9, 172n47

Van Der Slik, Jack, 73–74, 157
voting behavior
   career changes in, *105*
   distance in voting scores
      following selection, 82–85
   estimates of leaders' voting
      behavior, *88*
   expectations of majority leaders,
      72–74, 82–89
   at first Congress, 76
   influence of constituency, 72,
      85–89, 135
   at selection, 77, *78*
   as Senate majority leader, 2,
      72–74, 77, 82–89, 116
   stability, 72–73, 77, 82–85
   trends of Democratic majority
      leaders, 75, 82–89, 157–158
   trends of Republican majority
      leaders, 57, 77, 82–89, 157–158

Warner, John, 97
Watson, James E., *59*, *76*, *78–79*,
   83–84, *101*, *163*
Weinberger, Casper, 144
whip, 4, 6–7, 17, 50–51, 56, *59*,
   61–62, 68, 73, 155, 157, 173n61,
   173n65
White, Wallace H., *59*, *76*, *78–79*,
   83–84, *101*, 108
White House, 33–34, 38, 42, 50,
   96, 104, 107–108, 113–117,
   119, 122, 144, 146–147, 159,
   181nn166–167
Wilson, Woodrow, 33–34, 65, 97,
   99, *101*, 103–104, 119, 121,
   158–159
Woods, Randall, 176n94

Zeckhauser, Richard, 73, 173n65
Zweben, Murray, 32